Presented To:

_____

From:

_____

Date:

_____

Sweet DREAMS

HEALING *at the feet of* JESUS

DENA HOOVER

DESTINY IMAGE® PUBLISHERS, INC.

P.O. Box 310, Shippensburg, PA 17257-0310

"Promoting Inspired Lives."

This book and all other Destiny Image, Revival Press, MercyPlace, Fresh Bread, Destiny Image Fiction, and Treasure House books are available at Christian bookstores and distributors worldwide.

For a U.S. bookstore nearest you, call 1-800-722-6774.

For more information on foreign distributors, call 717-532-3040.

Reach us on the Internet: www.destinyimage.com.

ISBN 13 TP: 978-0-7684-3924-3

ISBN 13 Ebook: 978-0-7684-8949-1

For Worldwide Distribution, Printed in the U.S.A.

1 2 3 4 5 6 7 / 15 14 13 12 11

Dedication

To God, for showing me sides of Himself that the world has tried to distort and for being true to His Word.

...No eye has seen, no ear has heard, no mind has conceived what God has prepared for those who love Him (1 Corinthians 2:9).

Contents

Introduction

It was like any other morning. I had enjoyed my coffee and cereal with my husband, and now it was time to kiss him as he headed off to work.

I gathered my stuff to retreat to the lanai. Lanai—I find that word odd. In North Carolina where I'm from, it is called a screened-in porch. But as I quickly learned when we moved to Florida, this area of the house is a lanai. So off to the lanai I went.

Usually my weight-challenged, 11-year-old cat, Annabelle, would have already ventured out to select her seat. To know me, one would know that I love her, but not her shedding hair. I would like to say that I have trained her not to sit in my chair, but she runs the show, and we know it. I can thank my husband for that due to his pampering of her.

This is how I start my mornings—not to outwit my cat to the chair or to debate lanai or porch—but to sit at the feet of Jesus. I pull up my pillow and like Mary, gaze into my Lord's eyes, waiting in great anticipation to hear His voice. I have come to my Secret Place where God and I start our day together. I open my journal to the page I left off from the day before, greet Him with a "Good morning," and the rest is up to where He wants to take me. Don't get me wrong, there are a few "not so good" mornings.

I figure I had better be honest; He knows anyway. Besides, how can anything get resolved if I don't share with Him?

That is what our time boils down to: communication. We are building a personal relationship. I find that funny because this particular day we were talking about communication. How He waits in the Secret Place in hopes that His children will show up.

I have always believed that if He says, "all who have ears, listen," then He must have something to say. Mary sat to hear what He was going to teach. I want to learn, not just about life, but about the Maker of life. It is in those moments when I look back and realize that an intimate relationship between Him and me is evolving. He tells me things I do not know about Him *and* about me. Who more to know me than the very One who formed me in my mother's womb?

For several weeks, I had felt His prompting for what I would later learn was the beginning of a heightened awareness of our communication into a deeper relationship than I have experienced, but had long prayed for.

Our special relationship began as a fast, and before I knew it, it transformed into the very words you have so graciously decided to lay your eyes upon—this book. I started the fast like I had so many before: gathering materials on the subject matter He impressed, bringing my journal, a teachable heart, and His Word—my weathered Bible.

It was during this fast when He posed a question, "What do your dreams say about you?" I found that very intriguing, but had no concrete answer for Him. Little did I know that simple question would spawn an amazing journey with the one and only amazing God. His question was not a pursuit of dream interpretation, but a reference to what parents tell children as they are tucked into bed at night, "Sweet dreams."

"Many of My children do not sleep peacefully," God told me. "That is the direction I seek to share," He continued. "Why My children are not having sweet dreams."

As I penned the words, He spoke for the next couple of weeks; I had no idea that He would call it to print. I take His words in private time just as that, private. He spoke to me once, "Loose lips sink ships, unless the Captain says it is OK." He runs the show, and I am grateful to follow His lead. Just as if I would have lunch with a friend and she spoke something in confidence, betraying her or His trust is the last thing I want to do. So with His permission, I share our conversation at His feet.

-CHAPTER 1-

The Pillow

I will lie down and sleep in peace for you alone, O Lord, make me dwell in safety (Psalm 4:8).

Our time began with a vision of a precious little girl sitting at His feet on a pillow fit for royalty with her small hands clapping in excitement, her elbows resting on His knee. Looking closer, to my surprise, I recognized the girl; she was me. She had brown, shoulder-length, ringlet hair and big, blue eyes. She did not look like me as I had as a child, but somehow we knew each other.

"They are all My children. She represents them all. There is a place for them all," He explained to me.

Like a little one looking up to their parents in awe and amazement, waiting to hear the stories like the ones often shared at bedtime, she said, "Tell me about the cross," as she gazed upward into His eyes.

"Yes," I added, joining myself at His feet, "tell us about the cross."

"I had it planned long before you were born, little one, but it was for you," He said.

"A gift?" I asked.

"Yes, one you didn't even know you were getting or needed," He said.

"The cross," He continued, "was the most expensive gift—both physically and emotionally—I have ever given. But I am getting ahead of Myself. Long before I bought this gift, I created

13

a beautiful, most exquisite Garden. Oh, it smelled of lilac and some of the sweetest honeysuckle you can imagine. There was no such thing as hay fever, so no worries about allergy seasons. My children could run and play, dance and skip until they were happily tired. There was more love and happiness in the air than you could breathe in. I had made it for My children. It was safe. I would wander around the Garden with them. I wanted, from the beginning, to be a hands-on Dad. One who wasn't afraid to play with or enjoy His children. Time was all we had, and it was filled with love. I wanted My presence to make them feel safe because they were. I can still hear their laughter now. It is sweet."

He continued, "Just like any good parent, I had rules. 'Stay away from the tree.' I said it for their own good. Good parents have to do that, you know…set guidelines for their safety and welfare, even if they don't like it. Life was good. My children were so occupied with all the Garden had to offer that the tree was of no concern—until peer pressure," He said sadly, shaking His head slightly.

"See, I had a child who refused to listen, lucifer. He sought to destroy Me and My family. I will go to the end of time to bring back one missing child, but I will not allow one to ruin it for the others. I am a very protective Father. Something had to be done. I had to ban the rebellious child from the family," He said slowly.

"I think this is when My children became confused. Sin breeds confusion. They saw what happened to lucifer and began to fear Me instead of reverence Me. There is a big difference between the two. One fears out of being afraid of harm while another fears out of a longing to please."

With a heartbreaking tone, He continued, "I never meant for them to be afraid of Me. Instead, I longed for a strong bond that, because we shared such a love, neither would want to break. Between the confusion and their tendency to remember the bad instead of the good, things got out of hand—out of *My* hand. I want them back. Some feel since they are confessing their sins, they can wait. Yes, they can come back, just like My son, the Prodigal, found out, but at what expense?"

I asked, "Why do we do that? Why do we tend to remember the bad instead of the good?"

"Fear is powerful," He replied.

"But aren't You more powerful?" I questioned.

"Oh, yes," He replied with confidence. "It all boils down to where their eyes are. You don't know him, but I had a very zealous child named Peter. Oh, I loved him. He lost focus once—well, three times to be exact," He said, chuckling at His own inside joke.

"Peter looked away, and the fear became stronger." He continued, "It can take only a moment to lose your focus. His eyes followed his ears. That is why I say *'fix* your eyes on Jesus, My Son.' This takes practice and time. Peter didn't get it the first time either. But he kept coming; trying. I worked with him, and I'll work with you," He said assuredly.

He paused to take a deep breath and began again, "I won't be mocked by lucifer or anyone. Therefore, I had to keep My word. I had to let him go. He is an example of the extreme, not the normal. I want My children to know I am love who comes with discipline, but also great joy. Sometimes that truth gets forgotten."

"This really seems to trouble you," I said.

"It does," He answered. "I never planned it to be this way. But like a good parent, I had to do what was right for the better good. And that was the cross. I had to make it final. Before the cross, there was no way to unite My family. Peer pressure separated us. I could see them, but could not touch them. I wanted My babies back.

"Other gods were doing it as a continuation. They said, 'Do this, and then I will...whatever.' They couldn't live up to their conditional promises. I had to set Myself apart, because I am the one true God."

"How did Jesus react?" I asked.

"I never made Him go to the cross. It was completely up to Him," He answered.

"What about when He asked You to take it from Him?" I wondered.

"Haven't you ever had something you needed to do and deep down you wanted to do it, but when it came time, you got a little worried?" He asked.

"Yes, but I try to do it anyway," I replied.

"That is exactly what My Son did. He did it anyway. It was just His way of asking Me for help. I am so proud of Him, just like when My other children succeed. Jesus had a plan, and He knew it, and He saw it through. I have a plan for each of My children. All it requires is time with Me to learn and be taught how to accomplish that plan. Jesus spent many hours with Me. He was ready."

I had to stop the Lord to thank Jesus. I had often before, but this moment seemed different.

After a few minutes, He asked, "Do you know what I lost that day when My first two children ate from the tree?"

"No," I replied.

"Their hearts; another suitor came and stole their hearts," He said with a look of loss upon His face.

The very words from His mouth broke my heart. Our God hurts over the loss of us. We left Him. The thought kept playing in my head over and over like a scratched record.

"They are led by their hearts because they were made from pure love, but they got confused and fell for an imitation. Such has been humankind's story ever since. Over and over, I offer My purest of love to them only to have them reject Me, only to try yet again, another imitation love. I touch My people, I speak to them, there is My Word…but they continue to suffer needlessly."

I heard Him cry out in frustration. Not in anger, but a plea filled with sorrow. Sorrow for us. Sorrow for Him and all that we are missing. I didn't know what to say. I was so stunned that I became speechless. After minutes of trying to compose myself, I asked, "Why are You telling me this, Lord?"

"Because they need to know, and as long as I have children willing to tell them, I will keep trying. They mean that much to Me," He answered with conviction.

"Why, Lord, why would we leave such a wonderful place as the Garden?" I asked. "Why would we leave You?"

"They did not know what they had. You know, the grass is greener thing," He said.

I began to cry. It was so painful to hear that we caused this and that it wasn't supposed to be like that. A scream came out from a place I did not know was in me. My heart ached, and I couldn't control the hurt anymore. I wanted my Father back, and I would do whatever was necessary to get back to the Garden.

I want a family reunion. I want all who are His to come running down that long, narrow, gravel drive that leads to our Father standing on the front porch where He has been waiting since we left the Garden. Oh, I can see Him hanging onto the porch post with such an anticipation of hope on His face. *Will this be the day they return?* He asks Himself with hesitation, because He has so many times been let down. Crushed. Could He bear to ask the question again? Will His heart take the possibility of rejection again?

I had to cry out, "Please, Lord, ask one more time. Don't give up on us. We are coming." I can see the porch screen door opening; the angels are hurtling out. They have heard the voices of the long-awaited children. All the prayers and times when the angels were posted over us were not in vain. "They are here," He says, "they are here. Get the best vegetables, the best to drink, and line them up. I want to hug every one of them. No child will go without knowing that their Father is glad to see them." The angels will begin to cheer. There will be a feast like never before.

"Oh, dear Jesus, I want a plate at my Father's table." I holler out, "Shotgun." I want the seat right beside my Father, just like the Beloved. I want to rest my head on His shoulder. Run; run through the tall, grassy meadow up to the warm, welcoming house. The land we left is dry and barren. Yes, green grass is leading to a Father who never gave up hope. His children will return. I want to be one who returns.

I sat in numbness, barely able to type what I had just experienced. How do I go on knowing what is waiting? I heard His sweet voice tell me, "That is how you can go on. Tell all who will listen that I have a place set for them."

I began to cry as He whispered that He loved me. My fingers could barely move. I was still in disbelief that He had allowed me to witness such a spectacular reunion. A table of hearts.

It was time for our story time to end for the day. But what I learned about God was that He is always up for a story. "Sweet dreams until tomorrow," I said as I blew Him a kiss. As I rolled over to drift off I realized the pillow in my vision at my feet was now cushioning my head. He is always there to call on. That would be comforting in the nights to come.

CHAPTER 2

The Candy Store

The body is a unit, though it is made up of many parts; and though all its parts are many, they form one body. So it is with Christ (1 Corinthians 12:12).

Late one evening, I heard Him whisper, "The chain. The chain is broken."

"What do you mean, Lord?" I asked as I turned around.

"Remember in the Garden where everyone played?" He asked.

"Yes Lord, I do," I answered.

"There was a family line, a chain, that was the lineage," He said. "Me, My children, and then more children came along. When peer pressure entered and sin came between us, the holy chain became broken between Me and My children. What was created to hold us together was now broken. This panicked some, and they tried to reconnect it themselves. What was meant for good had now been used by satan, therefore creating a chain of bondage. The chain could only be made whole again by the cross.

"But unfortunately, peer pressure still exists, and some do not know the news of the cross. Still others don't believe it. They are deceived. The enemy, My fallen child, knows that if they realize the family chain connects them to Me, he has no power over them anymore. He knows he is defeated, but as long as they don't know this or don't believe it, everything is good for him."

"What do we do?" I asked in horror.

"It is not what but who. Remember those plans I talked about?" He asked.

"Yes," I replied.

"If My children who know they are free will spend time with Me, then I can send them to the ones who are in bondage. The only way to share the news that the chain has been repaired is to send My protégés. I work with wood, clay, and machinery. I fix things with My hands. I need others to be My hands. But even some who are free will not come."

"Why, my Lord?" I asked in disbelief.

"Many reasons, Child," He began. "They forget their time in bondage, they are afraid they'll return to bondage, or they've lost their will to go. They become worn out because so few are willing to help. The field is ripe, but the workers are few."

"What do we do?" I asked again.

"Let Me tell you about a coin," He said. "There once was a woman who cleaned her house diligently searching for a coin."

I knew He must be speaking of the woman Luke had spoken of. "Yes," I answered. "Please go on."

"Did you notice she had a broom?" He asked.

I knew she had swept, so it would make sense for her to have a broom, so I answered again, "Yes."

He continued, "There was so much dust and cobwebs that she had to clean before she could see the floor well enough to know if the coin might be there or not. All the dust had to be cleaned away before she could see the Truth. I am the coin," the Lord said boldly.

"When I am visible, then we can move to the house. See, first the house is your body. Once you are clean, the coin can be seen by the next house, which is the immediate family, then the extended family."

"Are you talking about generation to generation?" I asked.

He answered, "Yes."

"What about generations that are missed?" I asked.

"We will get to them. I send My coins in to help bring them back," He said.

"Who?" I asked, puzzled.

"New coins. Not in a new child of Mine but in age; the younger ones," He replied. "It is My hope that the younger can influence the older. Have you heard of Timothy?" He asked.

"Yes," I relied. "He was young, but very faithful."

"Yes, faithful and a bright, young coin," He added. "If a generation is missed, I send in the next generation, hoping they will listen. I do not wish for any to be left behind," He added, "but some refuse to see."

He continued, "Back to the cleaning. Cleaning is a lot of work, but just as the woman had a reward, you will be rewarded too. Every family needs a coin. I need more coins. You asked what you can do. I need more coins—My children who reflect Me, My truth. I need ones who have accepted My Son as their Savior and desire to set the captives free, ones who love others more than themselves and will not settle for salvation alone, but want to be a line in the sand, standing in the gap for future generations. I need more coins," He repeated.

I want to be one, I thought, *but how could I?* It seemed like such a big job, a tall order to fill, one larger than myself.

"With Me, all things are possible," He said. "You would be amazed at what I can do with a willing heart. Take My hand," He said as He offered His hand and a purple, plastic bucket with gumdrops painted on the side.

"Where are we going?" I asked, taking the bucket in one hand and His in the other.

"To the candy store," He said as He took my hand and began to skip.

Taste and see that the Lord is good; blessed is the man who takes refuge in Him (Psalm 34:8).

The Candy Store

"The candy store?" I questioned, skipping alongside Him. I had loved chocolate as a child, but being an overweight little girl had taught me that candy was not my friend.

"The candy store we are going to has no calories, but twice the fun," He said, smiling.

As great as that sounded, I would have to see it to believe it. That is what He showed me as gumdrops began to fall from my bucket. Strategically they fell to the ground, providing us with a brightly colored, sugar-coated walkway. It led us through the most beautifully colored forest. Candy corn hung from red Twizzler trees, while lollipop suckers lined the path. I could hear birds singing and saw yellow butterflies fluttering about. The sun peaked through enough to give light for our feet, but not hot enough to melt the candy. As beautiful as it was, I was not tempted to eat from the trees or pick the flowers. The scene was too gorgeous to disrupt.

"That is the whole premise of the candy store," the Lord said. "That it is so beautiful, a feast to the eyes, that you would not have the heart to hinder or disturb its beauty."

"Ugh!" I screamed. "What is that?" Looking closer, I could see it was a black snake slithering around the patch of Sour Patch Kid candies. "What is that doing here?" I screamed.

"Stealing the beauty," the Lord answered.

I looked around the forest, now seeing it from a new perspective. What had been breathtaking was now tainted. "What happened?" I asked, shaken by the changed view.

"Purity has been darkened," He answered. "What was pleasant to the eyes is now distracted by ugliness."

"Why did I see it first ahead of the beauty?" I asked. "Why was it prominent? Why could I not block out the ugly and focus on the pleasant? Why is it, Lord, that the snake was out-staging the candy backdrop? Why do my eyes no longer see the beauty first? What is it about our eyes?"

"You see what your heart feels," He stated. "You are afraid of sin, of what may hurt you, so you keep your eyes on it at the risk of missing the beauty around it. That is what he is hoping for anyway. That, at the bare minimum, you will be distracted by him and not focus on Me."

He was so right. Looking around the forest, all I could see was this slimy, black snake—not the gumdrop path or the beautiful white house we were approaching. No, my eyes were on him. "Oh no," I said as I realized that meant my eyes were off of the Lord.

"How do we stop this madness?" I asked.

"Go to the candy store," He answered.

It seemed kind of strange, but He had not steered me wrong so far.

"Let me help you," He asked as He took my hand, helping me step over the snake.

Wow, that was painless and somewhat easy, I thought.

"Yes, your fear of him makes it harder than it has to be," He added.

"What will he do?" I asked as we walked farther from him.

"He waits for the unexpecting person, one who does not see the beauty in the candy and will do his dirty work. He wants to overtake the forest."

It was so horrible to see such an ugly creature slithering in such beautiful surroundings. It had spoiled the whole forest. My eyes no longer saw the beauty for the sight of the snake. I didn't want to see it anymore. I wanted to go back to the time before I saw the snake.

"Then come with Me," He said as He opened the big, red door to a house covered in white, snow-capped candy, trimmed in red-striped candy canes. Hanging over the door was a chocolate sign that read "The Candy Store." As we entered the room, I noticed that it made a complete circle. Lined around the wall was a continuous Plexiglas box divided to house what appeared to be hundreds of different candies. The view of the colors and the smells were breathtaking, except for in the middle.

"What is that smell?" I asked, covering my nose.

"A broken heart," He answered. "It has soured and grown bitter, smelling like soured slime."

I saw a vision of a woman. She had trash going in one ear and slime vomiting out of her mouth. Her tongue was coated in green and tears rolled down her flushed cheeks. Her eyes were closed tight.

"She had heard enough. She had listened with her ears to all the advice and direction from others. They had been *in her ear*, resulting in slime coming out of her mouth, when she should have listened to the words of *My* heart," the Lord said.

"Does this have anything to do with the snake outside?" I asked curiously.

"Oh, you know it does," He said sarcastically. "He uses tactics like shame, deception, and the twisting of My words. Well-wishing children, some of My own, take those words and advise My children."

"But they have a choice, right, Lord?" I asked.

"Yes, but what if they do not know better?" He asked.

"They come to You," I said, thinking that was the right answer.

"Yes, come to the candy store," He replied.

Still not sure what the big deal was about this place, I nodded in agreement.

Suddenly I heard the woman in my vision cry out, "Open the eyes and ears of the new heart you have given me."

I turned to see her face as she continued, "I'm asking You to rid my body of this slime and replace it with Your direction and Your Truth for me, not what I have taken in from the crowd."

"Look," I hollered as I pointed to her. The slime that had covered her tongue had turned into what resembled a blue raspberry slushy waterfall. In her hand she held a white, rock candy lollipop. The blue slushy cascaded down the rocks of the candy sucker. She smiled. The bitter, foul smell of a broken heart was replaced with a sweet berry smell healed by His wellspring.

"That is what is so special about this place," the Lord said with His chest out and a large grin on His face.

Standing in amazement, I turned to the Lord, asking, "What is this place?"

"The conditions of your heart," He answered. "A magical place where your eyes reveal what your heart sees. A place where I take a broken heart and replace it with the pleasures of calorieless candies. Come with Me. I've been waiting to show you the arena of delights here."

One by one, He opened the plastic lids of the containers, holding each type of candy.

"Shall we begin?" He asked, holding up the first plastic lid with His right hand while waving the left in front of the clear box like a game show host.

"The first you have already seen, the bitter or sour candy. It does what it wants, says what it wants, because it didn't get what it wanted. It hurts and needs my attention, but too often it has been wronged to the point of hardening. That brings us to the next container," He said, shutting the lid of the bitter candy while opening the next box.

"The next is the hardest to work with, like the Jolly Rancher hard candy. It is solid all the way through because hurt has hardened it."

Closing the hard candy box, He paused to smile before moving to the next one. "Candy hearts," He said happily. "They dissolve easier. They say nice things," He said, holding one up with *I love you* printed in red across the pink heart. "People love to see them and love to get them because they are appealing. They make you smile.

"Next are the Bananas Fosters," He said proudly. "They are squishy on the inside once you break the thin crunch, they are burnt but retrievable. Life has not hardened them to the point of Jolly Rancher yet.

"Then, there are taffy bars. They are fun and everyone wants to join in. But they are deceiving; once invited, they stick to you. They join the party and then won't let you go.

"Bubble gum pieces are the smackers, the loose lips of the bunch. They love juicy gossip and aren't ashamed to tell what they think they heard.

"Here are the pixy sticks. These have been ground up by gossip, naysayers, and slander until their personalities are dry. I feel sorry for them because they have so much to offer. Their taste pleases others, but they have let what others have said sour their personalities. It really is a shame.

"This one is very special," He said as He opened its lid.

I leaned over to see what made this one so special. "Is it the ice cream that fell off the cone?" I asked curiously.

"Yes," He said. "A broken heart makes you want to cry, similar to the sadness a small child feels as he or she stands watching it melt on the ground. People can run to your side, but nothing makes the child feel better until a new cone with a fresh scoop is presented. Have you heard the advertisements for new and improved products?"

"Yes," I answered.

"They took the old products and made them better, fresher," He continued. "Like my children and their new cones, they are better because they know how to hold the cone now. You are more aware, more cautious—not paranoid. You take better care. You still eat the ice cream, just not as quickly or carelessly. When you know it can break, you are more careful about who you give it to. It doesn't mean you stop eating ice cream; you're just gentler."

I like that, I thought. *Just because one ice cream scoop falls out of the cone doesn't mean we should give up eating ice cream altogether.*

"Yes, you've got it," He cheered.

"Is there more?" I asked, looking around the room.

"Yes," He answered, opening the next box.

"Wait," I said, "those are the hard candies again. Why do you have two boxes of them?"

"Look closely," He said, "there is a difference."

Bending over, I could see that each piece was shattered within but still held together as a whole piece.

"They are crushed inside," He said. "They gave love one more try, but were crushed."

"That's horrible," I said.

"Yes, they put themselves out there one more time and someone stepped on them—again. Now they hang on hoping they can hold themselves together, but one bump, and the pieces will give way."

"Da-tah-da!"

"What was that?" I asked.

"It is I, the Holy Spirit."

"Allow Me to introduce you to the Holy Spirit," the Lord said, grinning ear to ear.

"Nice to meet You," I said.

He was dressed in a superhero outfit, cape and all. "How do you do?" He replied.

"Very well, thank You," I answered.

"This is my specialty," the Lord began, still grinning. "For those crushed pieces, I have a Son who knows just what to do with each broken sliver."

"If Your Son puts the pieces back together, then what does the Holy Spirit do? No disrespect," I said, addressing Him.

"The Holy Spirit gives you hope," He answered. "We are a team, each having our own roles in the Candy Shop, but neither being of any less of importance. Just like My Body. We don't compete, we support. We don't fuss, we love. And most of all, we don't undermine, we encourage. That is how it is supposed to be."

"How do we get back to that?" I asked.

"Join our team," He said.

"Da-tah-da," the Holy Spirit sang as He held up a blue and white jersey with the number 1 printed on the front and my name printed on the back.

"Why number one?" I asked curiously.

"Because I would leave ninety-nine to go find just one of My lost children," He said.

"Oh, how sweet," I said.

With a faint hint of blushing, He replied, "All of My children wear the number one. There is no favoritism."

"I love this place. Is there more?" I asked.

"Do you remember the time when you where a child and you slipped on the ice and fell down, crushing the bubble gum in your back pocket?" He asked.

"Yes," I replied. *That was such a long time ago,* I thought to myself.

"You thought you had to throw the chocolate bar away, but not here. We could have made it even better," He chuckled. "Like those television shows where they rebuild people to be faster, stronger, and able to leap tall buildings." His enunciation, like that of a sports show commentator, made me laugh too.

"And the reason why we would not throw it away is…"

…He has sent Me to bind up the brokenhearted, to proclaim freedom for the captives and release from darkness for the prisoners (Isaiah 61:1).

MOSAIC

I heard a drum roll.

"A mosaic. It looks like a jar of jelly beans—smooth, bright colors all nestled together. That is what My Son can do with crushed, hard candy, smooshed chocolate, or dropped ice cream. It is quite the piece of artwork, if you ask Me. There are many colors represented by My Body, all working together, playing off of each other's strengths and lifting each other's weaknesses. Yes, a magnificent piece."

"This is fun," I hollered with glee.

"Just like our next candy," He said, running over to another bin, taking out a plastic, slender holder, and tipping the top open to reveal Pez candy.

"Hee hee," I giggled.

"Yes, they make you laugh. They are fun. A heart that is fun is a treasure," He said.

"Come on," He said excitedly, "there are more." The next container held candy dots. "They come in a sheet, just asking you to share them."

"There are so many different candies," I said.

"Yes, My children can have many different hearts at the same time. But there is no combination that I cannot, no, *we* cannot heal. Oh, Child, I want My children to get this. There is hope, love, and repair.

"Then," He began, speaking with a loss of excitement, "there are the Sour Patch Kids candies."

"You didn't open a container this time."

"No," He replied sadly. "They are confused, not knowing whether to be sweet or sour. That is why they are still outside."

"I remember passing them on the path by the snake. What do you do, Lord?" I asked, feeling sad, too.

"I keep returning to the path, praying they will take Me up on My offer—the same one I gave to you, *to visit the Candy Store.*

"And when they do," He said excitedly again, "we open the Pop Rocks container. Yee ha!" He hollered. "It's a party in your mouth. We can have so much fun together even when we have to step over the snake. Do you know that I place My foot on his neck to hold him down when you need to pass by?" He asked.

"No, Lord, I didn't, but what happens when things seem not so pleasant and we get bitten?"

"Oh, sifting," He said, nodding His head.

Then I saw a wire sieve with a wooden handle. The flour in the sieve was being sifted delicately while being gently shuffled from one side to the other, then cascading into the bowl below. The bowl was no ordinary kitchen vessel, but His hand cupped, ready and waiting to caress the fallen flour.

"Sifting is a good thing," He continued. "The snake has to ask Me, and if I bid him the opportunity to bite you, it is to make you more resistant. When you have been bitten, your immune system is strengthened."

"No, no, let me, let me," the Holy Spirit interrupted with excitement.

"Go ahead," the Lord said, laughing.

"You get mighty people of God," He said, clapping and dancing around.

"I love that," I said while joining Him dancing. I felt like Pop Rocks candy myself.

We danced and clapped until we were exhausted. It was fun. Hearts mended could dance and cheer, I knew, because I was doing it.

"Come back outside with Me," the Lord said.

Why? I thought, *We are having such a good time in here.*

"I want to show you the ones who are lost," He said.

Our mood changed as we stepped back onto the gumdrop-lined path.

"Did you see the sticker bush hidden in the gumdrop patch?" He asked, pointing to the side of the house.

I had not noticed it because of the beautiful colors of the candy that sat in front of it. "Those hearts are afraid, so they hide behind and wish they could go in. The saddest part...they could come in, but they stay outside because of their fear. I don't give you candy of fear. Being afraid grows into fear; and like slime, it covers and coats you and gets in your eyes. It is hard to wash off; and if others get too close, it can get on them too. Go back into the Candy Store. That is the answer. Use fear as a detector to know when you need to come back in, not a condemnation to stay out."

The thought of people missing out on the fun inside the Candy Shop made me sad.

"Sad are the ones who don't have any candy," He added. "Those are the ones who have melted away."

"What can You do?" I asked.

"Let me, let me," the Holy Spirit asked, jumping up and down.

"OK," the Lord said, chuckling.

"We have X-ray vision. We can see even the smallest speck of candy. We can make you whole again. A little healing here and there and voila, a brand-new, shiny piece of candy," the Holy Spirit said smiling.

"You do bring such hope," I said.

"Thank you," He replied.

"I don't like it out here," I said.

"I don't want them to be out here. There is more than enough to share inside," the Lord replied. "Which brings Me to the Garbage Pail Kids candy," He said, taking my hand and walking me to the end of the path.

"See them?" He asked, pointing to the ground. "A jealous heart is like the spoiled child who wants all the candy in the store, but doesn't need it, just doesn't want anyone else to have it. They frustrate Me," the Lord said. "They start at the beginning of the path, spewing discord into My children's hearts. My prayer is that they will see Me waiting on the front porch and that they would be willing to come in. These are my children in need of discipline. I hate to do it, but a good parent knows that the way to teach includes correction. Oh, if they would just come in themselves, they would see there is no need for jealousy. I have more than enough."

"Why don't they give You a chance?" I questioned.

"They are often the products of nervous hearts. They have tried to open a package of candy. You know the ones with the pre-cut slit? Well, it didn't work and it spilled all over them, embarrassing them. Or maybe it got on the counter, causing someone else to get angry. Whatever the case may have been, they are nervous to try another package.

"That leaves Me with the wrappers, the ones I often find wadded up in the trash or tossed off on the side of the road. Those are the hearts that need CPR. If they will let Me, I will breathe new life into their numb hearts. I love them that much. I will not rest until I have combed every inch of this world looking for them, hoping that when I find them, they will give Me that chance.

"Our trip to the candy store has come to an end," He said, "but the store is always open. It is never too late or too early to bring your heart, no matter what combination you have. I love you, Child."

"I love You, too," I said.

"Until tomorrow, My precious one, sweet dreams," He whispered softly.

I found it comforting, yet optimistic to believe that I would have sweet dreams. See, bedtime had always been a scary time for me. It was a gamble if I would actually have sweet dreams or even sleep, for that matter. It was not unusual for me to wake up in a panic sometime between 2:00 and 3:00 A.M. Over the years, I had learned to talk myself down from it, praying one day that it would end. But I was willing to give those sweet dreams a try tonight.

"Good night, Father," I said as I hurried off to bed.

He said: "In my distress I called to the LORD, and He answered me. From the depths of the grave I called for help, and You listened to my cry (Jonah 2:2).

CHAPTER 3

A New Day

*See, I am doing a new thing! Now it springs up; do
you not perceive it? I am making a way in the desert
and streams in the wasteland* (Isaiah 43:19).

It had been a repeat of so many nights before. Go to bed optimistic, but wake to a heartbeat that was skyrocketing. Having
my husband beside me gives great comfort. But it would be nicer
to have it all stop. However, for now, I will hold onto his arm and
calm down until I fall back to sleep.

Mornings always seemed to come too early, and this one
was no different. I got up and began my morning routine: coffee
and cereal while I watched *Saved by the Bell* with my husband.
Hey, no laughing, it is clean and funny in a simple way. Shortly,
he showers, dresses, and heads off to work—and I retreat to the
Secret Place. I needed time with God more than normal today.
Last night's "upset" still had me a little shaken, and I needed His
comfort. Just as He is great with bedtime stories, He is equally as
wonderful with *get you going stories*. I wish I had done that with
my child, started her off more often with an encouraging parable.

As the sun rose, I found myself in the presence of the Lord.
"Good morning, my Lord," I said, with sleepy eyes and coffee
in hand. I began our conversation with a question. "What do my
dreams say about me?" I asked. He had mentioned that very question in an earlier prayer time. I found the question intriguing and
asked Him to elaborate. I loved learning why I do the things I do
and felt this might shed more light on that subject. When I did

not get a reply, I continued our prayer time with other topics. But now it had resurfaced in my mind due to another sleepless night.

"I feel very overwhelmed today, but I will keep doing what I know to do. What is out of balance, Lord?"

I often do this: ask another question before I give Him a chance to answer the first.

"Your heart is hurt by things and weighed down," He replied.

"What do I do?" I asked out of desperation.

"Let Me have it," He said with confidence.

"Lord, I hand You my heart," I replied, motioning my hand to the air. I believe He is sitting with me in our Secret Place, so I find myself interacting with Him.

"The antidote for a heavy heart is joy. I will bring you to joy. I will be gentle but stern. Thank you for trusting your heart in My hands," He said.

I felt safe in that moment. Where or what was going to happen, I had no idea. But I had tried so many things, and I wasn't getting anywhere. I needed Him to work. I needed Him to be all that I had preached, shared, and thought to myself. I needed Him to be my all in all.

"Dreams tell you where you have been or where you are going," He said.

"I didn't know what was happening. I didn't understand," I admitted.

"I know, My child," He comforted.

"What do I do? It makes me panic now. I don't know what is going on."

"That is *your panic.* You are worried and frightened," He added.

"Will You please reveal what is necessary to stop this panic? I don't feel well today. I feel overwhelmed and tired."

I waited but heard no answers.

"Why don't I hear, Lord? Why, Lord, do sometimes I wait, yet hear nothing?" I asked.

"Your ears are clogged. My children often don't really want to know, or their motives are not pure…and sometimes it is not the right timing. Or maybe," He added, "I just want to be with you. Sometimes I just like having time together with no pressing interest, just Me and My child enjoying each other's presence. It can be so sweet."

But then, He added, "It is never because I am not there. Do not take it personally if I do not answer right away. It may not be any of your business, I may not be ready yet, or you may not be ready. It is all in the timing."

"Is there anything else, Lord?"

"Nope, it is that simple."

AND AGAIN…

In the second year of his reign, Nebuchadnezzar had dreams; his mind was troubled and he could not sleep (Daniel 2:1).

"My night was bad again. I have about lost hope. Please free me of this panic!" I begged.

"I had a mighty ruler," He started. "Night after night, he was tormented by his past. He had seen some horrible things as a child, many he did not understand. That is where I came in. The sins of his father had been passed down by way of his eyes. He had seen things. Now when he slept, they replayed in his head. His father lost it all, and now what he feared was coming upon him. Often we must lose everything to gain. He needed cleansing."

"Lord," I replied. "Why in our dreams?"

"Because it is there when you are most vulnerable. Your guards come down, and truth, or at least what you believe is the truth, can rise to the surface. It catches you off-guard. That is the panic."

"What do I do?" I asked.

"Let it rise," He stated. "Nebuchadnezzar sought meaning for his torment. He looked in all the wrong places and suffered worse. Bring it to Me. Bring it to my coins."

"I need to," I replied.

"No, you need *Me* to tell you the truth. Your mind thinks what you are dreaming is true, and it is to you; but I, being the *real* truth, don't torment—you are being deceived by false truth."

"Lord, I'm so tired. Night after night, no sleep. It wears me down."

"What goes in must come out. Mediate on that which is good, pure, and lovely," He said.

"What about the past?" I asked.

"We will get to that," He answered. "Now who is getting ahead?" He asked with a grin.

"So what it is about the future I will know from my dreams? What to do or not to do? A kind of head's up?" I asked.

"Yes, you got it!" He said.

"Lord, I will go through this for You." I said this to make myself feel better and give the pain some purpose.

I thought to myself about how often I had prayed to be like Daniel and to dream great dreams that I would then interpret. I had never given Nebuchadnezzar a second thought. He was one I would help, not one I would relate to or be like.

I heard Him reply, not in a mean tone, but to remind me that He could hear what I thought. He began by saying with a sympathetic voice, "Don't disregard those in My Word who appear to have done the wrong things. Are you not able to learn from them too?" He asked. "Besides, you do not always know the whole story. They may have gotten it right the next time," He added.

This made me think of so many of the great ones to whom God had given second chances. I was grateful for their stories as well. I was also grateful that He still gives second chances today. I knew this to be true because He had given me some.

"Thank You, Lord. I needed that, and I pray to appreciate their sacrifices." I felt I needed to repent of my judgment of them. So, I did.

Lord, I ask Your forgiveness. They are Your children. To speak against them is to speak against You. Forgive me, Lord. For it wasn't until I have fallen desperate to my dreams that I paid attention to Nebuchadnezzar. I had always focused on Daniel. Thank You that I can come to You, knowing You are both a gracious and forgiving God. In Jesus' name, amen.

"Yes, you are right. They are both my children," He said. "One means as much to me as the other. Both need different things from Me, just like all parents even today love each child, but in unique ways that highlight their gifts. A good parent recognizes the gifts and needs of the child individually and prays to encourage. I made you all individuals, no cookie cutter children here, so why would it be OK to treat them as such—"

I had to stop Him mid-sentence. "I am overwhelmed," I said with a shaky voice.

"I know you are," He said comfortingly. "I will not tell you more than you can handle. But you are ready. I have prepared you for such a day," He said with a glow. "Yes, you are ready."

"You obviously have more confidence in me than I do in myself," I said with a nervous laugh.

He chuckled, asking, "Do you know how many times I have heard that? Oh, you should have heard Moses! He was the worst, not in a discrediting way. He meant it in a way showing he needed Me. He continually tried to convince Me that he was not ready." He laughed as He said, "But I knew better."

I got up from my desk chair, fell onto the bed, and began to sob, asking, "Are You sure?" I must have appeared weak or even as a baby, but at this moment I was confused. I mean, here I was writing as fast as I could the words that *God*—not a neighbor or someone behind a pulpit—was saying, and He tells me I'm ready.

"Ready for what, Lord?"

"Oh My child, do you remember Abraham? I told him to go before I told him the details. Did you hear Daniel say, 'I am the writer of mysteries'? We are going on a trip together, dear child. Our journey will have all the great components of a best-seller: mystery, love, comedy, and a few thrills that will put *Transformers* to shame." He must have thought that humorous from His chuckle.

"But Lord, what about the dreams?" I asked, as if to get us back on track.

"Relax, you are going to miss the comedy. Don't be so serious that you don't have any fun. Isn't that why you go on a journey in the first place?" He asked. "We will get to the dreams. They will be revealed. I will trade the pain of the past with real dreams for your future. You will see the plans that I have for you and live them out—and part of that plan is to hear you laugh."

I flashed back to a time when I was sitting with my earthly father. It was a cool day in the South; I could see the garden that he planted every year. He was very good at that gardening thing. Me, I have no green on this thumb. My dad and I sat on the steps to his "building"; that is what we Southerners call sheds that house lawnmowers and in daddy's case, every tool you could possibly need. As we sat there, he told me that he loved to hear me laugh. It made him smile. In retrospect, that was a very special moment, just like hearing my heavenly Father say it today. So, laugher it shall be. *But wait a minute,* I thought, *some things are not funny.*

"Oh my goodness," He said, jumping into my thought. "There is more in life to laugh about—if you don't take everything so seriously. If you laugh more, you can handle the seriousness better. Dear child, just follow My lead. You will know by My tone," He assured.

OK, I can do that, I thought.

"Now, darling, pack your bags. We are going on a journey," He said with excitement.

I sat back and reflected on what He had said today. I was ready. A miracle had happened as He spoke. All I could say was, "Let's go!" *My Lord had offered me a trip, a journey, and I wasn't going to pass up that opportunity, even if that meant going with butterflies in my stomach and a lump in my throat.*

"You can bring them, too," He chuckled.

I laughed too.

"What shall I bring?" I asked.

"You," He answered.

"I meant, what shall I pack?" rephrasing, like He might have misunderstood me.

"We are going to go light," He said. "With the cost of baggage these days, I recommend going light."

I found that funny coming from Him. I mean, He is God. But I guess He would know. "Ha ha, OK then, what is light?" It made me think: *His yoke is light; and when the apostles went out to disciple, He told them, too, to pack light. Maybe there was something to this thing we have with carrying so much stuff. Is a heavenly strength to be light?* I wondered.

I was curious because some might say my packing was not technically light. I could tell I was beginning to rattle on in my mind and that He was ready to answer me. I turned my attention back to Him.

"What was the question again?" He asked with a puzzled look on His face.

We both laughed. I had gone on so long that we had lost track of the question. I repeated, "What is *light* when packing?"

"Need-to-know basis," He said. "We are going to many places with many different requirements, just like My children are unique, so will the things you need be for each place. So each time, I will let you know. I never send My children out unprepared."

A little confused, I asked, "But what about places I have been to that blindsided me?"

The Lord quickly said, "I did not send you there."

"Then who did?" I asked

"Often My children go without asking, or they decide on their own, or unfortunately they allow another to lead them. Whatever way, I am usually blamed if things don't turn out the way they expected."

That seemed so sad, but so true. "Lord," I said, "I am sorry." I knew I had been one of those who blamed Him.

"You are forgiven. Know better in the future," was all He said.

"It's a deal," I said as we shook on it.

"Love you."

"Me too," I answered and smiled.

-CHAPTER 4-

The Rain

"For I know the plans I have for you," declares the
LORD, *"plans to prosper you and not to harm you,
plans to give you hope and a future* (Jeremiah 29:11).

I felt the mood change in the air. Neither He nor I were joking anymore. This was serious, and we both knew it. He began, "It is like the rain. I created rain and the very ground it falls to, but many factors influence where it lands. Wind, trees, and the birds all may alter its course. It is the same with My children. I created you, and you are to land on the ground, but many people may interfere with your course. Your course was interfered with. It broke my heart."

I could tell He meant it, but I had so many questions going through my mind, like, "Why didn't You stop the person? Why not just place me on the ground? Why not stop the interference?"

I heard Him softly answer, "Free will." It almost sounded as if He was sad it even existed. I knew I was.

It was raining the morning He spoke this analogy to me. It may sound silly, but I felt sorry for the drops of rain as they fell to the ground. I had such a greater appreciation for the drops that made it to their intended destination.

"You are getting it," I heard Him say.

"Getting what?" I asked.

"Understanding," He said.

"It may seem foolish, but understanding of what?" I asked.

"Appreciation for the ones who make it, who endured; endurance my child," He said.

I said with great conviction and almost without forethought, "I want to be one who makes it! I want to make it to the place You want me to land—no matter the interference attempts that try to block my path. I want to make it."

I heard Him clap. He was proud; I could see it in His smile.

Smiling too, I remembered how I wanted to see His face. Almost as that thought came, I thought, *I can't wait to see it in His eyes.*

With a crooked smile and the shaking of His head, He said, "Never satisfied."

My eyes got big and an, "Oops," slipped out of my mouth.

Then I heard, "I like that. As long as it is for Me. Worldly things, not so much, but for Me, keep it coming."

"Whoa," I said.

Before I could get my question out, He said, "I know the slang, like the saying, "Not so much," people say today. Remember, I am past, present, and future. I know My audience because I created them."

I thought, *That is so cool.*

He continued, "I know what will be *hip* before you do." He seemed quite proud of Himself and honestly, I was too. In that moment my love and respect for Him grew. I felt as if a flower was blossoming within me. I was closer to the ground. What had started as a panic-ridden morning had now become a calm, hopeful day. He really does change our tears to laughter.

The rain was coming down harder now, I noticed.

"Do you see all the drops?" He asked.

"Yes," I answered.

Boldly He said, "My Body interferes with my children."

I looked closer at the rain as it was coming down; the drops were running into each other, knocking them off their paths.

DAMASCUS

Your word is a lamp to my feet and a light for my path (Psalm 119:105).

"Put on your gladiator sandals; the pavement we are going to travel on is going to get hot. We are going to the road to Damascus."

Excitedly, I asked, "To see Paul?"

"I wasn't so excited with him at first," He admitted. "He was so busy with everyone else's path that I couldn't get him to stay on his until…"

I heard a drum roll in the distance.

"…the road to Damascus." The surface was a gray-tan cobblestone visibly rough in construction, but smooth on the edges, winding on and on into the distance. I fell to my knees. I had always known, if given the chance to stand on the road to Damascus, I would be overtaken by one of the greatest changes or transformations in history. The magnitude of it put me on my knees—not for the one who walked, it but for the One who changed him. I wanted that transformation. "Change me, Lord," I cried out, "change me."

"Pick up your cross and let's walk," the Lord spoke with such authority.

To speak with such confidence, I wanted that too. If it had to do with Him, I wanted it. That, I had settled in my mind, often saying, "When I get to Heaven and there is a basket sitting beside my Lord, I want it to be empty because I had received all and done everything He had prepared for me on earth. Let there be nothing left in my basket."

"Paul," the Lord said, "please come here."

The man was tall, but I believe it was due more to his demeanor than his height. He carried himself well, but came across as a little self-righteous. His countenance was stern, his stride controlled, almost arrogant. I thought this not in judgment, but shock. This was Paul, who had called out the followers of Christ before me with an air of cockiness. How could such a man of God be so forthright? His hair was light brown and his eyes a deep blue. There it was… in his eyes, there was the humility I had missed. It was in his eyes. Had I mislabeled him? Was his stern approach a mask for his own insecurities? Could such a man of God even have insecurities?

"Give him time. He will grow on you," the Lord said, nudging my side. "Let me just say," the Lord resumed, "he wasn't too happy having to travel, but even he could be persuaded."

"Wait a minute…timeout. I have a question," I said, waving my arms.

"You said you couldn't keep him on the path. You are God. You can do anything."

"Anything except interfere with free will," He said, stomping His feet. "Do you remember Jonah and the whale?" He asked.

Paul and I answered yes to His question at the same time.

"I aligned circumstances and situations so that Jonah could go to Nineveh to share My love with the people there. But although he initially chose other than My plan, even as he stepped over the anterior, mandibular incisors of the whale, I was with Him. See, your dental education didn't go to waste," He said with a sparkle in His eye.

I had been in the dental field for years, and then God called me to write. My husband and I had been concerned about all the time and money we had put into my dental career and wondered if it had been wasted. This showed me that every step in life can be applied when journeying with God.

"Oh!" He laughed, like He'd made the joke of the year.

I had to admit that it was funny.

"Oh my goodness," I said, "You are crazy funny."

"I know," He agreed, laughing even more.

"Oh, OK, Jonah's in the whale's mouth. Now who is rattling on?" I asked jokingly.

"Oh, yeah. Jonah could have said no and turned around and hauled himself back home, but he didn't. Just like the transformation moment of Saul-turned to-Paul, he realized that he had to do the right thing. I like to refer to those times as their Damascus Road experiences." He laughed again as I shook my head and grinned ear to ear.

"You weren't finished, were you?" He asked while looking at Paul.

"No. No sir," Paul answered with respect.

"Paul, do you remember when you would get in trouble as a child and your parents would call you by your first *and* middle names?"

"That is so funny," I said.

"Yes, maybe to you...you weren't the one in trouble," Paul said bluntly.

The laughter quickly turned to *oh no*. It was serious.

The Lord said, "No, but the world used my name in vain. Your name was being used for correction, when Mine is being used..."

I had to swallow hard; I was scared. He was more serious in His tone than I had previously ever heard.

"...it is out of hatefulness and stupidity," He continued. "That fear you have right now," He said.

I wasn't aware He even noticed the fear I was feeling, because He was so involved in His message.

"Yes," I said with wide eyes and short breath.

"That is good," He said.

I breathed a sigh and said, "Whew," like I had dodged a bullet.

"No," He said, "not a fear of 'dodging a bullet,' but a fear of respect. The others have to have respect too, for their Damascus day is coming. I love My children too much to leave them on the wrong road. I just hope they choose as wisely as Paul did."

I saw Paul breathe a sigh of relief as well.

I could have cut the tension in the room with a knife. I like the God who just a few minutes ago couldn't compose Himself from laughter way better than this serious one. I felt small beside Him.

"It is not to belittle you, My child, but to remind you that I am God. But there is hope even for the rain drops that are in the way. Even the hardest, most interfering rain drops can become soft and helpful, like Paul. When they know from which cloud they have come, they can help other drops in their quest to endure to the ground."

I saw drops, one after another, fall from His hand, bumping into other drops as they made their way to the ground. "It is similar to bumper cars. Do you like bumper cars?" He asked.

"Oh yes." I had fond memories of my husband, daughter, and son-in-law riding together at the amusement park.

"That is how it can be: laughter, accomplishment, and endurance. As the cars go around, one bumps into another, causing the other car to slide across the way."

"But what about the ones that get stuck?" I asked.

"Send me another car," I heard Him shout. I saw a yellow car come from around the corner. There was laughter. They hit. All three went their separate ways, but as they slid off, the laughter continued to echo.

"Lord, there is a lot of laughter," I noticed.

"I wish it so," He replied.

"Joy and laughter. My Body needs to laugh," He said.

"Why aren't they laughing?" I asked.

"Because they are too angry, so they get stuck. Let each other bump you out of the collision," He said.

"But what if they were hurt? What if they met Saul before he was Paul?" I asked.

"Good question. It has a one-word answer: grace. All were Sauls before they were Pauls. All were drops that hindered when they should have helped. Plank or toothpick...which is in your eye?" He questioned, raising His right eyebrow.

I was sure now. Just as God had said, Paul had grown on me. It was not arrogance that I saw in him. It was reverence. His love, respect, and gratitude were worn on his exterior like a fine-tailored suit. The remembrance of Damascus Road made him uncomfortable, not because he wasn't forgiven, but because he wished he'd not been that other man—the man who didn't know Jesus as his Savior.

I could relate. I had done things in my past that I'd rather not revisit, but like Paul, I would go there again if it helped a brother or sister in Christ. That was the humility in his eyes, the willingness to go for another because of what his Father had done for him. He had grown on me like my Father had said.

"Don't judge a book by its cover," the Lord whispered to me.

"Paul," I began as I looked into his eyes, "I'm sorry for my assumptions."

Humbly, he bent down and kissed my check. "My Father gave me more chances than I deserved. Who am I not to extend that same love to a member of His Body?"

I will never forget how graceful he looked as he turned to walk away down Damascus Road. There goes a true example of God's grace. He was living out his transformation. *What a class act,* I thought.

The Lord and I just sat there along the road. I could sense He was still fuming over the name-calling. I took a double take to make sure what I was seeing was true. There was a single tear running down His face. He was hurt.

"Oh, my Lord, we have hurt Your feelings."

"No child, My heart. Each one has a piece of Me, so I hurt when they blaspheme Me. Oh, it makes the memories of the Garden come forth. Oh, how I wish we were back there. That is where My endurance comes from—the thought of getting everyone back."

"I don't know what to say. I am sorry. What can I do?"

"You are doing it. Just keep writing."

"I love You so much, and I am sorry for all the times I have hurt You." My words didn't seem enough to me. My heart ached for the both of us. At that moment, I decided that with His care I needed to endure. I loved Him too much not to.

The room was somber, but I could tell plans were being made. Another trip was on the way, but I needed to sit on this one for a while. I wanted to remember how much I loved Him at this moment and that He hurts too. I want to know Him personally. I want to know what makes Him laugh, sad, proud, and happy. I wasn't going to waste this opportunity. He obviously had things to say, and I was going to write.

"I love You, Lord," I said as we hugged. I could sense His comforting nature in our embrace. We both needed each other. Although He is God, He wants and desires His children. I felt that. Before I left, I prayed.

Dear Lord, it breaks my heart that You have been hurt. I pray no more! No more name calling. I pray we wake up and see what we are doing. No more excuses!

I couldn't continue. The emotion was still too fresh. My Lord was hurt. This wasn't something I could just run through. I needed to chew on this for a while.

Lord, as the days follow, create an awareness of where I have and do hurt You. Forgive me, Lord, amen.

Respect; He deserved it, and I wanted to give it to Him. Not because I had to, but because I wanted to—and not because He said to, but because I love Him.

I had to go about my day, but I would take what I had learned with me. It was part of me now.

-CHAPTER 5-

Technology

See, I am doing a new thing! Now it springs up; do you not perceive it? I am making a way in the desert and streams in the wasteland (Isaiah 43:19).

"Here I go, writing on my laptop computer," I said.

Before I could get the words written, I heard Him say, "No, here *we* go."

I am almost in tears before we even start, for many reasons. It was another night woken by a racing heart that led to a conversation with myself until eventually dozing off. And to top it off, He wants me to change from writing in my journal to typing on my laptop. I can honestly say that I am not a big fan of some new technology, but my problem with this way of writing is that it seems so impersonal. I miss my paper journaling.

"Child, you remind Me of Abraham," He began. "I asked him to leave all he knew. He too was unsettled."

"I'm afraid I'm going to miss You by using this computer," I said.

"Oh Child, he was afraid he had missed Me, too. Think about what I had asked of him, 'Pick up and go.' 'Where?' he asked. My reply was, 'I will tell you when you get there.'"

"Not much to go off of," I said as I thought about how I had heard something similar from Him a little over eight years before. I was content living in a house located in the same neighborhood where I had grown up.

In mid-thought, He interjected, "Same."

I had an idea what He was alluding to, but I wanted to make sure from His own words.

"What do you mean about 'same'?" I asked.

"It is like this laptop," He began. "It is different and therefore will require change. My children do not like change. Oh, they cry out for things to be better, but that will mean change. You can't stay in a bad situation and expect it to get better without some form of change. It will be better in the long run, but you have to trust that I am right and that it will be worth it," He said. "Abraham moving from all that he knew gave him the opportunity for life to turn out better, wouldn't you say?"

"I have to agree," I said. "I mean, his bloodline reigns supreme."

"Just as I asked Abraham," the Lord began, "are you willing?"

"Yes Lord, I will," I replied.

"Now, what about this conversation last night?" He asked.

"Upon waking, I thought about King Nebuchadnezzar," I began to explain. "You had mentioned him yesterday. I wondered how he handled his nightly torment. I find great comfort in the touch of my husband's leg. That seems to be the first thing I do… reach for his leg. It is calming to know he is within reach. I wondered was there a Mrs. Nebuchadnezzar, and did he find solace in her touch? Or maybe he had a royal servant who stood in the hall guarding the door. If so, did he call for him? I had hopes for him. I wouldn't want anyone to suffer alone. My heart is heavy for him and myself—not in a pity way, but a *will this ever end* way."

As I am writing, I wait for the Lord to interject, not hearing anything other than my air conditioner kick on. *This is not normal,* I thought. "Lord, where are You?" I asked.

"Child, I am broken that you or any of My children ever feel they are alone," He said.

"Lord, I am broken that we feel that way," I replied. "What do we do? Was Nebuchadnezzar afraid to go to sleep," I asked, "because I am?"

"Turn with Me to Hebrews," He said. "We started to take a look there yesterday, but as friends do, we got sidetracked when engaging in conversation. I like that," He interjected, "that we are becoming so close we drift off into many areas to discuss, not caring where we end."

Smiling, I agreed and reached for my Bible as I held back the tears. I could understand why Nebuchadnezzar began to search for any and everyone to get an answer to his torment. Someone to explain; no, better yet, someone to make the suffering stop. At some point it became too much to tolerate any longer. A good night's sleep. Was that too much to ask for? I mean, he was king. If there was anyone in that town who had the resources, it was him. "Then why couldn't he make it stop?" I asked.

"Honey," I heard Him repeat, "the faith chapter."

"Yes, Father," I answered.

As I turned to Hebrews 11, I heard Him whisper, "All of them had something they wanted to stop. David wanted the giant to stop; Joseph wanted the lies to stop; and Abraham wanted his children's unwise behavior to stop. All had pleas and cried out to Me. All had sleepless nights," He concluded.

"I had never looked at what might have kept them awake, only what they had accomplished during the day," I said.

"It takes both day and night before Me for things to actually stop."

"Are You saying that we are to be before Your face 24/7?" I asked.

"No," He chuckled. "Not necessarily, but those who over-came their torment kept their eyes on Me," He said. "They knew where to stay—under My wing. You cannot soar to the heights I have set for you without the undercurrent of My wing span. Stay in My flow," He added, chuckling to Himself.

I joined in. True His words were, but His arrangement of the words was funny.

HEBREWS 11

"Good morning, Lord," I began as I normally did. I have to admit I have put off and honestly avoided our time this morning.

"That is OK, at least you came," He replied.

"It seems all I want to do is cry when I sit down with You lately," I admitted.

"Honey, it is a season," He said. "We all have them. It is here that the fire comes and the strong survive. I don't mean the strong in physical strength or like the world views strength...I mean heavenly strength," He said.

"Please describe that strength to me, Lord," I asked. "I want to know what I am striving to look like."

"Oh, My child," He began, "you are strong. I view all of My children as strong. The problem comes because they don't see what I see. I know their potential; they don't. If I could just get them to see My Son in them," He said.

"What about the transformation that takes place?" I questioned.

"That is for you to accomplish," He stated. "I know the whole story. I have the bird's-eye view. It is you who needs to see the transformation as it happens—all in good time, My time. Although some would like it to happen instantaneously," He said in a matter-of-fact tone.

"I would be one of them," I said admittedly.

I heard Him giggle, "Hee hee.

"Everything works together in a designed order," He said. "Allow Me to show you."

"I know," I said, "Hebrews 11."

"Yes," He replied. "Can we get there today?" He asked, grinning.

This time the *hee hee* came from me. As quickly as the laughter came, the tears began to well up in my eyes. "Lord, I was up again last night," I cried. "Again, I have to ask, will it stop?"

Although I would not threaten the lives of others over what seems to be an endless pattern of sleeplessness, I could in some sense sympathize with Nebuchadnezzar at his last-straw moments of desperation. I have to admit, I found myself hesitating from what I realized was a fear of finding the answer and it being my thorn to bear. What if He told me I would always wake in a panic? What if I just had to accept this as part of *my plan?*

The thought made my stomach ache. What if I didn't like the answer? I try not to live my life in the *what ifs.* Truth, be it gentle or with a sting, is always better. I knew the truth is the only way to be free. So whatever that was would be freeing, even if it wasn't what I wanted to hear. I sensed He was waiting, so I began reading Hebrews 11.

"Do you see that, My child, in verse 2?" He asked softly.

"The word *commended?*" I asked.

"Yes," He replied. "You asked what heavenly strength was," He said.

"Yes," I replied. I remembered.

"They were commended for their *faith,*" He said. "That is the cornerstone of a strong child."

His words did not impact me like I wanted them to. I had heard so many things about *doing,* that to *have* faith seemed too simple. Or was it? I mean, it seemed so difficult.

"It is complex," I heard Him interject.

"Lord, I'm confused," I said.

"You hit the nail on the head with that one, Child," He added.

I giggled and blurted out, "Lord, You crack me up with Your sense of humor."

"You haven't seen nothing yet," He chuckled. "I created laughter, so why wouldn't I make a funny? Oh, you have so much to learn about Me. Thankfully we have eternity," He stated.

"Yes, Lord, thankfully," I said. "Now about faith," I asked.

"Something I created to be easy has been contorted into this great work," He explained. "A striving for something others have described as either unobtainable or leveled. Yes, that is what I want to say, they have put levels on it."

"I am still confused," I said.

"I would say so; it has been presented that way. Do you know what faith is?" He asked.

"I thought I did, but I'm not sure now," I stated.

"It is something you believe in your heart and say out of your mouth," He said. "That is it in a nut shell," He said with confidence.

"But what about the *levels* You mentioned?" I asked.

THE PRODUCTION

I had no clue when I typed His words that they would show up here, in a book. He truly is a mystery. That made me wonder, *Was the show a mystery?* Before turning to Hebrews 11, otherwise known as the faith chapter, He said, "Everyone listed here lived the production of their lives.

He had spoken about a production earlier, I remembered.

"While each had their own plot," He continued, "all of the plots together were a play. It took each one to produce the production.

I love to watch the stories of My children unfold. There is love, romance, hardship, endurance, and triumph woven into each."

I noticed the sequence He mentioned. It prompted me to ask, "Lord, why did You order those concepts in that particular way?"

"Oh my, you noticed that," He remarked.

"Yes, I love detail," I replied.

"Me too, My child. Notice love falls into to romance, but often that romance, if not nurtured in Me, becomes hardship. But if followed by endurance, triumph will follow. What saddens Me— too often My children get stuck in hardship. They become bitter, angry, and revenge sneaks in."

I could sense a twinge in His eye, like a twitch, almost an unpleasant concept that brought an unhappy tone to His face.

"What is that, Lord?" I asked.

"Displeasure; I am displeased."

I knew He was referring to revenge, but I wanted to make sure. "Are you referring to the revenge part of some people's lives?"

He answered with a flat, "Yes!"

I could tell He wanted to elaborate, but before I could comment, He said, "But this is a happy time. Let's focus on the ones who endured, not revenged. We'll be with them soon enough." I felt I should do as He asked and leave it alone, so I waited.

He was frustrated, and He wanted to take a minute.

To myself I had to admit I was surprised how aggravated revenge made Him, but I wasn't going to press Him. In due time I heard, and He asked me to focus back on Hebrews.

"The composer of the modern-day Bible calls this chapter 'examples,' I call them My children. This is My brag book, if you will," He said.

I could completely relate because I am only a few months away from the birth of my granddaughter, and I can guarantee

I will have a brag book. My mind must have run off about the prospect of her arrival because again I heard, "Focus, My child." It made me laugh.

"Allow Me to introduce you to a few of My babies," He said with great joy in His voice.

Babies—how sweet that sounded. We are His babies. "Why do you think I am so protective? Like a mama bear watching over her cub. As you are already watching over your granddaughter," He referenced.

A flame shot through me at the thought of someone harming her or any grandchild of mine.. *Not on my watch*, I thought.

"Not on Mine either," I heard.

I hated to ask in such a passionate, sweet moment, but He already knew what I was thinking. So I said it out loud, "But what about…" I stopped. Honestly I was afraid of the answer. See, I need Him to give me peace. I was harmed as a child. Where was He? I felt guilty for even questioning.

Then He began with tears welling up in His eyes, "Child, do you fear the raindrops?"

"Yes," I said with a pain in my heart.

"All of those water droplets were not My children. Mixed within them were my tears. They were from what I knew, but was unable to stop. I wanted them to cushion your journey. I was right alongside every love, romance, hardship, endurance, and triumph you experienced," He said.

The tears were more than I could hold back any longer. I removed my hands from the keyboard and cupped my face as the tears ran between my fingers. There was something comforting knowing that He had been there through it all. I had more questions, but for now I just wanted to live in the awareness of this news; I had not been alone.

I kept hearing, "As a mother bear cannot be everywhere her cub goes." At some point, what she has taught him has to be tested. We switched to a mama bird pushing her chick out of the nest. This is where endurance comes in.

"Is what you have been taught enough? The difference between the bear and the bird; I could go with you, but like the cub and chick, you too had to be tested. This defines the meat eaters from the milk drinkers. Who is weaker, the bird that never leaves the nest, or the one that, out of a mother's love, is pushed out? Hebrews shows some of the ones who, when pushed out of the nest, flew. I wasn't worried, because they always came back. As the saying goes, 'Let the one you love go, and if he or she comes back...'" He stopped there. He was reflecting, I could read it all over His face.

I believe He was proud. I thought to myself, *I hope to cause that look to come over His face someday.*

I heard a gentle, "It does."

"I love You, Lord," I replied.

"Me too," He replied.

There was a peace in the air. A contentment as if all was right in that moment. I wanted to slow down and allow it to soak in. I never want to rush these times. I sat back in my recliner and let the peace fall over me like a soft blanket.

FOR THE LOVE OF HIS SON

"There was a man," He began, "who loved his son very much. His son had been sick many, many years. He sought all that was available in hopes of finding a remedy for what had ailed his boy, but with no success. That was until a man named Jesus passed through his city. He was afraid of many things—rejection, embarrassment, and once again being disappointed that he, the father of his ill son, could not find healing for his boy.

"But," the Lord said, "he stepped up to level one. He walked up to My Son, Jesus, and began to explain the medical history of his son. Yes, he stepped out of the crowd and asked."

I could hear cheering in the background. "What is that?" I asked.

"The angels," He answered. "They love a good story and never fail to cheer a child who steps out in faith. It happens when they accept and believe My Son is the Savior that He is and every time thereafter. We realize and appreciate the trust it takes to step out. I just wish My Body would. They too often condemn and pressure those who do not move or act in the speed they have determined to be accurate and then hold it over their heads. As long as they are moving forward, I am happy. It is the back stabbing and stagnation that can become troublesome," He explained.

"Yes, faith is in levels. As one foot goes forward, trust is built, and then the next foot hopefully will follow," He concluded with a happy smile on His face.

"But Lord, what about the word *believe*," I asked. "How does it feel? How do you know?" I asked.

"Very good questions," He said with a grin and a twinkle in His eye.

Now that I looked closer, His eyes had the reflection of stars. It was a beautiful sight. They radiated a perfect white glow. I could have gazed into them for hours, but I really wanted to hear what He had to share with me about believing.

"Thank you," He said.

"For what?" I asked.

"Noticing My eyes," He answered. "Most do not stay long enough to see them."

I felt a girlish grin come over my face. He noticed that I had noticed. It was a sweet moment. I didn't want to rush it, so I sat there and soaked in His presence. But I needed to get back to

Hebrews. There was more, I felt, that He wanted to uncover; yet the questions of belief still hung in the air.

"When the man stepped out in faith, he then believed My Son would do what He said. They work in unison," He said.

"What unison?" I asked.

"Faith, belief, and trust," He answered. "They all build upon each other. One can have the faith to believe what I say and then trust I will put those words into actions. This would be a good time to explain to you that I work in layers. I hear the church refer to it as *peeling an onion*. I know you are tired of hearing that analogy," He said.

"Lord," I shrieked, "don't say that out loud." He was right, but I was not used to having my dirty laundry thoughts aired aloud.

"Transparent," He whispered.

"What?" I asked, not hearing Him clearly.

"An onion," He repeated. "When you peel away the layers of an onion, the thinner the layers the more transparent they become. Heavenly strength is not afraid of being transparent."

"Wow, I didn't see that one coming," I admitted.

"I've been known to throw a lesson in there without them seeing it coming," He admitted. "I find My children learn more that way. No one really likes to be lectured. Don't get Me wrong, I will if the situation warrants such discipline, but I prefer to teach with a story versus coming across preachy. As a whole, I like the onion analogy. It describes how I heal—in layers. That is why it appears to you that it is taking forever for the sleepless nights to stop. The children in Hebrews endured until what they prayed would stop, did stop. A strong child of God has stamina. Oh, I love how that rolls off My tongue," He said as He did a little jig.

Yes, our God did a little jig. I don't know why it surprised me; He does call us to dance.

"Speaking of dancing, have you heard of My son, David?" He asked.

"Yes," I replied, "but I would love to know more." There is nothing like hearing parents tell stories about their children. A glimmer comes over their eyes and an excitement in their voice. I know from experience. I love to share childhood memories of my daughter when she was a baby. I could tell as God began to speak, He was no different. This Parent was about to pull out the brag book of stories and lay them on me. And I was eager to hear.

"Want to talk about an onion? Boy was he," the Lord said. "Layer after layer. But My boy David is the epitome of heavenly strength. It gives Me goose bumps to think about him," He replied as a true father would. "That boy was a chip off the old block."

Off the top of my head, I could not remember if David was mentioned in the list of God's children who He proudly said endured. As I ran down the names listed in Hebrews 11, there was David nestled between the greats like Samson, Jephthah, and Samuel. I wondered, *With whom would my name be listed?* I wanted to be heavenly strong—one who my Father spoke highly of because I too had endured. I want to be an onion.

"Where I had previously disliked the onion analogy, I now wanted to be an onion, to be transparent, naked before You. Where there is dark, bring Your light. Where there is deceit, bring Your truth. Where there is hurt, bring Your healing. Where there is hate and brokenness, bring Your love. Let there be no stone unturned. Give me the courage I need to stand honestly before You. I will tell You up-front...I'm afraid," I admitted.

CHAPTER 6

Let the Peeling Begin

But we all, with unveiled face, beholding as in a mirror the glory of the Lord, are being transformed into the same image from glory to glory, just as by the Spirit of the Lord (2 Corinthians 3:18 NKJV).

"Good morning," I said as I sat in my chair on the lanai.

"So you want to be an onion?" He asked as we began our morning together.

"Yes, Lord, I do," I answered.

"When much is given, much is asked," He stated.

"I believe I understand," I replied.

"Do you?" He asked.

Because He felt the need to ask the question, I must not. "So," I asked, "please explain it to me. Where do we start this morning? I do have a question, Lord. Last night I had a good night's sleep. At least from my perspective; there was no waking in panic. I, however, did not sleep all the way through. Why is that?" I asked.

"Do you remember Nebuchadnezzar?" He asked.

"Yes I do," I replied.

"It wasn't until the dream that he began to be tormented. I am the Keeper of all dreams. I do not create bad dreams, but I will allow them to pass through My hands if it will peel a layer," He began to explain. "This is where much is asked. Once the layering becomes uncomfortable, most choose to bail on the peeling. They never go deep."

Then He asked, "Have I ever told you about the well?"

The grin on my face had to reflect the fact that He had. The part that made me smile was realizing that when He shared it with me, I didn't know it would be for this time.

I could hear Him chuckle as He said, "I have many tricks up My sleeve, but no one just seems to want to stay long enough to see the whole show. But tell them what I said about the well first, then we'll talk about the show...or shall I call it the production of your life."

I was so excited to hear that story that I wanted to get right to it.

THE WELL

I had a vision of a runner running by with a cup skimming the top of the well water, never slowing down, leaving splashes and violent ripples as water drops fell on the concrete below. The Lord had a look of hope that this one would stay. He is standing beside but toward the back of the well. He looks hurt and disappointed—sad.

"Draw deep into the well. Don't settle for the top," He says. "There is much to learn and healing to be dealt."

"I want my own cup, not only what others' drank from the well." I reply. "Share with me my own delight with You! To hear from others is wonderful, but it is their testimony. I want my own," I repeated.

"Deep calls unto deep," He states. "The deeper you are willing to go, the lighter you will feel. You can reach the weightlessness of soaring like an eagle, but you must be willing to stay first. Come to the well and I will wash you," He says.

"Do I bring anything?" I asked.

"Don't bring anything. I have all you need. I am all you need," He answers.

"I pray for clarity and understanding. I want to go deep," I declare. "I want to be one who stays!" I still am shaking my head in amazement, saying, "I want to be one who stays."

"Oh, My child, I want this too," He said tenderly. "The well is where the real cleansing begins, and it leads you to the cross, where it is finished."

"I'm not sure if I completely understand," I admit, "but if it is closer to You, I want it."

"The well is like an underwater village. You can get to anywhere from there. We may visit a grandparent or a friend. It all depends on what you need. See, it is personal. I am a personal God. No blanket paths here," He said.

I was not sure what to ask. I sat trying to comprehend the village. He interjected as I was thinking.

"Think about a fish tank. You can have a treasure chest, fancy plastic sea weed, or maybe a lighthouse all for the fish to swim around in," He said.

Somehow I felt this analogy was cheapening the well.

"Honey, there is great magic in this well," He said.

"Wait, not *magic*," I blurted out. "You can't say *magic*, Lord," I said.

"Dear, magic is a descriptive word. It means exciting and beyond spectacular. It is not a spell someone with ill-intentions places on an enemy. No, it is beautiful colors and beams of light. It is a feeling that two people in love share. Please don't allow the enemy of this world to distort things that I created as beautiful," He said.

I thought for a minute and realized from my own experience—what my husband and I have is magical. It is special. Television and the media had made it...He stopped me mid-sentence.

"You are questioning Scripture with what I am telling you. Look with Me—at what my prophet Ezekiel wrote." I turned as He had asked and began to read. "There it is," He shouted, "your magic charms with which you ensnare people like birds. Can you see the difference?" He asked.

I thought to myself *yes,* but I wanted to make sure, so I asked Him to explain.

"The difference is in the use," He began. "Magic as a descriptive to a feeling or a child watching a rabbit pulled out of a hat is fun, but when it is used to trap my children…" I could hear the tone in His voice go serious. "…it is not OK. I will not tolerate such actions. As it is stated in the last book of the Great Book, I will deal with them harshly."

I knew He meant it. I could tell by His tone.

"Yes, Child, I do," He continued. "I watched My Son pay the ultimate price so My children would be free, and someone with their hocus pocus thinks they are going to come along and bind them again? I don't think so," He said assuredly.

This tone was different. He was angry, and I didn't want to be the cause of that.

"Child, I have said it before and I will say it again. I am a very jealous, call it a protective, God. I love My children, and no one, I mean no one, will harm them, except themselves," He finished.

What? The conclusion to His statement caught me off-guard. "What do you mean 'except themselves,'" I asked. I was afraid of what I was going to hear.

"Let's go back to the Garden. Eve was the apple of My eye. No pun intended." I heard him give out a halfhearted "ha," almost like He knew the comment was funny, but the circumstance took all the humor from it. "Eve was created to help Adam, not hinder the Garden. She was deceived, but she made the choice. That is what I mean when I said, 'except themselves.' Every minute of every day that I give you is full of choices. What you do with those choices can determine your need of the well," He explained.

"How did we get back to the well?" I asked.

"It always goes back to the well, or should I say the choice should be to always go back to the well," He said.

I still was not following His point. "Lord, please spell this out to me. I just don't get it."

"I love when My children ask for clarification," He said. "I want them to understand. Let's look at Eve. All people seem to remember about her is the forbidden fruit incident. I am not taking away from the catastrophic repercussion that one act started, but she redeemed herself. Or at least in My eyes. She came back to the well. She and Adam started the chain, the family lineage. She made a mistake, a poor choice, but she came back to the One who could cleanse her. I am very proud of Eve. She could have given up after such a poor choice, but she chose not to. That is a heavenly strength; persistence. Eve is still the apple of my eye," He said proudly.

I saw Him smile. My attention went back to a question I had thought, but had not spoken yet. "Lord, what about those choices that are placed upon us against our will?" There was silence, then what sounded like a growl. This subject obviously hit a nerve.

WOE!

"Have you heard what I will do to those who harm My children?" He asked.

I knew what He was referring to. "It is better to be thrown in a lake with cement tied to you," I replied.

"Yes, but I don't think they get what judgment they will receive," He added.

"Lord, no disrespect, but what about the young one who was harmed?" I softly asked. I knew about the young one harmed. It had been me. I didn't ask for what had happened to me. Unlike

Eve, I didn't make the choice; it was thrust upon me. I wasn't asked or consulted. And to be perfectly honest, I was too young to even know what the word consulted meant. I wanted to know about them, the ones who weren't given a choice.

I felt a level of healing in just asking the question. By no means was it complete, but it felt like a start. So, I waited. I could see His face and what appeared as a ring, similar to the pictures I have seen of the ring around the planet Saturn, was spinning around His head. Within this ring were emotions spelled out: confusion, sadness, hurt, pain, and the word *fault* stuck out. He was feeling them all. I could see it on His face. I sat and watched; His eyes were open, but as if in a daze. He was there, yet I dare not interrupt. It would be offensive if I tried. It appeared as if, although He was in a state of shock, He wanted to experience it.

I watched in disbelief. I waited. This went on for what I thought was hours. Out of respect, I continued to wait. It was as if the room began to spin and I got caught up in the ring. The ring began to expand, and my breath was taken. I caught it just in time to grab a hold of one of the emotions. I couldn't tell which one, I just knew I needed to hang on. We spun around and around until I felt nauseous.

Just as quickly as I had been sucked in, I was spit out. Across the room, violently I was thrown. I laid there limp, on the cold floor. I didn't want to be there. I was not sure how I got there, but I was learning I was there. Slowly, with some pain, I lifted my head. My eyes began to squint from the light. It was so intense I had to shield them. I thought they would adjust, but I continued to squint. I wanted to open them wider. I felt this need to see all I could see. There was comfort in that light. There was harmony and love. I needed it, but I couldn't get my eyes to cooperate. I cried out for help. I was frustrated, yet no one heard me.

"Yes, I did," I heard firmly. "Yes, I did. I was there. I heard every word; I felt every emotion, every plea. I was there," He said.

Before I could control my tongue, I blurted out, "Then why didn't you stop it?" I fell to the ground hyperventilating. I had to ask. I couldn't contain it any longer. "WHY! You are GOD. You are supposed to protect me." Every fiber in my being fell farther to the floor. I had no energy. I was broken. I covered my eyes and sobbed, not like I had skinned my knee, but like my heart had just been ripped out.

"You are right. You did have your heart ripped out," He said softly. "There is a battle for your heart," He said with a soft tenderness.

I lifted my head, no longer caring if the light would hurt my eyes, and softly asked, "Why did You let him take it?" I stared up at Him with lost eyes. Questions like that people say God doesn't answer. He has a plan and bad things happen to good people. Well, today I wanted to believe He would answer. Anger began to rise up, and my tone was no longer sweet. "Lord, PLEASE answer me. What do I need to do…" I stopped mid-sentence.

I had for years come to the well. Many tender moments filled my memory. But to this day, I had not been given an answer. Reflecting, I could see how many heavy layers had been removed, and I had been given the beginning of an amazing personal relationship with God. Over time He had been healing me from many choices I had made and some that I had no choice in making.

But here we were, at what appeared to be a crossroads. No, I would not stop loving and praising Him if He chose not to answer my question, but I knew deep down I would be disappointed. Not just disappointed for me, but for others who would come my way and, just like I had, needed the answer.

He jumped in. "There is the key; you don't need the *answer,* you need *Me,*" He explained.

I have to admit, I begged to differ. "How can I trust You to protect me in the present if I know you didn't in the past?" I asked.

"How do you know I didn't?" He asked.

"Because it happened," I replied. I had never been so honest with Him, so transparent. I waited. I was not sure where we would go from here. Guilt came over me in the form of questions such as, *Who do you think you are that God would tell you?* I realized that the emotion that I had held on to from when I was flung from the ring was GUILT. *You are not good enough. I mean, look what happened to you. You must have done something.* I was not surprised. I had thought that for a while, but I had not allowed it to be said. Now I was hearing it echo over and over. Almost like it was making up for all of the times I had denied it to speak. It was out now, and it filled the room.

Then He said, "You have a choice now. You can toss that guilt in the well, or you can hang on to it. Which will it be?" He asked.

I knew in the back of my mind that He had not answered my question about not stopping the incident. But it seemed this guilt thing was more pressing at the moment. I knew I wanted to take it to the well. But I thought to toss it would be too light of a word. *Maybe **heave** would be more precise,* I thought.

He broke in as I finished my statement. "Heave is a strong word and fully understandable. But with a strong word anger hides," He stated. "If the guilt is thrown, but the anger remains, there will be another choice pending. What will you do with that anger? It will take on a life of its own if not tossed itself. Here is where big problems cultivate. My children either choose to hang on to the guilt or whatever negative emotion that flung with them from the event, or they bring it to the well, not recognizing another emotion lingers, such as anger," He explained.

I have to admit when He called us "His children" I felt a twinge within my body. For the first time I thought, *No, parents take care of and protect their children.* As soon as the comment played through my mind, I heard the question posed by a dear friend of mine, "Are we blaming the sins on our earthly father or our heavenly Father?" Wow. That blindsided me. I felt a rush of compassion fill my body. It was like a wave that needed to reach the sea. That compassion needed to reach my heavenly Father. He needed to know I was sorry for the anger I had been harboring toward Him. I knew what it was like to be blamed for something others had done. Yet, I had done it to Him. I was sorry, truly sorry. Where do we go from here? I could tell I was tired. I was exhausted from the roller coaster ride of emotions and revelation.

"Being transparent is draining," I heard Him say. "Yes, to whom much is given, much is expected," He said again.

I still did not completely understand or have my big, pressing question answered. But at this moment I had a peace—a peace that healing had taken place and that He would answer my question in due time. I believed He would be faithful if I would be patient. *Thank You, Lord, that I can speak my pain and You still are there.* He didn't leave me today even though my words were harsh. Already I was seeing He isn't like us. He sticks it out. There was that guilt again. I needed another trip to the well.

"Deep! Go deep! We will go deep!" I heard. "Much will be asked as we go deeper during the following days."

In Need

I felt uneasy with a hint of anticipation. I knew what I wanted to open with, but again I was afraid of not getting resolution. That in itself caused apprehension because it was a sideways admittance of unbelief. But had He not helped the man who had blatantly confessed to a very strong sense of doubt? I was on this journey; and unless asked to get off, I was going to pursue my Lord like there was no tomorrow. I needed Him, and I wanted to be healed. No more Band-Aids or temporary facades of what on the outside resembled a possible solution until unwrapped and the ugly comes oozing out again. No, I had had it with fake, both from myself and others. Could I possibly start a call to truth? Not truth like we see it, but Truth like He knows it? I was going to see.

"What is this uneasiness?" I asked.

"It is the panic," He replied. "When you don't know why or you don't have the answer, it manifests as panic. Why do you think everyone fights for control?" He asked.

I could feel my heart begin to race.

"Stop right there," I heard. "Do you see that?" He asked. "It has gone from an act, and in your case, even as a child, you cannot have a conversation without the fear exposing itself as panic. It has grown," He said.

"I am still confused," I said.

"That is still the panic," He replied.

"It is bigger than..." but before He could finish, I broke down into tears.

"I just want You to replace this fear with Your perfect love," I cried. "Your Word says that love will fix it. I want that perfect love. How do I do it?"

"Faith," He answered.

I cried out, "No," as I sobbed like a child. Again I could sympathize with Nebuchadnezzar for being at his end with the tormented nights. I had been faithful, or least I thought so. Night after night I would lie there hoping and praying it would end. But it hadn't, and now He wants to tell me that I have to have faith.

"I am tired," I said as I continued to wail with tears streaming down my cheeks. "Can't You just come get me?" I cried.

"I am trying," He replied.

I felt like I was 2 years old, and I just wanted my mother to hold me and make it all better. But I was an adult, and I couldn't make it stop. Why? What had I been doing wrong? I could no longer see the computer screen for the alligator tears that were cascading from my eyes. The pounding was still there, and the tears hadn't stopped—and all I had was faith. I wasn't being hateful, but what was faith going to do? How would anyone buy what I was selling if in the midst of their pain I said, "Just have faith"?

I wasn't getting it and I surely wasn't going to offer it to others at this point. "God," I cried out, "we need help. We need healing, and darn it, we need *You!*" I don't know that I had ever been so enraged and fed up at the same time. I had learned and believed that God healed and would never give more than we could handle.

Although I knew that I could *handle* the sleepless nights if I had to, I wanted to understand why I would have to. I mean, I recognize from time with Him that I fear sleeping, and scripturally He had the answer. Why then or who then is the hang up? That is when it hit me like a ton of bricks—*I am.* I am the hang up. I had been so focused on *make this go away* that I hadn't thought to ask what do You, Lord, want to accomplish with this? Everything works for the good of those who believe. What is the good You want to come from this? So I stopped and asked, "Lord, what is it that You want to come from this?"

Without one missed beat, He replied, "That no other would lose another night's sleep."

I was stopped in my tracks. I watched the prompt marker on my laptop blink on and off as I sat there questioning if I had heard correctly. *Was He asking what I thought I heard? Dare I ask Him to repeat Himself?* I sat there questioning what to do next.

"Yes, My child, I am asking exactly what your heart is telling you," He said, breaking the silence. "If you will allow Me to walk you through this time, others may, if they choose, be free. That is faith."

It was like the wind was knocked out of my chest when the word *faith* came from His lips. I had not believed Him, yet He still asked me. No one had done that before. Most people I had experienced would have gotten fed up with me long before I had a chance to get fed up with them. But He was still here.

"I want to explain one more thing to you before you give me your answer," He said.

I guessed He was waiting to hear if I would take Him up on this faith thing. Honestly, I thought I had when I accepted Jesus. *I must have been wrong,* I thought.

"No, you were not wrong," He stated. "Accepting Jesus is by faith, but it is not the end of your faith walk. I lose a lot of My children with that mindset. Your journey is a step of faith every day. Take up your cross every day," He reminded me.

"Oh," I said. It was starting to come together.

"Notice your heart rate," He said.

I realized that it had slowed down.

"You are in faith," He said. "In faith, confusion cannot stay."

"How did that happen?" I asked.

"You focused more on Me than the fear," He said. "Remember Peter?" He asked.

"Oh my goodness, I had done it. Never again will I think *why did it take Peter three times?* I just hoped I wouldn't set a record for the most," I said with a half-serious smile.

I heard Him laugh and correct me, "It isn't the number; it is that you keep trying."

I took a deep breath; His response took some of the pressure off.

"Child, I have much to tell you about faith, belief, and love. All I am asking of you is to hang in there, or better put, hang on to Me. I want to talk to you about layers of belief and levels of faith," He stated.

"Lord," I began, "I sure could use that lesson."

"Yes, you could," He replied, "but not right now."

"With tears, I will wait," I said. "It seems that is required a lot."

"No," He said, "it is strength. And to get stronger it will need to be exercised. It is painful now because your flesh is used to *right now*. You can do this," I heard Him say.

"I sure hope so," I responded. "I guess we will see."

"You cannot nor are you meant to do this alone," He said with compassion. "Isolation is a breeding ground for fear. It is like a Petri dish left in a warm, moist environment. Before you know it, you have more mold and bacteria than the strongest antibiotic can kill. But I am the Holy Exterminator," He said, smiling.

I had to laugh and ask, "What?"

"You heard Me. I can kill anything." He chuckled as if he had made the biggest funny.

"I love You so much," I said. "Lord, I felt this was the time to just get it out there. I want to do this," I said. "I want to endure."

He was silent. Then the tears trickled down His nose. He didn't need to say a word. I knew someday I would be thanking Him more than He was thanking me. We were a team now. He was my Superhero, and I would be His sidekick. Together we could knock out sleepless nights. Or at least I would try to help. I knew deep down He could do it all on His own. I mean, does Batman really need Robin? God was willing to let me be part of the Kingdom's business. I wanted to be the best employee I could be. Again I said, "Here I am reporting for duty," as I saluted. "Amen." It seemed appropriate.

OH, IF ONLY TO SLUMBER

Later that evening, my husband and I headed to the hot tub. In the community we lived in, there is a community pool with a hot tub. We often liked to end our long days with a relaxing dip in the pool topped with a calming sit in the warm water of the hot tub. This evening would prove to be no different. After a few minutes in the jetted-water retreat, we voted to recline in the lounge chairs. As we both laid back, I wished, as he nodded off into slumber, that

I could just fall to sleep at will as he did. It impressed me so that at the drop of a hat he could fade into a peaceful dream state. The evening's backdrop was the perfect setting. The sound of the waterfall and the cool breeze through the palm trees invited a siesta. But there I was, not able to answer.

As I watched him sleep, I was reminded of a not too far off time when something else that may have seemed simple to the average person was an obstacle to me. At one time I could not go to work without crying all the way to the office door. I have since found out it was a repercussion of the incident I had suffered as a child. But too, I had watched my husband leave for work day after day, year after year, and never miss a beat. I wanted to be like him. Now, I was finding the same request. I wanted to rest like him. I knew in that instance, I would conquer this sleeplessness, just like I had the crying before work.

The apostle Paul came to mind. God has helped me in the past; He will help me now and in the future. I knew God had *onion-peeled me through that situation,* and I knew in my heart He would see me through this, too. One day, as silly as it may seem to those who sleep like babies, I too would drift off to sleep on a lounge chair as water trickles down the rocks and into the hot tub.

"You have hit upon something; sleep like a baby," I heard the voice of the Lord say.

CHAPTER 7

Truth Begins

*Then you will know the truth, and the truth will set
you free* (John 8:32).

"Lord," I began, "I come humbly to You this morning seeking
answers that will free us; Your children. Needing to know the
One who knows the answers—for what good is freedom if we
just fall snare to another lie? We need to know the Truth so that
we are wiser to the traps that are laid before us. We need knowledge *of* Your Word, but also a relationship *with* the Word. Today,
Lord, I feel a boldness stirring, a presence unlike I have felt. Your
will be done. So, without any further delay, I ask You about Your
Son, Jesus."

He jumped in, "Oh, I love to talk about Him."

There was a sparkle in His eye. I hoped that the question I was
about to ask did not put a damper on His Spirit. But He had told
me before that He liked boldness. Not arrogance, but confidence.
So here it goes, "Lord, in the Book written by Mark, Jesus cried
out, 'My God, My God, why have You forsaken Me?'"

With a lump in my throat and fighting back tears, I waited.
I almost felt like I had hurt Him, but I needed to ask. I knew
where the question was coming from—yesterday. "Why didn't
You stop it?" still stuck in my heart. "Why, Lord? Why have You
forsaken us?"

I sat in the deep silence and cried. Waiting, hoping He
wouldn't give up on me. I mean, I wasn't trying to make Him
angry; I just wanted to understand. Deep down, I wanted that

knight in shining armor to ride in and save the damsel in distress. But was that realistic? Did it happen only in the movies? Where would our relationship go from here? He had made it very clear not to test Him, and I wasn't. I was coming as a child to her Parent, broken over a painful experience. There was no ill-intent, but pure innocence.

Many thoughts flooded my head as I allowed my mind to run rampant. *What ifs* overtook my mind. *What if* He says there is no hope? *What if* you are on your own? *What if* He says I can't help you? All of these I knew scripturally not to be true. But today I needed evidence of Him. I was asking for an experience with Him.

"Dena…" He said. This was different. He never calls me by my name. It is usually Sunshine, or some silly pet name.

"…I wanted your attention and for you to know I am serious," He explained without me even asking.

I knew the seriousness, not a *you're in trouble,* but rather that He takes this topic very seriously. He knew the question I had asked and was about to address it.

"Child," He said with a tender look, "I know the answer you seek. But over that, I know the Truth you need. I have every intention of answering your question. But even though you believe you need it now, there is a better time. Look back at what Jesus cried out again," He said.

My eyes went to the pages of my beloved Bible. "My God, My God." He stopped me there.

"Do you notice that He called out to Me as 'My God,' not as 'My Father'?"

I hadn't noticed that before. It made me wonder of other times I may have missed who the writer had purposely identified.

"I noticed you used the word *purposely,*" He said. "That is a very important word to Me. I have a purpose and a plan for each of you. Notice the sequence: purpose and then the plan. Dena," *That still sounds strange hearing my name coming from Him,* "it is times with Me that you learn your purpose, then comes the plan. I am responsible for everyone," He said.

I thought, *I cannot even begin to conceive the volume of people that must include.*

"And although every individual child is of the utmost value, I have to make sure they are ready to go," He stated.

MY VOICE

"My people get agitated because things don't move fast enough," He began. "Hearing is not just for the prophets. There is a prep time. If I sent you out before you knew My voice, it would bring disaster. You have to remember, I am trying to save the world. There is enough disaster without My own going ahead of Me. You know the saying I said to Moses, 'Where I send you, I will go'? If I send you before you are ready, then it is on Me. I delay, as you see it, for your own good. I have and know the timeline that is not of your concern. I take your training very seriously. I do not rush My children from milk to solids. They have much to learn, and I am the only One to show them.

"Allow Me to use a child's mother as an example. A baby learns the presence of his or her mother by recognizing her voice. The child then matures and begins to turn his or her head when she comes into the room. Then the child learns to understand the word *Mama* and repeat it. Then, after a while, sentences to full conversations become second nature. This learning process is effortless to the child if he or she pays attention.

"Just like Mary, who sat at my Son's feet—all she had to do is pay attention. Hearing is difficult to do with distractions. Just watch a baby. If someone shakes a rattle, it will distract the child's focus from the mother. This is what I meant when I spoke *off of milk.* I can spoon-feed you, but I can't make you chew. I can draw you to the well, but I can't make you drink. Coming is up to you," He said. "You wouldn't give your baby to someone you just met; why would I entrust My children at first?"

This made me think of the Scripture that says He knew us in our mother's womb. I wanted to inquire about that.

"Now, that is not for you to worry about right now. You are only responsible for what I teach you. If you get into other things, it is on you. That is not to say I won't help you," He said.

I didn't want to be rude or show any disrespect, but I asked, "Lord, what does this have to do with my question?"

"Everything, Child," He answered. "You will get your answer, but it will be in My time."

There it was, I thought. *He is going to answer me when He is ready. Here goes transparency, and it is painful.* "Lord, help me with my pride." I could feel my heart pounding. It was unpleasant; it was bitter. I didn't like it.

"Neither do I," He agreed. "But if you are willing, we can do something about it."

I knew the moment He mentioned that He would tell me in His time that I had a pride issue. No, the word *issue* is not strong enough—I had a disease. I want what I want when I want it. Yuck, that has an odor to it that most cow pastures couldn't create. The stench was nauseating, and I was not a happy camper to admit it, but to get peace I had to lay it out. "So, what do we do now?" I asked.

"Hmmm," I heard. Not like I had caught Him off guard, but like He was sizing me up; almost as if wondering where to start. *Wow, it must be worse than I thought,* I thought as I grinned.

"Well, one might think," He said as He grinned back. "But I know you know that nothing is impossible with Me."

"Well," I observed, "I am *with* You."

I heard Him chuckle. "Yes, My dear, that you are. Stuck with Me like glue."

"I could not bear for You to leave," I admitted.

"I can't, I am *in* you," He said. "We are attached like superglue. You are stuck with Me."

Hilarious; I laughed so hard. "Thank You that You care so much that You don't want me to worry," I said. Ha ha, you are stuck with me. I loved it. I thought, *I think I am about to see how much I need it.* Appreciation covered me. *A step to humility,* I thought. I wondered if humility was a heavenly strength.

"Wonder no more," I heard, "it is a must."

A must, I thought. "Maybe we should start there," I suggested.

"That would be a good idea," He agreed.

"I have some homework for you," He said.

What? I thought. This had not happened before.

"Oh," He stopped me, "yes it has. The difference is I am telling you ahead of time on this one."

All I could do was laugh. I felt such a love and appreciation toward Him. Either way, what He wanted to teach me was good with me. I loved my Teacher. Then it hit me; in this moment He was my teacher, like in that moment He was Jesus' God. There has to be something to this.

I heard the sweet sound of His laughter. "Never doubt that there is hope for you, My child," He said assuredly. "You are My sunshine, and your willingness brightened My day." We both smiled.

"What about that homework?" I asked. This made me think about my daughter kidding with me about being a teacher's pet in school. I remember my son-in-law joking one night at dinner, acting as if he was me in class raising my hand to ask for more work. I am not sure if their perceptions were correct; but right now, yes I had my hand raised and wanted that work. I wanted to learn. As sweet Mary sat at the feet of Jesus listening to hear what He wanted to share, I too was on the edge of my seat waiting. "What would You have me learn?" I asked eagerly.

"Humility," He said plainly.

My first and only response was, "OK." He must have sensed that I was perplexed.

"Meditate on it, and read what I say in My Word," He suggested.

I thought, *Why?*

"Because," He replied without missing a beat, "no one can or should be asked to do what they don't understand. I want you to know what it is so you recognize when you are not doing it."

"Wow, that's smart," I blurted out.

"I have My moments," He replied with a laugh.

"Hee hee," as I joined in. I didn't want to miss a minute of His laughter. I treasured that sound. He really is a fun God. But I knew just as true, He also meant business when necessary. I respected that. I appreciated that. I appreciated Him.

CHAPTER 8

As Children

And He said: "I tell you the truth, unless you change and become like little children, you will never enter the kingdom of heaven (Matthew 18:3).

"Good morning, Lord," I began. "Where do we start today?"

"Tell Me what you learned yesterday afternoon," He replied.

"First, I just want to tell You how much I love You. My heart hurts. I'm not sure why, but I know my sleep still torments me," I said.

"In time, dear one, in time," He replied.

I knew there was a bigger picture. He had shared with me before that if I rushed things, I would miss Him. I was beginning to understand what He meant. Although I would prefer this process to be faster or even instantaneous, if I tried to speed it along, I would miss all these special moments. I could see now that He used my nights to reveal Himself. Not because He needed to be seen, but because I needed to see Him.

My attention turned to something He had spoken to me earlier that morning: "I comfort as well as command." He loves us and love encompasses comfort. We are missing Him in His Word if we read all of the text as a command. I now look at His words like, "Don't be afraid," as an endearing Father, not a heavy-handed God. Where I thought I was not doing something wrong or lacking in my character for being afraid, I now see that it was to help, not condemn. I cannot say that I am thankful for the nights of restlessness, but I believe I can say, "I will be."

So for right now, I am going to enjoy this time and believe that joy *does* come in the morning. This is the day that the Lord has made, and I will be glad in it. And I am glad to have this to share. As I was meditating on Scripture on humility as my homework assignment, I ran across Matthew 11:29—He reveals things to the children and hides things from the wise. I knew from this revelation that the things were hidden from the wise because they were in this text, proud—*know it alls,* if you will. They thought they had it all figured out, so why attempt to teach those who believe they have it all down pat already?

But what stuck with me was what He revealed to the children. The question began to flood my mind, *Why the children?*

He replied, "They are teachable. They are like sponges who want to learn and soak it in when instructed. They enjoy learning."

Was this a strength? I wondered.

"Yes," He replied, "most definitely. Teachability; a heart that wants to learn and enjoys the process. They have joyful hearts."

As would be expected, another question was raised. "Lord, what does a child's heart look like to You?" My reasoning was, I can't seek something if I don't know what it looks like. I need to know what I am looking for so I will know where I am and when I get there. I continued my question, "Not by appearance, but by heart." See, God looks at the inside, not the outside. So I knew He knew what it looked like.

He began with one word, "Pure."

"Please elaborate," I said.

"Your mind can not comprehend it because it has been touched by sin," He stated.

"What do we do?" I asked.

"Replace sin with My Truth," He said

"Is it that onion again?" I questioned.

"Yes," He answered, chuckling. "It is back again to peeling back one layer at a time. Renewal means to make it better than it currently is. I am not replacing your mind or your heart. I am making it better. It was sick." Then I heard Him say, "Ask Me if there is a doctor in the house."

I thought that odd, but I asked, "Is there a doctor in the house?"

"Well, yes there is," He announced, "in your house. There is no waiting list, no co-pay. I am on-call year round."

I had to laugh to myself, I mean, with all the talk about health-care recently in the media. As the world promotes our current system as hopeless, He was announcing such hope. I wanted Him as my medical doctor on speed dial.

I could have gone on for a while with my doctor-related one-liners, but He jumped in with, "Seriously, there is an epidemic."

"Epidemic?" I questioned.

"Yes, if you think the locust or the frogs were bad, it doesn't touch the heart disease among My people," He said.

I noticed that this time He called us *people*, not His children. "Why is that, Lord?"

"My children's hearts are fine; it is the adults who have me concerned."

I was a little confused. I knew children whose hearts were heavy. What did He mean? So, I asked Him, "What do You mean?"

"I am not talking about chronological age. Age is irrelevant to a heart," He stated. "I am talking about the condition of the heart. Everything is done to bring you back to a child's heart. The condition of whether that is at age 20 or 80, as long as we get there."

"I see," I replied. Out of nowhere, I sneezed. I happened to be in the library at the college I attend, where no one said, "Bless you." So in the midst of the silence, I blessed myself.

"Why do you say that after you sneeze?" He asked. I really hadn't thought about my sneezing being part of our conversation, but He asked, so I would answer. I rolled my eyes, not out of disrespect, but because I realized in the moment, I didn't know.

He responded with a puzzled look, "Why would you bless a sneeze?" The way He asked made us both laugh.

It did seem ridiculous when I thought about it. I realized that I am beginning to love those moments of laughter we share. He has such a sense of humor. He knows when the mood needs to be light and when to be serious. He is the total package. I love Him.

After our sneeze talk, we were back to our discussion about hearts, "Do you know how much strength it takes to go back while moving ahead?" He asked.

I thought I knew what He was referring to, but I wanted to make sure. "Go back while moving ahead?" I repeated with a puzzled look.

"There is a place where sin was introduced into each of My children's lives," He began. "This is the place where we need to return. But it has to be done very meticulously so that you have the strength to keep moving forward. It is when those two points meet that purity is reached."

"Wait Lord," I blurted out. "Is that even possible?" I asked. "When we are moving forward, we are still in a sinful world."

"Good question," He remarked.

I waited for the answer, then said, "Yes, how?"

"Not *how*, Child, but *when*," He said. "When the bride and groom reunite," He said proudly.

His statement made me think of the wedding gown. A long train with elegant beading that sparkled. Not from the sheen of the material, but the glow of our face seeing our Beloved.

"He is preparing for that special moment when He will sweep you off your feet and parade you around because you are His treasure," He said, smiling.

I thought of the Scripture, where your heart lies there is your treasure.

"Yes, yes you have it," He said with excitement. "He already has a heart that treasures you. The key to the treasure is renewing your heart to treasure His."

"Oh, Lord," I gasped, "make it so."

"Honey, I made your heart," He started, "but I will not nor can I make it treasure Him. As much as I desire it to be, I cannot."

"Oh darn," I replied, "it's that free will again."

"Yes," He said.

I was beginning to really dislike that aspect of our makeup.

I could sense He stopped me in that thought. "You will learn to use that free will to your advantage."

I wasn't too sure about His meaning or even the verbiage He was using.

"But that will be for another day," He said.

I was glad, because I wanted to get back to the wedding.

"Again," He said, "I cannot force you, but I will help you, if you desire."

"Oh, I do, I do," I said. Those words resonated, and my mind went to the wedding. "I do," I heard Him say and everyone rejoiced.

"I do," I yelled as if no one had heard me.

"Child, they are waiting for you," He whispered softly.

"Then why are they cheering?" I asked.

"They are practicing," He replied. "They want to get it right. To make sure everything is perfect. They all are on the edge of their seats with excitement. Oh, if I could just get My children here to be that excited."

"I want to help," I blurted out before I even knew I had said it or even that I had thought it. It was out there now, and I did mean it. *I love to throw parties. Decorations and God's Word go together just beautifully,* I thought.

"I think so too," He interjected.

"When do I start?" I asked. I saw myself salute as if I was reporting for duty.

He let out a playful laugh and said, "Hold on, My little filly." His laugh was now a full-blown, bent-over stomach buster.

"Little filly?" I questioned. "Are we on the ranch, and I didn't notice?" I asked, laughing.

"No," He answered, laughing so hard that I thought He was going to cry, or wet His pants. (I can't believe He had me write that.) The way He said "little filly" had been animated to say the least.

"I wanted to say it that way," He said. "Don't you ever change up your voice to be a character you like?"

"Yes," I answered. I immediately thought of how my family loved to quote funny lines from different television shows. I was beginning to see there were a lot of opportunities to laugh in this world, even though it is not our home. I think I have been taking things too seriously.

I heard, "Do you think?"

"Yes," I said as I smiled. "Yes."

I could sense it was time to wrap up, but before I went about the daily events, I heard Him say, "Pack your bags, My child, we are going on a journey."

"Oh, I love journeys," I replied. "Where are we going?" I asked.

"Mountain climbing," He replied with excitement in His voice.

"Yeah!" I cheered.

THE MOUNTAIN CLIMBER

"It is an adventure; put on your gear, we are going climbing," He said.

"Lord, why do You use the word *climbing?*" I asked.

"Because climbing takes planning, preparation, and patience. Lean on Me. I am the poles in your hands."

I found myself in a vision of a climber going up the side of the mountain. The climber was animated like the one on *The Price is Right* game show. I could tell that it was animated because even though it would be work, it would be fun.

"Carry My Word in your backpack and the Holy Spirit will be your shoes," the Lord advised me. "Jesus has plowed the mountain before you by the cross."

"Lord, what is the mountain?" I asked.

"Adults' hearts," He replied. "Up top is a cave of entry," He stated. "Landslides start up top. Along the way up, we will chip away at the hard rocks until we reach the top where my entrance will start an avalanche of emotion. I will love them to pieces. You get to watch. It is beautiful. They will love you, too."

"Lord," I asked, "will You tell me something? What will You do with those pieces of love?"

"I will do one better," He said. "I will show you; just stick with me and watch," He said, smiling.

"Why is there warm snow on the ground?" I asked. I could feel it through my boots. It was not wet but soothing.

"Snow melts in My presence, like a bride and a groom melt when they see each other," He explained.

All He wants is for us to love Him, I thought. *No strings attached.*

THE TIDE SO OFTEN CHANGES

It had been such a great day, but now night approached. The thought of laying my head to rest created a daytime panic. I didn't want to face the torment that I had grown to know night brought. "Lord," I cried out, "what do I do?"

"You have become afraid to sleep," He said. "My children dread to go to bed and dread to get up. Oh, how they suffer needlessly."

"What do we do?" I asked about in tears.

"It is all in the onion," He assured me. "Together we will peel away what is necessary so that you and others can rest at night and enjoy the day, not fearing the darkness. I said the night was good. But fear has made it bad. Let's take the night back," He said.

CHAPTER 9

Reporting for Duty

For our struggle is not against flesh and blood, but against the rulers, against the authorities, against the powers of this dark world and against the spiritual forces of evil in the heavenly realms. Therefore put on the full armor of God... (Ephesians 6:12-13).

I woke up this morning with an almost *mission* mentality. I saw a vision of a woman in her dress military blues, her crisp attire showcasing medals of courage and honor. With her right hand at attention touching her cap upon her head, she gave a salute. I knew I had been given a job, a purpose, and I wanted to begin. Overnight, I had received information that someone I loved had been up all night because they too could not sleep. This was after yesterday when the Holy Spirit had reminded me of others who recently said they were having sleeping problems. Maybe this was more common than I had considered.

"Yes, they suffer in silence," I heard the Lord interject. OK, then, in a line from the *Mission Impossible* movie, He said, "If you choose to except this mission..."

Before the sentence was complete, I yelled, "Yes, I accept!" Like the movie, I had no idea what all was to come. I considered only the outcome. Maybe it's a good thing not to know all that's involved in the process—or maybe I should have asked more questions. *We would find out together,* I laughed softly. Either way, I wanted in. My heart was broken for my loved ones and those I do not know. We need sleep. We need peace. We need Him.

"OK, Lord, where do we start," I asked.

"Start?" He asked. "You have already started."

"Huh?"

"The day I posed the question, 'What do your dreams say about you?' you started this journey," He explained.

"Why didn't You tell me?" I asked.

"Why did I need to?" He questioned.

It seems a little like trickery to me. There was silence. *Maybe I said the wrong thing?*

"No, you are fine. I just wanted you to slow down a minute," He said. "See, I didn't have to tell you to slow down, I showed you in being silent," He explained.

"What?" I questioned.

"If I had told you that day, you would not have had all the facts. That would have been more trickery, as you put it. By allowing you to go through the past days, you built a closer relationship with Me," He said. "You saw the need within yourself and now have a passion for others to be free."

THE FIVE-LETTER WORD

"Really, all of that?" I questioned.

"Yes; as we peel, you will see your healing, the desire to help others, and our relationship will flourish," He explained.

"I don't know how You can do all of that, but it is true," I said smiling.

"I didn't do it," He stated. "You did."

"How?" I asked.

"Faith," He replied. "You are coming as a child with a teachable heart and having faith in Me," He said.

"What?" I blurted out, "Not that word again."

"Do you know why you do not like that word?" He asked.

"No," I replied.

"Because you have no control over it," He said. "There is no measuring stick to gauge where you are or to compare it to where others are. But My people try," He stated. "They strive to make themselves feel better about their walk with Me by comparing themselves to others. It will not work; and honestly, if they would stop, their lives would be more peaceful."

"But what about those in the Book of Hebrews?" I asked.

"What about them?" He replied.

"Didn't they have great amounts of faith?" I said.

"Yes, but each one of them had different purposes asked of them," He said. "So how can one be compared to the other?"

"It is apples and oranges, as they say," I stated with a question undertone.

"Who are *they?*" He asked.

"Lord, I do not know, but *they* say a lot, it seems," I commented. We both laughed; but underneath, I was anxious to move on. It would be night soon enough, and someone I loved would toss and turn. I wanted to get on this.

"Whoa, hold your horses," He said. There was another reference to the old corral. He laughed, but this time I didn't. I was serious, and I wanted Him to be.

"Stop," I heard. "No one is more serious about the freedom of my children than I am. Do you remember the cross?" He said sternly.

I started to cry. I didn't mean to be disrespectful, but my heart was overflowing with compassion for those like me.

"Honey," He began, "I understand and am so proud of you for your desire to help others, but this is a process that I will insist we follow. Here are some ground rules: stay with Me. If you get ahead or move too quickly, you will miss Me."

I had a feeling that in itself was a clue to this sleepless thing.

"You are right," He said. "Learning to stay with Me is strength. Anyone can get ahead or lag behind, but children need to stay with their parents."

I thought of a time when my daughter decided to hide in one of the standing clothes racks in a department store. It scared me, as well as her, almost to death. I needed her to stay with me when we shopped. "Is this what you mean, Lord?" I asked.

"Yes, I know your path, so who better to lead you?" He stated.

"Now," He continued, "ground rule number two: listen. I will tell you if you are veering off the path. And ground rule number three: pray."

This one threw me for some reason. *What does prayer have to do with sleep?* I wondered.

"Prayer connects you with Me and the heavenlies," He said. "It puts things into motion that you have yet to see. Yes, that's it," He said with excitement, "to stay a step ahead without getting physically in front of Me, you pray. I will tell you things you do not know, and you are to pray. And only, I stress *only,* tell those who I led you to tell."

I could tell in His voice that was very important. "That is the key to staying with Me. If you get ahead, it is not just you who may step off the path, but others who you may influence," He said seriously.

Influence, I thought.

"Yes, influence," He repeated. "My children have great influence over each other and when used carelessly can set others back years. Well, what seems like years," He said.

"I pray, Lord, to stick to You like glue," I said. "Where do we go from here?" I asked. I sat and waited in excitement. Wow, I was excited. Not too many days ago, I was at the end of my rope. Now I was eager to get the show on the road.

-CHAPTER 10-

Burdens

Carry each other's burdens, and in this way you will fulfill the law of Christ (Galatians 6:2).

"Remember," He said, "that Paul says, 'I have learned to call it all joy.' Trials come, but hopefully My children realize that the victory is not just conquering the trial, but enjoying the process."

"You have used that word *process* several times now," I noted.

"On purpose," He said. "I want it to stick. This sleep problem has been going on for generations. I keep chipping away at it. Some are freed, while others need a little time. There is no *poof* and it is all cleared up. It is a process. Not just for you, but everyone who is not sleeping. They have their own path and purpose. You are merely an example. No more can I do it for them, than can you. Don't take that on, child," He warned. "I have lost good warriors in My battle due to their need to carry everyone else's troubles."

"But Lord, You told us to carry other's burdens," I pointed out. I felt I should look up that Scripture.

"This does not imply that you take on their burdens," He clarified. "There is a big difference between carrying and taking on. I was referring to a fellow brother or sister who had sinned. My children have to read the whole context, not just the one-liner," He said.

I sensed a little frustration, but didn't bring it up.

"If someone sins, be careful, help them, but don't take it on," He said. "That is how you can fall into your own temptation. If they are doing drugs and you take on their habits of going to the dealer, you will be tempted," He explained.

"How then are we to carry each other's burdens?" I asked.

"Hang on," He said, "I want to explain one other thing. If you think that you are capable of carrying others, you are, as the Scripture says, fooling yourself. I am the only One who can do this without falling into sin. On the other hand, if the person sees you as the savior, then they will compare themselves to you. We have already discussed that," He said. "They have to see that *I am* their Savior. If My people start presenting themselves as Me instead of a help to Me, then more burdens are created. Do you understand?" He asked.

"I think," I replied. "Let me see. I can help, if that help is to direct them to You."

"Basically, yes," He replied.

"OK," I said, "back to my question...how do we carry each other's burdens?"

"First and always, pray," He began, "either together or just with Me. Pray," He repeated. "Here is the tricky part—showing them Me. That may be by sharing the Word, it may be introducing them to your pastor...but the key is *gently*. They are in pain, so be gentle. A heavenly strength is knowing how to be gentle," He shared.

"But Lord," I began, "are there times when You need to be stern?"

"Definitely," He said, "but even when I need to be stern, it is done gently. Firm but not harsh." He said, "There is a difference. This would be a good point to bring up a comment I mentioned earlier to you," He stated. "Do you remember I said I wanted to show you weary versus tired?" He asked.

Yes, I had remembered this even though I thought it was odd.

"Look at Galatians 6:9 since we are so close already. Do you see 'let us not become weary in doing good'?"

"Weary needs rest, tired needs unloading. If you are weary, come to Me, and I will give you rest. Whereas if you are tired or exhausted, we need to check your inventory. You have taken on burdens, or someone else's troubles that are not yours, or you have taken on responsibilities that I did not assign for you," He said. "When you help others with their burdens, you can become weary if you have not done it properly, just as I described to you. It is draining to help. The difference between tired and weary is tired means you took on that person's burden. You are doing something that you were not called to do, and it wears you out."

"I'm not following You," I admitted.

"OK, look at it this way," He said. "You have your own burdens, sins that you are working out…correct?" He asked.

"Yes," I replied.

"If you add to those the sins of others, you are carrying more than you were supposed to," He stated. "I will not give you more than you can bear. So if you have more on your plate than you can handle, then you put something on your plate I did not assign."

I had known this to be true because many times I had more to do than I could possibly juggle. But since I knew each job He guided me to do, I was busy but it was manageable.

"My people are taking on more than is their responsibly," He said. "They are tired. Did you know that being too tired can keep you from sleeping?" He pointed out.

Oh how I know it well, I thought. Many nights I had gone to bed thinking as soon as my head hit the pillow, I would be out, only to get there and I was wide awake. "Why is that, Lord?" I asked.

"Believe it or not," He said, "you were created for a certain amount at certain times."

His comment made me think about the seasons.

"Very true," He agreed. "One season is preparing for the next," He said. "If you take on more than you are supposed to, the next season suffers too. It accumulates and overwhelms. It torments your mind, just like Nebuchadnezzar. Think about the last time you were over-booked. Where does it play? In your mind, over and over. It won't shut down; therefore, you have trouble getting to sleep."

"What do we do?" I asked.

"It is simple," He began. "Make sure you know that where you are headed is where I am leading. A good way to make sure is to check your motives, even with carrying each other's burdens. Ask yourself, 'Why am I helping this person?' If it is for any other reason than to see the person be free, then spend time with Me so we can sort it out. That is why I said, 'Each one should test their actions.' Why are you helping? If some were honest, they may not be the ones to help. There is nothing wrong with knowing your limits. That is a huge heavenly strength. Do not take on things you are not prepared to handle."

I saw a sad look come over His face.

"What is it, Lord?" I asked with concern.

"I almost hate to say this even though it is truth," He replied.

"Why?" I asked.

"Because some will use it as an excuse not to help at all," He admitted.

I saw that sad look get sadder, if it could even be so.

"Not helping is almost worse than helping when it is not your call," He started. "At least the person in need knows that someone cares. But oh the ones who have been passed by, by the ones who have opted not to help. This troubles My heart," He said, placing His hand over His chest.

"If I am honest, when I look back in my life at the times when I was exhausted and wearing myself thin, peer pressure comes to my mind. There was that phrase again," I said.

"Well, we might as well get into the responsibility topic since you brought up peer pressure," He noted.

"No better time than the present," I said, grinning.

"If the enemy can keep you busy, he keeps you off your calling," He said. "That is not to say you will not accomplish your purpose; you just may be delayed or not do it as well. Or worse, you won't enjoy it. What a tragedy that is," He said as He shook His head. "You were made for your very own purpose; so even if it is trying, you will have joy doing it. If you have taken on roles that peer pressure has placed on you, you won't enjoy them. You will just want to hurry through to get whatever done."

A light bulb turned on in my head. That is exactly what He had tried to show me earlier today. If I didn't slow down, I could miss Him and inadvertently because I wanted to rush, I would miss the joy.

"I want to slow down," I announced. *That is good stuff,* I thought. "Thank You," I said. "You had started to talk to me about the ones who use excuses to keep from helping," I remembered.

"Now, we want to be careful here not to judge," He began. "It would be very easy to say, 'I won't...or how could they....' Do you remember when My Son spoke to those who pulled the woman out of bed and displayed her in front of a crowd to accuse her of adultery?"

I could see His chest rise, like He was proud of His Son. "He told them, all right," I said.

He smirked, and I just grinned. He is a proud Papa.

"Anyway, be careful not to cast a stone. You may be in front of a window," He said.

"Yes, Sir," I said, taking in His wisdom. I knew I had better heed this warning. I was sure I had excused myself out of something in my past, and that is where I wanted it to stay. So, I laid down my stones and sat at His feet.

"Continue, Father, I'm all ears," I said humbly. I thought, *It must be aggravating for Him to have some who want to spin the meaning of His Word to fit their own needs, present company included.*

"Stop right there," He said. "I will not have one bad apple ruin the whole bunch. The great ones far outweigh the bad, and I still have hope for the bad. So, in reply to your statement," He continued, "it is all worth it. I would have done all that was necessary for one, just as I am doing for them all. They are all My children, and I love them equally."

"Well, I guess You told me," I said, grinning. But as He had spoken earlier, His correction was gentle but firm; there was no harshness. I could feel His love and conviction. I was not offended in any way. I felt loved. He cared enough for me to help me understand rather than to leave me in my own conclusion. *What a Dad!*

-CHAPTER 11-

Follow the
Yellow Brick Road

Your word is a lamp to my feet and a light for my path (Psalm 119:105).

"Y ou have come a long way, child," He said.

I knew that was a good thing, but I also knew I had a long way to go. My mind went to a vision of Him and me skipping down a yellow brick road. As I watched this vision, I heard Him say, "I am going to give you a renewed mind, a bigger heart, and more, abundant courage." I was in the movie *Wizard of Oz*. We began to sing, "Follow the yellow brick road, follow the yellow brick road..." I thought of Toto. *Where is he?* I wondered.

"Toto is you as a little girl," He began. "You may not understand now, but you will. This I promise."

I trusted He would keep His promise.

"For now, let's enjoy skipping and singing," He joined in.

I knew this had to do something with being a child. But I just wanted to enjoy and not over think it.

"Ah ha," He said, "that is what children do. They enjoy without bogging things down with thoughts. I want to talk to you more about that, but it is recess right now, so let's play," He said.

"Recess has become a timed event," He began. "Do you hear that?" He asked as we skipped. "That is what freedom sounds like," He answered.

What shall I ask? Then the question came to me, "How is my time today?"

"Ticking," He answered, smiling.

"That sounds like panic to me," I said, "like I'd better hurry because it is running out."

"No," He said, "that is all it is…a sound, not a deadline. The end is near, but I want you, and them, to come because of Me, not time *ticking*. Do not fear them into coming."

I keep hearing "time is running" out. It is, but it always has. I hear the tick, tick.

"View it as time lost from being with Me, not a deadline you must hurry to meet."

"How should we hear it?" I asked.

"As a heart beating," He replied. "As anticipation of being together. I can be with you when you write your paper, do your laundry, or sit on the front porch. We can garden, care for your children, and even grocery shop together."

I knew that was true because He had helped me in the past remember what groceries we needed and what was healthy for our bodies to digest.

"Time is a heartbeat, not a tick tick," He continued. "I have given time so you would choose to reunite. Do everything like we are together," He said.

I knew in the back of my mind, as great as all this insight on better sleep was, there would come a time when we would have to go deep. I mean, I am afraid to sleep, not being restless. But for now, I was going to skip and rejoice in the Lord. I knew I would need the energy later. I prayed, "Fill me with joy and laughter to give me the strength to endure what is to come. For I want the prize, my Lord. Amen."

I swallowed hard and reminded myself of the purpose. We need to sleep. We need to sleep. We are going to sleep.

THINGS YOU DO NOT KNOW

I had been in a relationship with God long enough that I knew it wasn't as much the question as it was how the question was asked. When I typed "We need to sleep," I knew what I needed to do.

"Lord, why don't we sleep?" *Oh boy, the can of worms is opened now,* I thought. But so be it; what is in the dark cannot be dealt with until the light hits it. So let in the light.

"Just a minute," He said. "I want you to realize what just happened. You were willing to open the top of the can so the light can come in. That is strength and faith. YAY!" I heard Him cheer. "You were not afraid to open the can, and you had faith it would be OK. Bravo. Bravo," He said, bowing as if at the end of a standing ovation.

THE ARMOR

It hung from the air as if suspended by the universe. No strings or cables, just thin air. It was the most brilliant piece of armor made of iron that I had ever seen. The light that shone down made it beam more radiantly, if it was possible. There was something about it that made me know I needed it, but to hold it seemed unobtainable, beside the fact that my fingertips would smudge this magnificent piece. No, I couldn't; I would just look. Even if I wanted to touch, there would be a fight with the perfectly constructed protection that appeared to be some type of Plexiglas.

"There is a handle," I heard.

I had not noticed the silver, interlocking chain that dangled from the right side. I moved closer. He was right; there it was, a hand-sized metal handle similar in shape to a mallet. This alloy device was dull, causing the eye to dismiss its presence. All I could think about was how the sun appeared to highlight this masterfully made garment, and I needed to touch it.

"Then touch it," He said. "Go ahead."

"I couldn't; it's too magnificent. I would ruin it," I replied.

"You can't," He said, "it is indestructible. It is a breast plate. It hangs there day after day as people walk by, yet they don't touch. I appreciate that they are respectful, but it was made for them. I am not even sure how or when it became an idol. Something that is reverenced and thought of so highly that it is put on a pedestal has the marking of a god," He explained.

I was confused; a breastplate that was a god. *What?* I had no idea what He was talking about; and to be honest, I was getting a little annoyed. It had been a long night, and to say the least, I was irritable. The day was full of things I had to do; but due to little sleep, I was not in the mood to carry out my tasks. I could sense I just had a pity party, and as I looked around, not a soul had shown up. "I want to sleep!" I screamed.

"Child, I am fully aware of that," He said, almost agitated. "So open the box," He directed. "Just do it already."

"Open the perfectly crafted protective casing for this absolutely stunning vest?" I asked.

"Yes," He insisted. "What good does it do for my people if they just admire the garment...if they are not willing to put it on? I appreciate the reading and the meditation. It is all very necessary, but if no action follows, then the knowledge stops there. Have you met four of my children who I called kings?" He asked.

I had an idea about whom He was referring to. I had studied them years ago. They had stuck in my head as reminders to share what God teaches me with my daughter, so that curses of one generation would not continue to the next. I could pray, learn, and change my actions, but if I did not pass this wisdom down, my family tree would continue in the bondage from which I had been freed.

"Communication and action has to follow insight," I heard Him say. "If you do not share what you know, then what you know dies with you."

Wow, that seemed officially straightforward, I thought.

"I am not holding anything back," He said. "We are in this to win this, as they say. I have heard your cries, pleas, and the frustration in your voice. I want to help you, so it is *game on*," He said.

I sensed pity parties were out of the question from here forth. It was time to get down to business. *I sure like the joking side of Him*, I thought to myself as I continued to listen.

"Now about the kings," He returned. "Four generations of sons to be exact: Uzziah, Jotham, Ahaz, and Hezekiah. All with great potential, but some more than others chose to build upon it."

I sat and listened.

"The first of this clan, Uzziah, took it upon himself to enter My temple to burn incense. This was a no-no in this time. He knew better, but let his pride get the best of him. Now his son Jotham repented of his father's sin, but kept his wisdom to himself. He basically cut off the new blessing that allowed the old curses to creep back in. He did not communicate. He allowed his people to worship in the high places. Can we say *peer pressure?*" He asked.

"The need to please others over what they know I have asked. I see it so much, over and over. Oh, how I wish My people would be hearers and doers. New knowledge must produce a new action to follow or history will repeat itself. This opened a whole can of defiance. When Jotham's son Ahaz comes along, sin is rampant. Idols were made, sacrifices were made. Not just any sacrifice, his sons," He clarified.

His eyes shut as if in pain.

"It is still an image that brings a jolt of anguish to mind. It wasn't supposed to be that way," He insisted. "If they call it preachy, then so be it—preach. They need to know," He said with such conviction.

I could hear compassion in His voice. I thought about the images I had allowed my eyes to view and the times they had flashed forward into my line of vision. I couldn't imagine His pain.

"But hope came in a new birth—Hezekiah. No, he was not perfect, but he repented for himself and his family," He noted. "He communicated to his people and put his words into actions. He tore down idols and laid down the law."

I heard Him chuckle.

"What's so funny?" I asked.

"He laid down the law," He repeated. "People hate the law, but despise the robber. They want justice but no rules. What is a ruler to do?" He asked.

I hoped He was speaking in general, because I was not prepared to answer such a question. I waited, hoping He wasn't waiting for me to answer.

"I am not asking you such a thing," I heard.

I motioned my hand across my brow as to show the relief I felt.

"I give them armor to protect themselves," He said, "though they opt to leave it on a shelf. I have written commandments to make their lives easier, yet their rebellious nature causes them to defy." Again He asked, "What is a ruler to do?" This time there was no pause. He continued, "Be patient. That is what I do."

I smiled at His answer.

"A good ruler communicates and leads by his actions," He said. "He never calls his children to do what He would not do himself. He loves at all times. He is patient and kind. That is what I do."

Love radiated from His presence. He loves us, I could tell. Although He had to be stern, it would be out of love. He loves us, and I was grateful. All seemed right at the moment. No, I had not gotten more sleep, but I was at peace. I wanted to learn to soak in those moments. They were becoming a refueling time for me—a recharge of my internal battery—and I was appreciative for the boost.

"Put on the breast plate," He said all of a sudden.

I thought, *I haven't broken it open yet. How am I going to put it on?* As the words formed in my mind, I felt the cool, hard metal touch my arms. I turned to find Him handing it to me. My mouth dropped as I stood in disbelief. *Should I take it?* Even if I wanted to, I was frozen. I could not move. There I was with my mouth opened wide and arms stretched out, but I couldn't move. *How pathetic,* I thought.

"No, no," He said. "It shows your reverence of the glory this piece represents. I am sad, though, because I sense that you do not feel worthy," He added.

How did He know that? That was a dumb question, I thought. *He is God, after all.* The tears poured down my face. He was right, and I could not pretend otherwise. I continued to stand there frozen; but now, sobbing. I wanted to feel worthy. I wanted to matter. And Lord knows, I have tried everything under the sun I could think of to be worth it.

"Whoa, whoa," I heard. "Whoa. Oh dear, stop, stop." There was such sympathy and sorrow in His voice. He cupped my face in the palm of His hands and looked me in the eyes. "Dear child, you *are* worthy, you do not *do* worthy," He said. "Oh my," He said as if He needed to fix something.

"There is great confusion about *being* and *doing.*" He shook His head as He muttered, "Where do I start?" He looked up at me and said, "Let's go back to the Garden. Remember my dear Eve?"

"Yes," I answered. I had such new respect for Eve. I would love to hear more about her.

"Shortly after the forbidden fruit incident, she and Adam knew they had sinned against Me," He began. "They, like so many today, tried to hide from Me. I asked them where they were, very well knowing already. But I wanted them to come out by choice, not by force. I don't work that way."

I know, I thought. *Although I could stand a little shove every once in a while,* I thought, laughing to myself.

"I heard that," He replied as He grinned. "Before eating the fruit, we walked together. We were just hanging out, being together. Then came the work: he in the fields, her in labor. That was the *doing.* The same applies today. I called all to love Me and then love their neighbors. To keep things in balance, there has to be a *being* with Me, then the *doing* for your neighbor will be cheerful. When My children get this mixed up, they begin to seek their worth from the doing and forget it is from who they are that is known from being with Me."

I shook my head. I had been a Pharisee; wise to the Scriptures, but working to enter the Kingdom.

"Yes, dear, and that will never work," He said. "It takes my Son's selfless act, and yet they say it is not enough. Some believe they have to work at the church cake sale and paint the sweet lady's fence down the street instead. I call My church to do those works, but not in the place of My Son. You are a daughter of the King; that is enough," He pointed out.

That is enough, I repeated in my head. "I want this one to stick," I said.

"It will," He replied. "It will."

"When?" I cried out. I felt I had so much to learn and at times like I was dog paddling in a funnel. All I could seem to do was keep my head above water at best. This could not be the way it was meant to be. I knew all things were possible with God—then why was I having so much trouble?

"Levels," I heard Him say. "Remember the levels to belief. Each layer of onion skin peeled offers an opportunity to develop another level of belief. One level at a time, dear; one at a time."

LOVED ONES

To My Grandma

*They may not be here to touch or to feel
But that does not make them any less real*

*They have gone on ahead to rest with the Lord
But they are still loved and greatly adored*

*One day the Lord will take us home too
And then we will see those special few*

*That while here on Earth made our life so sweet
That now live in our hearts as memories*

*The ones who held your hand when you cried
And never seemed to leave your side*

*But for reasons only God knows
Their loving souls had to go*

*But hold those thoughts close to your heart
Close your eyes and you will start*

*To make them real even if it is just to you
For always remember they still love you too.*

CHAPTER 12

Good Morning, Giant Slayer

So David triumphed over the Philistine with a sling and a stone; without a sword in his hand he struck down the Philistine and killed him (1 Samuel 17:50).

Oh happy day! That is all that seems to come to mind this morning. Great night's sleep! What a difference a good night's sleep can make. This popped a query to mind this morning as I was skipping about my day. I was amazed at the level of productivity I had mastered and all by 9:00 A.M. As I sat down to begin my greatly anticipated time with God, I began with one question: "Lord, why do we sleep well some nights, yet others seem to be filled with fear, panic, and yes, torment?" Instantly, I was prompted to David.

"Oh my dear one," He said with excitement, "I have been waiting for this day. The day I would get to share with you a man after My own heart." He seemed tickled to speak of this man. "Do you know why he was a man after My own heart?" He asked.

Earlier in a prayer time God had spoken that I might ask Him about *His* heart instead of posing the questions about *my* heart. I thought this might be what He was referencing, but as always, I like to double check. I mean this is God, and His Word is mighty. So I said, "Lord, I believe I do, but please confirm."

"Formal this morning," He replied. We laughed.

I had been working on a research paper earlier that morning, and I guess the formality of that paper had crept into my conversation with God.

"That is a very interesting point," He added.

"What point, Lord?" I asked.

"That what you had been doing previously has found its way into our time. That leads well into My dear son, David. Throughout his life he sought Me, but in the times that he allowed other influences to creep into that time, he would sway off the path," He noted.

I knew a little about David and one thought came to mind: what about the jealousy King Saul had for David? "That was not any fault of his, was it?" I asked.

"Oh no," He began. "You are right, Saul was jealous, and David was reaping the joy of his victory over Goliath."

"Then how do other influences creep into our time with You?" I asked.

"They creep in because you let them in," He answered.

I was confused and felt we were talking in circles. I had often felt that way when reading the parables, so maybe there was a hidden meaning that I wasn't getting.

"No, no," He said, "you are assuming I meant David. What Saul did caused David to bring it into our time. Saul was jealous of David's popularity. He had been the big man on campus, then here comes along this spunky, young fellow who, to Saul, appears to have stolen his thunder. Attention, or shall I say the need for it, can drive wedges between the best of My kids."

That was strange, I thought. *He referred to them as kids.*

He replied abruptly, "Not just them—to all as kids. Not just David or Saul, but you as well," He explained.

He said it with a straight face, and to be honest, I was not surprised or offended. He was right. I had been jealous of my brothers and sisters in Christ, and often I had wanted the notoriety they had received. It was true, and I had better swallow and grin because He had called a spade a spade. "So what do I do?" I asked.

"I believe the best answer can be found through a glimpse of My dear son, David," He answered.

I had heard that now several times, "My dear son, David" and I sensed a stir of—

He stopped me mid-thought. "Acceptance," He finished the sentence. "Your stirring can be calmed with acceptance. If you are secure in who you are, then others' success will bring you only joy because you can rejoice with them instead of against them. A heart like Mine loves others to be all I created them to be," He said, smiling.

That's easy for Him to say, He had not been... This time I stopped myself in mid-thought. *Yes, He had been rejected, worse than I will ever experience. He is rejected by those who know better, not to mention those who do not.*

"Thank you," He replied. "It is nice to be appreciated. But rejection is not scaled. A broken heart is a broken heart. I know; I feel the pain every time I see My children rejecting each other."

So much was rolling around in my mind. *Had I not been appreciative of Him? Had I made Him feel unaccepted?* That had not been my intention at all. Then, I thought about His words, "See My children rejecting each other." He not only sees it happen but sees it coming. It must be horrible to know, but because of our free will, not be able to stop it.

"Unfortunately, all children are unappreciative of their parents on occasion," He commented. "That is why I like to thank those when they do come around. I appreciate them, just like David. See, it isn't because I love him more or think he is all that and a slice of bread," He said, chuckling.

His sense of humor never senses to amaze me, I thought to myself.

"I am grateful for all of My children, but I do reward, and yes, brag about those who endure," He said. "There is an opportunity for each one to be everything I had hoped for them; but whether they pursue that opportunity is up to them."

I was beginning to understand. David had pursued Him and inadvertently became all His Father had hoped. This had made His Father proud; but the bonus is, I have the same opening. I wanted to seize that opportunity. As I said before, when I get to Heaven, I don't want there to be anything left in my basket. I want to have become and conquered all I was sent in this specific time to accomplish.

"Then do whatever it takes," He said with a confident air. "David wanted Me beyond all else. He did some things that were not pure in My eyes, but he always came back to Me. I wish My children to stay on the path that I light, but a well-taught child knows how to find his or her way back to that path if he or she steps off. David stepped off the path, and I am sure if you asked him, he would agree it happened more times that he'd liked."

I must be seeing things. This cannot be true. Was it David? No, it couldn't be.

Then God suggested, "Ask him yourself."

I didn't know whether to cry or kneel. I was beside myself with disbelief.

"No," God replied, "I wouldn't bow." They both giggled.

Did I just hear that? David giggling? Still in a daze, I heard David speak.

"To reiterate what my Father said, yes, I stepped off the path far too many times."

He had a very deep, yet honestly handsome tone to his voice. He stood up straight and often looked over at his Father, as if seeking His approval. He was mesmerizing, the kind of man who takes your breath away because you admire him and would like to be like him.

"I wish I hadn't, but I do not regret the things I did," David continued. "For from them I grew to know my Father's heart, and I hope to say, grew a heart like His."

This shepherd's boy is no boy at all. He spoke and carried himself like a man; a man of God, I thought. He did it again, I saw Him look toward his Father.

Why is that? I thought. *Dare I ask? I mean, this is the giant slayer. Does he have two stones in his pocket?* I laugh to myself. I could tell I was nervous. I tend to make silly jokes and laugh this way. *Why am I spending time thinking to myself when the David, Jesse's son, is right in front of me?*

I heard God say, "Yes, why are you?"

"I have to remember He knows me and my thoughts," I said, chuckling.

This brought a grin to His face. Then He interjected, "I believe you had a question for David."

No, He didn't just throw it out there like that, put me on the spot, I thought, semi-blushing.

Nonchalantly the Lord said, "I love bold. It is a quality I find very attractive in My people. David was bold in spirit, but humble in heart. Both are heavenly strengths," He added.

I saw David's face turn a ruddy shade. I could tell it made him feel good to hear those words of praise from God. I knew it would to me. I figured I might as well ask my question. It is always worse to back pedal out of an on-the-spot moment than to just go ahead and ask. "David," I said, "I see that you look often to your Father when speaking; why is that?"

I saw a glow come over him as he began to speak. I could see what God had seen in him as a boy when Samuel was sent to his father's house to look for the anointed one. He was kind and gentle, but stood firm with the boldness God had spoken of.

"I look to my Father for everything," he said, "because I am not capable without Him. I learned this in the places of desperation; the cave, when I lost my best friend, and when I slept with a married woman. I cried out for Him, and He always came through. I look at Him out of gratitude and appreciation. But most of all, I know that when I look away too long, I get into trouble."

His voice changed. He sounded like a little boy, so innocent, yet mature to realize that when he looks away he gets into trouble. Oh, it made me adore him even more. The purity he displayed created an admiration for him. I wanted to be me...but learn from him.

"You have it," I heard all of a sudden. "That is how I pray My Body will work," the Lord said. "They will look at Me to become themselves, but learn from each other. Oh, hang a banner...yell it from the mountain tops, 'Be who you are, and learn from each other.'"

"I have to be going now," I heard David say.

"No, no, please don't." I felt a lump in my throat and tears welling up in my eyes. "I have so many more questions. We just got started. Please not yet."

"I have to. I have streets to walk and songs to sing," he replied.

That did it; the tears came flooding. There were streets and people were singing. I thought of my grandmother.

"She leads the choir," the Lord shouted.

That was all I could stand. I began to sob uncontrollably. The tears ran down my face like a raging waterfall. My heart sank, and I was flooded with her standing there in a beautiful gown with her hands raised, praising her heavenly Father. I could not contain myself any longer. I broke. She was happy, singing, and in love with God. Oh, how my heart needed to see and hear that.

"Thank You," I said as I fell to the feet of my Father. "Thank You," I said as my tears dropped on His feet. I had loved that woman more than life itself. She had been taken away too soon; at least my broken heart believed that. Now I see she was needed in Heaven. She had a job to do, and I was so proud of her; so proud. *You go, Grandma,* I thought as I continued to sob. *You go.*

When I looked up, I saw David looking at me with a tear in his eye. He said with broken words, There are very few things greater than a family reunited. I wish no family would ever separate; but like myself, we often have to learn the hard way."

I thought so highly of him for his transparency.

"He has heard the onion analogy, too," God said with a laugh.

"Oh, do not get me started on that," David said with his words back together. "Do you know how annoying it is to talk about peeling an onion while you are hiding out in a cave?"

I could not help but laugh. At least I had been in the comfort of my home when I got the teaching.

"OK, OK," the Lord said. "No ganging up on the old Pops. Run along, David, I am sure you have mischief to get into, and I know Dena has things to do," He said like a proud parent of multiples.

I felt like part of the family. It felt good. It reminded me of when my daughter and nephew were young and they would gang up on me. It was fun, but a time would come when I'd have to round them up and direct them to the task at hand. I recognized that feeling, like being part of something special.

"Maybe the word is *accepted,*" the Lord said.

Speechless; I had not put the two together. I belong. Would it be enough? I was willing to stay to find out. I will never forget that day. I spoke with David, the giant slayer, the man who is funny, kind, bold, and loves His Father's heart. I was given a gift of a vision of my grandmother leading the choir, mouth wide as words of praise filled the heavens.

As miraculous as both of those experiences were, neither compared to the feeling that I belonged. I pray that feeling blossoms into a garden of knowledge of who I am. May it penetrate my heart. Yes, it had continued to be a happy day!

I heard God say as He walked away, "To whom much is given, much is expected."

No fear; I had been given much. "I love You," I spoke, as I walked away.

-CHAPTER 13-

Chewing on Some Meat

There is a time for everything, and a season for every activity under heaven (Ecclesiastes 3:1).

Another good night's sleep; but much to my surprise, before I got to my cup of coffee, I felt panic. When I say panic, it doesn't touch the intense night ones that I am prone to experiencing.

"Hold on a minute," He said. "I don't like that kind of talk."

"What, Lord?" I asked. I thought I knew, but always made sure.

"Prone to," He repeated. "You are healed from all *prone tos*. We are just working them out in the natural. I already see them in the spiritual," He stated.

Hmmm, I thought. *Put down the milk and pick up the fork, it's time for some meat.* I made a funny to myself when I thought, *But I'm a vegetarian!*

However, I don't think the humor was shared because He said, "Any other time I would be laughing along with you, but not today. We have serious things to attend to."

"Then so be it, Lord…let's dig in," I said.

In a very serious tone, He began, "I want you to meet someone this morning."

I had not heard this demeanor from Him before. He wasn't angry, but He appeared to be all about the business at hand. Surprisingly, I wasn't afraid, but a little concerned. The first thing that came to my mind was the comment He had said the day before about much being given, then much is expected. He had said that multiple times. Was now the time I was going to be expected of something? I had now talked myself into being scared. "What is it, Lord?" I said with hesitancy.

"Child, child, child," He said as He shook His head. "You always think it is about you."

Whoa, that hit hard; right in the gut. *What?* I thought. *I love others and want the best for them.* I felt the hair on the back of my neck stand up.

"No," He said, "you are doing it again. This is not about Me pounding the hammer down on some outrageous or miserable demand that I am expecting you to pay Me back for the good I have given you. No, no," He insisted.

I could tell He was taking a time out to compose Himself. I stood in silence, wanting to understand.

He began slowly, "My Son hung on the cross so that..." He took a breath, and then continued, "...so that we could have a relationship. I give because I want My children to have—but in return, I expect them to be responsible with the gifts I have given them." He stopped as if to ponder what direction was best from this point.

"Lord," I stopped Him, "may I speak?"

"By all means, dear," He said with a loving tone. "You are always welcome to talk to Me. I prefer communication, but talking is a start. But that is a subject for another time. Please, tell Me what you want to share."

"I have to confess," I began. There they come again, the lump in my throat and the tears in the corners of my eyes. I began again, "I have to confess, I have wanted the blessings, but have been afraid of the requirements. I believe I have looked at the latter as punishment."

I saw His head drop. I wanted to finish, but before I could, I ran to Him and hugged Him. I could not stand to see Him so crushed; so distraught. "Father, I see now. You give because You love us; but just as we parents expect our children to accept and use gifts in a positive manner, You do as well."

Hmmm, I thought, *mature words, or at least for me. Positive and manner, had I actually bitten into the meat?*

"Child," He said, "I want you, and *all* of My children to have all of your hearts' desires, but until your heart desires what is good and pure, I cannot answer those wants."

"That makes sense," I interjected.

"But there is more," He said. "With a heart on the way to its spiritual representation, there will be gifts given. I have to know, no, I *hope* they will care for those gifts."

I thought about my daughter and the many things my husband and I had given her over the years. She took good care of her things, but as God was suggesting, I did not know if she would until I took the chance and gave her the gifts. I had prepared her the best I could before the gifts were given, and then it was up to her.

"Sweetheart," He called me. "That is it exactly."

I found comfort in His words.

"But there is more," He said again. "Great joy is found when children display the heavenly strength of responsibility, but some fall short. That is OK because as long as they are trying, I will step back in and assist again."

"That must be when I feel like I have gone around the same mountain again," I said.

He laughed. "You are right. I will allow people and situations to come around to provide an opportunity to try again."

I thought, *I am going to try harder at these mountains from now on.*

"That is a wonderful idea," He said, smiling, "but some of those mountains are not expected to be moved the first time around."

"What do You mean, Lord?" I asked.

"I don't hold My children responsible for what they do not know," He said. "If I have not taught them, then I believe they deserve grace. Some mountains are unknown territory and are there to prepare you for future mountains. They are made as learning tools. Now, when one has experienced that mountain, then it is My hope one will know what to do when a similar mountain is presented. But either way, I am right there with them. We are a team."

What pressure His words took off me, I thought. I had so often climbed and climbed until exhausted, thinking I had better get it right, and beating myself up if I didn't. It also made me think about being a parent. I could not prepare my daughter for every mountain that may come, but hopefully the lessons learned from previous ones would give her enough knowledge to apply in the future.

This made me think about the subject of math. I didn't understand why the teacher would explain one problem and then send me home with homework, knowing I was not prepared. Learn on your own from the simplest example I can give you is what I'd think the teachers must say to themselves as assigning the homework. But I am very tainted over this subject. Math was and is *not* my happy place.

"No, no, no," the Lord interjected, laughing. "The mountains you face help build upon the next one you must face; but whatever is new holds the same philosophy. It is new, so you are not responsible. You are responsible for staying to learn…or leaving, that is called choice."

I liked this, I thought, *but where does God come in this?* I had instilled in my child to always seek God in times of mountains or pits. Some called them valleys, but from the places I had stood, valleys were just the grassy paths to the pit I was about to find myself in. With that being said, maybe you can tell I do not like the word *valley.* If all held true, maybe He would tell me why.

"Oh, you want to play that way," He said with a Cheshire cat grin. "Well, I will tell you, Miss Smarty Britches," He said, still grinning. "You don't like valleys because you find them weak. You want to climb, and they don't provide that option for you."

"OK, then why do I want to climb so badly?" I asked.

He got quiet. "I know the answer, but you may want to sit down," He said.

My stomach dropped. "What is it, Lord?" I said worriedly.

"You are trying to matter," He said bluntly, but with compassion. "In your attempt to *be* somebody, you are running from yourself."

I knew what He had said was true, although all of the rhymes and reasons were not clear. It was as if He had held up a mirror in front of my face. I thought my heart had stopped because I had forgotten to breathe. This was raw, and all I could do was fall limp. "I want to stop running Lord," I said softly. "I want to stop." There was silence in the air. It wasn't awkward, but in some sense necessary. Yes, I needed to stop.

With His arm around my shoulder, He whispered, "Let me tell you about My son, Saul. He can help."

I remembered He had mentioned earlier about wanting to tell me about someone. I was humble and ready to listen.

"Humble lives in the eyes; it looks with concern for the other because it has needed concern from others," He said with great wisdom. "Saul," He began, "was a mighty King. He had great popularity and power, until David came along."

David, I thought. *How could sweet, smart, and handsome David cause this king any trouble?*

"He didn't," He answered. "Saul just believed it that way. I had sent David to be a support and a friend to Saul. But David had been victorious and that drew attention and praise from Saul's people. This is the first common mistake My people make; they try to claim ownership of others. People are not to be owned. My Son, Jesus, paid for them to be set free. But I am getting off track. Had Saul's heart been pure, he would have realized that David's victory was his victory. They were to be a team, but popularity and insecurity overtook Saul's thoughts. See, he thought David was out to steal his kingdom, which was but a gift I had given him to use. Instead of talking to Me or David, he allowed those thoughts to consume him, and then his actions followed. What was meant to be an A team, now began to crumble within itself," He concluded.

I couldn't believe my eyes, but standing in the distance just beyond God was who I assumed to be King Saul.

The Lord turned to him and motioned him to come forward. "Dena, this is Saul," He introduced.

I noticed he did not move until spoken to. He came closer. He was a rough-looking man, not by his clothes being wrinkled or leather and chains, but he looked it on his face. He appeared to have had a hard life.

"Yes, he did," the Lord spoke. "Would you like to share, Saul?" He asked.

"Yes, Sir," he replied with humility. "Dena, my rough appearance, as you describe it, was brought on by myself. I made things harder on myself than they had or were supposed to be. Looking back, I know now that God's plan was of joy in my life. But the biggest one I missed was to share. I let my need for others' approval blind me from the family God was creating around me. David was to help me live in the abundant life God had planned for me, but I thought he was there to steal it from me. Sadly, in my attempt to stop David, I lost me."

His head dropped as in slow motion.

"May I ask you a question?" I asked Saul.

"Yes, please," he replied. "Anything you can learn from me helps take the sting out of the bite I have taken."

"Why is it that you stood so far back from God until He spoke?" I asked.

With a half grin, he began, "I wish I had done this in my heydays. I stand and wait because I got in trouble as a young ruler when I ran ahead and didn't wait for God's commands. He tried to slow me down and show me the straight path, but I let my stubbornness get the best of me."

I could tell he still ached over this. *Wow,* I thought. *How tragic.*

"Yes, it is," the Lord agreed. "It happens all the time between non-believers and my own Church. It is tragic. The saddest part is it is preventable. I give the gifts, be they spiritual or in human form, to My children based on the plan I have determined in their lives and how responsible they have been with the gifts. If you gave your child a brand-new sports car with no regard to the sacrifice you made to provide that car, and he or she went out and totaled it, would you be eager to give the teenager another?" He asked.

I had to admit, "No. I really wanted my child to enjoy the gift, not wreck it."

"That is exactly how I feel," He said. "I give them gifts to enjoy and to share with others. If a car, I expect they would want to drive their friends around. But if the car is totaled, neither the child nor the friends get to enjoy the gift. That is what happened with David and King Saul. Saul had gifts I had given him, and with the gifts David was being given, they could have shared and enjoyed them."

"Lord, it appears that those two men were not the only ones who lost out," I added.

"Yes, that is true," He agreed. "The kingdom, the people, many others missed out, too. Families do this all the time; one squabble divides the family and sides are taken." He paused a minute and then said, "I am not here to take sides but to take over."

I was stunned. "Take over what?" I wondered.

"I want to consume My children's lives," He said. "Every crack and crevice; I want to be part of. I am not about separation but reconciliation. I want them to forgive."

Wow, that's a big want, I thought.

All of a sudden He stopped and turned toward Saul. With eyes full of love and true sensitivity, He spoke to Saul with words that spoke to my heart as well. "Saul," He said, "I want them to forgive themselves as well."

That was deep. I could see the impact it had on Saul's face as he held back tears.

"Let it go, My child," He said as He comforted him.

It was absolutely one of the most beautiful things I had ever witnessed.

Is this all possible? I thought. I knew some very hurting people, including myself.

"Yes, it is possible," He said. "But first I must see My son off."

He turned to Saul. I did not hear what He said, but I saw him wipe his eyes. He cared for Saul even after the things he had done. It was beautiful to behold. Saul walked off. I sensed he needed time alone, and I respected that. Nothing else was said about him, but I now knew what I had experienced earlier; humbleness. I could look at him with humble eyes because I had needed concern from others, and now I could feel concern for him. I prayed he would find that forgiveness for himself. He was a good man who had lost his way.

FORGIVENESS

I remembered His reply to my question about forgiveness; yes, it was possible. I loved His optimistic outlook.

"If you believe it, then it will happen," the Lord said.

Dare we go there? I thought. *I mean, should I?* So I did. "What about those things we believe, but never see them come to be?" I asked. There it was—out there.

"Everything does not have to be a production," He stated.

I knew what He meant. I did tend to over-emphasize things. I had to laugh.

"In response to your question," He started, "there are behind the scene things going on all the time that you do not see. All prayers are answered. I could not say in My Word, 'Ask and you shall receive' if it weren't true. I take My role as your heavenly Father very seriously. And with that everything comes by Me first."

"Take for example," He began, "when My fallen son asked to sift my son Job. He had to ask Me. All things come by Me first. If you noticed, I took much grueling time to process if this was the best answer. Now some may argue what is best, but I reply that they don't have all of the facts. I allowed the sifting, and Job was rewarded with a double portion. There is meaning and purpose to every decision I make."

His remarks made me think of yesterday when I had been given the gift of seeing my grandmother praising our heavenly Father in worship. For so many years, I wanted her back. But knowing what I have seen now, I could not ask her to give that up. In a peaceful way, I knew He had done what was best. She suffered so greatly in her final days on this earth. If I had a choice of that suffering or leading a choir on golden streets, I would take His decision. I respected what He had allowed now. I was thankful He loved her that much.

After that thought was resolved, another question popped into my mind. "Lord," I asked, "what about those left behind?" I shook my head as I asked the question because I had heard so many theories like ones that said He would not answer such a question. But one theory that I had held too was that you don't know unless you ask. *If He chooses to answer, I will rejoice; if he doesn't, I will try again later.* That made me laugh.

"For another day, dear," He replied. "It is getting late, and you need your rest."

Rest; that sounded good. I had put in a long day. I could use some rest. "Night, Lord," I said. "Please thank the guys for sharing with me." I felt such brokenness for Saul. He has been so kind to share his hurt with me. I hoped he would be all right.

"He will be, My love," the Lord replied. "He will."

Not a Door Mat

Ever since the Lord stated He wanted reconciliation, not division, I had a burning within my gut that would not subside. I mean, some people just won't. And as much as we try, they seem determined to block the reunion. Then there are those who just want to keep the peace. I could sense I was riled up now. "Yes, I would agree that a family reunion is ideal, but we cannot be door mats can we?" I asked.

"Forgive Me for the chuckling," He said as He held His hand over His grinning face, "but your temper tantrum was quite amusing."

I don't know why, but His seeming lack of concern for my rant did not anger me. This seemed odd since I was so miffed. *Wow,* I thought, and then noticed I was grinning too.

"Child," He began, "you have been with Me long enough to know that My children are far from being doormats. They are temples."

I checked myself; there was still no hostility or sadness over Him not being angry.

"You know," He continued, "that ideally I wish too that My Body all got along not for the sake of peace, but because they *know* peace, the peace that Jesus left them. I will not give up trying and sending those who are willing to go. And as serious as this matter is, I will not allow it to cause those who know His peace to be bogged down. That is why I chuckle. Life is fun," He said. "I will deal with them as I deal with you. If they choose to live in an angry state or a bitter mess, then time with Me is offered. If they choose the other end of the spectrum—to live in a martyr mindset of keeping a fake peace—I will wait in the room as well. Their lack of budging does not and should not keep you from the family tree I have for you. So grab your potato salad and picnic basket. I have many for you to meet."

I thought about the ones He had been so gracious to introduce me to this far and to think there was more. *So a few won't budge,* I thought. *I will pray and leave the Lord to carry their weight. I have relatives to meet!*

THE DREAM

"I am beyond excited. I can hardly stand myself. What a difference a good night's sleep makes. I couldn't wait to tell You," I said.

"Do tell," He said with a mysterious tone.

"Well," I started off, "I had this dream that my husband had decided he wanted to leave me. Now before you get concerned that I have lost my mind, allow me to explain. I have struggled for what feels like forever with the fear of being left alone. It all stems back to the incident. I was left alone when that happened. It was of no fault of anyone except the perpetrator, but as a little girl, I did not understand that. I've just come to believe that if I was ever left alone, this might happen again. So, it isn't that my husband may leave, it is the fear I have of being left alone.

"Anyway, back to the dream. When he said that he was going to leave, I did not react as I normally would have, or what was normal for me. I didn't wake in a heart-pounding panic, or I am realizing at this very moment, I didn't feel a sense of guilt. I didn't feel as though I had done something wrong. Yee ha!" I couldn't contain it any longer.

"So, I'm still asleep not panicking, and I begin to have a rational conversation with my husband about how he is feeling and presented my rebuttal. It was absolutely amazing. I was calm and collected. Don't get me wrong, I was explaining to him why he should stay, but I was not begging. Man, that felt good. I don't even know what to say besides thank You."

"Why are you thanking Me?" He asked.

"Because I know somehow, somewhere You had something to do with it," I replied.

"Yes, you are right," He said. "But do you know how?"

"No, I don't, but I would love to know," I replied.

"Things that you are afraid of come out in your dreams," He stated. "However, you are still afraid of them when you are awake. That is why you had that panic the other day during the daytime. You cannot run. You go where they are because you bring them with you. Are you with Me so far?" He asked.

"Yes," I said with concentration.

"Let Me tell you about a son of mine who was rather hard-headed," He said with a chuckle. "His name is Jonah. He ran, but he couldn't hide. He took himself wherever he went. Sadly, where he took himself others were there, too. I am getting ahead of Myself. Jonah wanted My help; but often when I offer help, My children run. So, a little wind here and big fish there, and voila! Jonah ends up in the mouth of the whale. Then he had to stop running.

"See, My children want things to stop, like you did with your panic attacks, but they won't take the time to stop and accept My help," He said. "Do you understand?" He asked.

"I'm with You so far," I said as I sat on the edge of my seat.

"You stopped it," He said, nodding, "because you stopped."

There they were again; the tears. "I had no idea that was what I was doing. I just knew I needed You," I said.

"That is the first step, My dear," He said, "when My children realize that nothing or no one else will do and that they need Me. Then the healing has a chance."

"What do You mean, a chance?" I asked.

"Sad to say," He began, "but it is a chance because throughout the healing process, there are so many opportunities for them to stop stopping."

It wasn't a funny subject, but the stop stopping made me giggle.

"There are so many layers to their hurts that it cannot be peeled away all at one time. Some get tired or impatient and stop coming," He explained.

"What do You mean, stop coming?" I asked.

"The Secret Place," He replied. "I wait every day hoping they will come, hoping," He said. "You kept coming, we built a relationship, and I pray it continues."

"Why do You say pray it continues?" I asked.

"Because so often when things get good, they stop coming," He said. "They believe they have things under control and they can handle what comes along in life. It is like watching a train coming, but no one is listening to the conductor blow the horn, to get off the track." He covered His eyes like He didn't want to watch.

"Lord, I don't want to be one who does that," I said.

"The choice will always be up to you. I will always be there waiting. I will always be there with and for you," He said.

"Why repeat yourself?" I thought.

"Because if you stray, I am always where you left Me, waiting," He explained. "I will never leave you or forsake you, remember?"

It made me think of a song written by Matthew West that I had given my daughter when she was getting married. The lyrics read, "If you ever need me, you know where to find me, I will be right by your side." I stopped a minute to reflect. *He was right. He had always been there, even when I didn't come. I love Him more and more every day,* I thought. *I cannot live nor do I want to live without Him. He is my all in all.*

I had to go now, but as always I would wait anxiously until our next time together. But as always, I wait anxiously until our time again. Things were changing. I could tell. I felt different, and I liked it. There is something comforting about knowing He is always there waiting to see me again. "'Til then, Lord, 'til then," I said, turning to go.

"Have fun," He shouted. "Can't wait to hear all about it."

I blew Him a kiss, and He caught it. He is love.

His Fountain

Through thick and thin
Through good and bad
Through what makes us laugh and what makes us sad

To have faith is what He asks
He can heal the brokenhearted
He can redeem your past

But to believe is our part
He can't cleanse your wounds
Until faith you do start

To grab his love and hold tight
He counsels our hurts day and night

So I tell you from experience and beg for you to know
There's no other way, no other way to go.

A jealous love I crave for you

To know the Savior as a Father so true

He's there for us always, awake and asleep
Search in your heart, He's there, His love is deep

Draw near to Him, He'll be right there
"Johnny on the spot" as if out of thin air

His love endures forever
His Word is true
You can't fathom the love He has for you

So open your heart; let him reign
I promise you'll never be the same

So remember the mustard seed that moved the mountain
Drink from "the living water,"
take love from His fountain.

-CHAPTER 14-

A Cry in the Night

Then they cried out to the LORD in their trouble, and He delivered them from their distress (Psalm 107:6).

I have been through a whole gamut of emotions: anger, confusion, frustration, and sadness, to say the very least. I woke in such a panic that I thought I actually could hear my heart beating outside of my body. This isn't fun anymore. I noticed that when I panic within the panic, it gets worse.

"Your observations are wise," He said.

"Thanks," I said somberly. "Is our conversation going to go somewhere today?" *Let me just get this out there: will all of this be for good? Stop candy coating,* I thought. "Is this going to pay off?"

"I would ask you the question, but I already know the answer: What are you doing this more for? The people or you?" He wondered.

My heart broke. I knew what He meant.

"For me," I said sadly. I wanted to show people I have done something. I screamed as I realized how transparent I had just been, and it scared me. I panicked and stomped back to bed. Which was worse, waking to a racing heartbeat or airing my deepest emotions and thoughts? I ran.

TRANSPARENCY

Did I really want people to know I was that vain? I mean, it was fine when Saul was being transparent, but me? That was different because people would know.

"If it is all exposed, then there is nothing to reveal," He said profoundly.

But was it vanity or something else? I wondered.

"It is something else," He replied. "You want people to like you...no, love you."

"Yes, I do," I screamed at the top of my lungs. So many had not, and I can't do enough to make them. The tears were uncontrollable now. I was sleepy, and my head felt like it was going to pop off. The pressure has been building, and I cannot contain it any longer. "Make it stop!" I screamed.

"You are doing it," I heard Him say. "You are making it harder," He explained.

"No, not again," I said. I remembered the words of Saul admitting that he too had made things harder than they needed to be. "What now?" I asked on the verge of exhaustion. The room was tense, and I had had it again.

"Why is it that after such a great day prior, it all falls apart so quickly?" He asked.

That would be a question I would ask, so why was it coming from Him? I wondered, but not amused.

"Because I have a side too," He answered. "My children seem to think that it is all about what *they* are feeling or thinking when I have a role in their lives, too." He wasn't angry; but He said His words with purpose.

"Well, what do You want or expect me to do?" I asked in an *outside voice*.

"Remember," He said. "Remember what I did for you yesterday. Don't be so quick to forget from where I have brought you, and give Me a little credit that I will take you there again. This is no game with Me. I love you, and if you will calm down, I can help."

"Calm down," I stomped.

"Yes, calm down," He repeated. "In those moments of panic, stay calm. You can do it. Too many times My people react out of fear. They make quick decisions that get them in deeper than they originally started. Instead of Me telling you, let me introduce you to someone. Elijah, come here, son," I heard Him yell.

I wasn't prepared to see him. I knew of his run-in with Jezebel and his tight bond with the Father, but beside that I was stumped.

"You know more than you think you do," I heard the Lord say. "You have prayed to be like him," He said, reminding me.

I could not think straight, I was so frazzled from the night before. The panicking, the sleepy body, and a mind that wouldn't rest. I knew there was a great opportunity in front of me, but I was so sick of the whole ordeal.

"May I?" I heard this older gentleman ask.

"Yes, by all means, please," the Lord replied.

"I ran," he began. "I ran when a very mean lady was after me. She had a plan, and I played right into it."

I could tell by his tone, he still wasn't pleased with that fact. I listened as he continued.

"God had a plan for me too, but I chose to allow my fear of man, or in this case a woman, take over," he said. "I panicked and ran. Just like our Father was saying, I made a decision out of my fear, and it ended up making things worse on me and others around me. I, too, had just been with my Father. We had a beautiful, loving time together. And then as quickly as that time ended, Jezebel waltzed in and I forgot all my Father and I had shared."

He sounded very much like the prophet he was called. He had a matter-of-fact demeanor. He wasn't like David who had boyish charm in a man's body, or Saul who, while slightly defeated in spirit, had a solder's pose. No, Elijah seemed flat. No dimension. I don't mean that as an insult. He just didn't come across bubbly.

Then it hit me; he was all business. Didn't he skip when he walked with God?

God interrupted, "Dena, have you not skipped with me on occasions, but found it necessary to walk in others?"

"Yes, I guess I had," I admitted.

"Then please do not judge My son," the Lord said bluntly.

"I am very sorry, I didn't mean it that way," I said apologizing.

"I know," the Lord said, "I was making a point. You are assuming that he didn't skip by this one meeting. He is all business because he wants to help you. We skipped."

"I'm sorry to have interrupted you, Elijah. Please continue," I said humbly.

"I ran," he continued, "when I should have stopped. I knew my Father would care for me because He had before, but I ran. May I give you a little advice?" he asked.

"Yes, please," I replied. I noticed he had very pleasant manners, something that I found appealing having been raised in the South.

"Listen to God and stay close," he said. "When those moments of panic come, stand firm, not letting your emotions dictate your footsteps. Don't rush yourself."

That hit home. I want to get to a decision quickly.

"If it takes ten minutes, take it; if it takes thirty, take it," he continued. "It will take less time in the long run if you take the time up-front than it will if you rush in the midst of the panic," he instructed.

"May I ask you a question?" I said.

"Certainly," he said.

"Do they stop?" I asked, hoping.

I saw him glance over at our Father as if to ask, "Do you want to take this one?"

After a time, Elijah turned to me and said, "Wait and see."

That was not enough for me. I wanted a definite.

"The only definite you have is that God is good," he said. "He will see you through."

"But I know that," I replied with frustration.

"Do you? Do you really?" he insisted. "If you knew, then what they did or didn't do would not matter. I will give you a little hint. It is really not about the panic; it is about the relationship," Elijah said.

I had to let that one sink in. They must have known that because there was silence.

"A good relationship has its ups and downs, with both bringing the relationship closer," Elijah said.

Then God spoke. He had been silent for so long that I was a little startled to hear His voice. "Marriage," He said, "was a gift, but what a dump it has become. I created it to be special, but it is treated as drudgery. If those who are one would see the trials as a beautiful trail that leads to each other's hearts, they would never leave each other. The sun shines at the end of a rainbow. But the rain must come. Noah—he got it," the Lord said.

With that cue, Elijah bowed and said, "I bid you farewell."

"It was a pleasure," I said.

"Mine as well," he replied as he shook God's hand and walked away.

As he left, I felt I had missed out on his stopping by.

"You did, My child," the Lord confirmed. "He is full of great knowledge and oozes wisdom. Yet, you let him walk away."

"Why, Lord, would I do that?" I asked.

"It isn't just you," He said, "others do it too. They are in such a hurry that they miss golden opportunities that I have laid at their feet. It is a shame," He said, shaking His head. "In their need to move to the next, they miss the present and often they miss Me."

He was right or at least as far as me. I remembered a time when He had told me specifically, "If you don't slow down, you are going to miss Me."

"I want to stop," I blurted out.

"For their cry of 'make it stop,' My children need to stop," He said. "Very good," He said as He smiled. "Very good. The key is not to rush. A heavenly strength is not to rush. Let me tell you about Noah…now he didn't rush."

TIRED OF BEING TIRED

"My first reaction is to tell You that I only woke up a moment with what I would describe as a mini-panic attack. I remembered what You said: stay calm. So I focused on that and soon was back to sleep. The attacks aren't gone, but I feel I handled it well. Somehow I don't think that is the goal here. I would think free is being free, not manageable," I stated.

"You are right," He agreed. "I want My children to experience complete freedom that was made possible by the cross. My Son didn't die for half freedom. It was finished, complete, abundant, and for everyone. I merely want you to be able to recognize and stay in control of the current situation until the onion peeling is complete," He said.

"That seems like a long time," I said, half discouraged.

"Not once you get the hang of it," He began. "It is new to you. Many of My people are accustomed to letting their flesh, their emotions, run their lives. That is why it feels to them they are on a roller coaster. Up and down, around and around. It gets tiring because the cart never stops at the station. They are trying to stuff down the panic and pretend everything is OK. That can wear out a person," He concluded.

"Tell me about it," I confirmed. "Lord," I said with a soft but hopeful voice, "I am tired of my day's enjoyment or lack thereof, being determined by how well I slept the night before. In fact, I don't want to begin our conversations with if I slept or not. It just seems it has way too much focus that it doesn't deserve.

"I am tired of being tired," I added. "What do You think?" I asked.

"What you feed will grow," He replied. "What you meditate on will lead your actions," He explained.

"What do You mean?" I asked.

"Do you remember Noah?" He asked.

"Oh yes, I was so excited to hear what you had to say about him, but I get distracted by the sleep or didn't sleep problem," I replied.

"That is exactly what I was trying to explain," He said with an ah-ha look in His eye. "You wanted to know about Noah, but you had been so focused, mediating on your sleep patterns, that your actions followed. What you think about will affect what you do...or in this case, don't do," He explained.

"Lord, I have to ask this question," I said.

"OK," He replied, "but it isn't being irresponsible."

I laughed. "I love that You know me that well. I wanted to know if I don't talk about the sleep, am I pretending it isn't there?" I explained.

"No," He said, "because it is still there, right?"

"Oh yes," I said. "That I know for sure."

"Yes," He agreed, "but you are putting it in perspective. We can begin focusing on what is causing it, which is what is really important about it, instead of it."

"I like that," I said with a big grin on my face. "Where shall we start?"

"Chipping away at the heart, or better put would be chipping away to get to the heart," He replied with excitement.

The very thought makes me feel sick to my stomach, I thought.

"That's not good," He said.

"I know," I agreed.

"I hope that knowing that we are underway gives you comfort," He said. "We peel away at the heart condition one layer at a time."

"How do we do that?" I asked.

"How do you know somebody?" He started.

"You communicate," I answered.

"Yes, and that brings intimacy," He added. "You have conversations to get to know each other. If intimacy is stopped," He continued, "you grow apart, creating distance. Then when each has things occur in their lives, the other misses being part of it."

"Lord, I don't ever want to be distanced from You," I shouted.

-CHAPTER 15-

Hearing

My dear brothers, take note of this: Everyone should be quick to listen, slow to speak and slow to become angry (James 1:19).

"With so much noise in our lives, how do we make sure it is You, Lord?" I asked. "How do we know it is You, beyond hoping?"

"OK, here we go," He began. "There once was a wolf who cried wolf."

"Don't you mean boy?" I questioned.

"No," He assured me. "This wolf cried wolf. The wolf talked about himself, did for himself, basically worshiped himself. That is the flesh. If your flesh speaks, it is all for it. Did you notice I used the word *all?* The flesh is unbalanced; I am balanced. When *I* speak, what I say helps you and others. Would I cut off My Body's nose to spite its face? No, I wouldn't. But the flesh would. This is why it is so important to listen carefully. Take time to process, to think about what or from whom you are hearing.

"That brings us to the enemy," He continued. "The enemy likes to have you rush into a decision based on what you hear before you discern. That is why, over time, I tell you things in advance—I want you to learn to hear My voice. I don't need or want you to rush."

"What do You do with people who won't make a decision?" I asked.

"Two things come to mind," He began, "One, I am patient, and two, I heal. Often they are limited to their decision making because they are not aware of their choices."

His answer made me think of a scenario He had shared to me once. He spoke of having the choice of three cars. One was red, one blue, and the third yellow. He had gone on to say that if you did not know there was a green car to choose from, you would not choose green.

"Exactly," He agreed. "Once," He continued, "they have made a decision, go forward. The enemy likes when you question your decision. Remember that I don't change. I am constant," He added.

"What is the second?" I asked.

"If another's indecisiveness troubles you, then let's investigate why," He said. "As far as the one who is indecisive, let's also investigate why. I am here to uncover the mysteries of *why*, since I am the One who knows the souls," He explained. "Don't venture out of the gate until you are comfortable with My voice," He continued. "Too often out of zeal My children run ahead, like sheep bolting out of the pen. A shepherd herds the sheep to where he knows he can round them up when needed. That is another reason why our Secret Place is so important. Learn to hear Me in the quiet before we step out into the noise. Hearing My voice is not meant to be hard," He concluded.

"Then why is it?" I asked.

"Because of doubt and deciphering," He replied. "If you know My Word, you will know Me. I never contradict it."

"But what about questions that do not go against your word but are unclear?" I asked.

"When in doubt, wait," He instructed. "I am the Clarifier."

"What if we wait too long?" I asked.

"I will catch you on the next round," He said, smiling.

"But I don't want to miss it the first time," I said, unsettled.

"I appreciate that," He said, "but maybe there is a need to be perfect, or not to disappoint."

"Or maybe I want all of you I can have," I added.

"Very good," He shouted. "When the *needs to be* are healed, the *wants to be* will be done. As the fears begin to dwindle, their voices go too, leaving it clearer to hear Me."

I thought about my math class; how, as my own fears had been healed, I could hear peace when in the classroom. I was no longer distracted by my flesh or the enemy egging it on making his voice more apparent.

"I will not holler over the other voices, but I will help you elevate Mine," He said. "I don't do screaming matches. No one gets heard there. I don't confuse, shame, or belittle. My voice follows Myself; My Word. Other voices follow their flesh, the enemy, or someone else."

"Lord," I began, "that is a lot of voices to decipher through. It's confusing."

"Yes, but child, when it is Me, you do not question. However, you may question yourself or others."

"That I have done, but honestly I have questioned, even thought it was You only for the circumstance to prove I was wrong."

"Wrong would be not trying. In fact, it is sad," He added. "Did you know *things* can distract you too?" He asked.

I recently had been almost obsessed with finding a lamp for my office. As silly as it may sound, I can get set on something that is a legitimate need and can't rest until I find it. "Yes, Lord, I can see what You are saying," I answered.

"*Things* can have a voice…if given too much attention," He noted.

"I had even resorted to making a list of *things* I need. I do love lists," I admitted, "but this lamp was beyond containable on a list. What is this craziness?" I asked.

"Yes," He laughed, "it can make you crazy."

I laughed. I thought about how the search was driving me bonkers.

"It can drive you to buy out of frustration," He said.

"So true, Lord," I agreed. "Over time, You directed me to the very one that sits in there now. I love it; it's perfect."

"Peace," He said. "When it is My voice, even if it is about a lamp, there is peace. Rest in knowing that I will bring what you need when it is the right time."

I took a deep breath. I had not realized how much energy the lamp pursuit had drained from me.

"You like lists, right?" the Lord asked.

"Yes," I replied.

Rather than waiting, I have the tendency to buy things just to have something that meets the need. My husband often says, "Don't settle; wait 'til you find what you really want."

"But I get impatient," I admitted.

"And waste money," the Lord interjected.

"Yes," I was sorry to admit.

"I know your heart and what you need, and if you think about it, I know where the item is," He said.

This made me think of our bathroom clock. I had been looking for one for months. Then one day when in my prayer time, God brought one to my mind.

"I can use things to help you hear Me clearer," He said.

I thought about the many times I would be in a store and would hear Him prompt me to get, or not get, certain items only to find out later that I did or didn't need them. "Yes," I said, "I like that, let the items serve me, not me chase the items."

I heard cheering.

"You got it," He said.

"What else can I do?" I asked.

"Change your viewpoint," He said. "Keep your eye on the prize; a peaceful night with a blanket of good rest. For example," He began, "when you complete an assignment for your class, your prize is completion. If you dread it until then, you don't enjoy any of it. To focus on the prize and enjoy the process leaves no room for dread."

"I don't want to dread," I stated.

"Then change your thinking," He suggested, "then your actions will follow. It is a process. That has to be expected. If you spend energy fighting the process, it only hinders the growth—stunts it, if you will—slowing it down, because it takes you off your focus. It all works together while we work on your heart through faith and actions. The heart is chipped away as you focus on the prize, and your actions will follow if you change them. Don't forget to change them," He repeated.

"How do I change them?" I asked.

"By the words out of your mouth and the movement of your feet and hands," He answered.

"Oh my goodness," I squealed, "feet and hands! The transforming of my heart will reflect in my mouth, feet, and hands."

He laughed and said, "That is the real prize." He chuckled, "So shall we start?"

"Oh, yes," I said with excitement.

A GARAGE

"Your heart is like a garage that over time has been packed with stuff you don't need. Things you have forgotten are there, and worst of all, items that are hazardous to your health. We may even run across items you didn't even know were put there," He added.

"Wow, it sounds like a mess," I admitted.

"You got it," He agreed, "but we are up for the job. Grab your rubber gloves and an old pair of jeans…we are going in."

We laughed. I thought to myself that my old viewpoint would have said, "Savor that laugher because it's going to be painful." And although that might be true, I want to focus on the laugher, not dread the pain. *Perspective; that is what I need, an encouraging perspective.*

"Oh, oh," I heard Him almost jumping as He spoke. "Encouraging perspective, oh," He said again. "Let me get someone." He left the room for a minute.

"Barnabas," I heard Him call, "Barnabas."

Out of nowhere came this man running from around the corner.

"Yes, Lord, what is it?" he said with a cheerful voice.

"I want you to meet someone," He replied.

"Great," he said excitedly.

"Barnabas, this is Dena. Dena, this is Barnabas," He said, introducing us.

"Very nice to meet you," he said as he shook my hand.

"Likewise," I replied. "You are one of my favorites of God's children," I said with a big smile on my face. "I have always prayed to be a Barnabas of my time—you were such an encourager to others."

"Well, thank you, my dear," he said. "That is very sweet of you, but I really cannot take all of the credit."

Hmmm, I thought, *very noble, but he does deserve some credit because I know we have a choice to view things half full or half empty.* "So," I said, "that is very humble of you, but you didn't have to be so encouraging toward others that you met."

"Oh yes I did," he said, as if he couldn't wait to explain. "Have you heard about the onion?"

I shook my head thinking, *Not again,* but laughed politely.

"What?" he asked with a slight confused look on his face.

The Lord stepped in saying, "Yes, she has heard about the onion and is not wild about the analogy," as He laughed.

"Well, I think it is absolutely beautiful," Barnabas said.

I thought, *But I bet it stinks.* I chuckled to myself and then returned my attention to what he had to say.

"My onion experience was great," Barnabas said. "I wanted to be the best I could be and if that was the method God deemed necessary, then I was onboard."

Wow, he is so upbeat. It was refreshing.

He continued, "The best thing about the onion is you get to share the results. By becoming all I could be, I wanted others to as well. It is gratifying to pass it on and see others blossom. There is something special when you see another person's light come on inside."

I loved that illustration. "The more lights that shine, the brighter the world," I added.

"Yes, oh, yes," he agreed. "You have a good one here," he told the Lord.

"Yes, I do," the Lord replied, "a little stubborn, but a submissive heart."

I stood listening to God and Barnabas speak highly of me, making me a little bashful.

"Why so red?" Barnabas asked.

"I'm not used to such kindness," I answered, seeing the fun drop from his face.

"What?" he asked. "This can't be. Lord, what on earth?" he asked.

"Barnabas," the Lord said, "negativity is at a catastrophic height. Back-stabbing and name-calling are the solutions to problems in many lives. Many even claim to use these methods as a sign of how much they love someone."

I thought Barnabas was going to cry, because he appeared to be so distraught over this modern-day revelation.

"What?" Barnabas said, speaking in sheer horror. "That is not love." But then he stopped. "What can I do, Lord?"

"Keep being you," He answered. "Just like I will tell all of my Barnabases of the current time to keep being themselves. I have to go after the one, and while I am gone I need the 99 to keep glowing. I need their lights to shine like lighthouses directing ships. The lost need beacons to guide them in. If the light goes out, they wander into things, things like jagged rocks and walls. They are blind; but with Me, they can see.

"Once they can see, my Barnabases can encourage them to keep looking in love, for those to help. Their first reaction will be to close their eyes again out of fear. Change scares people," He added. "They need smiling, bright faces to show them it is safe."

I looked over at Barnabas, who was tearing up. "Lord, I must go now. I have some praying to do," Barnabas said. "I need to make signs and billboards. People need to know that they don't have to suffer. I want to encourage them, share the love of God with them. Dena, it was a pleasure to meet you. I hope to see you again."

"I wish you didn't have to go, but I understand," I replied. "Barnabas," I added, "I really want to be like you." I looked at the Lord as I continued, "I mean, be me but a light like you are. You are every bit as nice as I thought you would be."

"Thank you, dear one. I bid you good day and a life full of light." He bowed and then turned away.

He was gone in a few swift steps. There he was, the Encourager. I hope to be one, too.

"Dear," I heard the Lord interject, "everyone can and has the choice to be an encourager. It is a choice."

I understood what He meant. I have gifts, a purpose that He had ordained, but encouraging others is a characteristic you amplify while living out your purpose. They were not separate, but in addition to. "I want to," I said out loud. "I want to encourage in addition living out my calling."

"Great—another light to the family," He replied. "Now, go shine and we will meet again later."

"Love You, Lord," I said as I waved goodbye.

"Love you, too," He replied.

THE OIL CAN

"You are a well-oiled machine," I heard Him say. "But even the best NASCAR cars need oil changes. Come in for service regularly," He stated.

"I like that," I said with excitement. "Change me, Lord, change me," I shouted.

"Life puts wear and tear on your body. Just like your car needs tire rotations and oil changes to keep them running, you need service too," He said.

"I feel like I am on a secret mission," I said.

"You are," He said.

"I feel like one of the 400 You had in hiding," I said jokingly.

"Yes," He said. "You are funny."

"I learned it from You, Papa," I said, laughing. "I want to be a spy and go undercover," I continued, "with a brown, bomber jacket and air force goggles. What else Lord?" I asked. "Will I be undercover the whole time?"

"Yes," He said.

"Cool," I said excitedly.

"But you will see others in different roles," He said. "So don't be jealous, you will be OK," He warned.

"Sorry," I said. He knew that my strong desire to be mighty in the Kingdom sometimes brought out the ugly green monster when others rose and I stood on the ground.

"We'll work on that," He said.

"Please do," I commented.

"Remember, you asked," He said, laughing.

Somehow I wasn't laughing as much.

"Lighten up," He said.

"I would love to," I replied.

"We will work on that too," He added.

"Yeah! That will be more fun," I said.

"It all can be fun, if you will just succumb to it," He said.

"To what?" I asked.

"To the process," the Holy Spirit said as if He were a cowboy about to lead His men into battle.

"What is this process You keep talking about?" I asked the Lord.

"I wondered when you would ask," He remarked.

THE PROCESS

"The Holy Spirit starts His work the moment you invite My Son into your life," the Lord began. "We are a package deal," He said, laughing. "He prompts you, similar to fishing. The Holy Spirit bobs around hoping you'll take the bait, just like the fisherman ties a fishing lure to the end of his fishing line. Neither the fisherman nor the Holy Spirit can or will make you take what He is offering. However, if you do, then I am the line. It connects us. This gives Me an open door to move into."

"Then what?" I asked.

"I take you off the hook and put you in a better pond, one that I oversee," He explained. "I feed you and care for you. Some try to jump back into their old pond because it is more familiar. I hate to lose them that way," He admitted. "There are those who stay, those who leave, and those who wreak havoc," He said.

"What about the ones who stay?" I asked.

"Well," He began, "the first thing they notice is the pond is clearer."

That sounds good though, I thought.

"Yes, but it shows them how dirty they are," He explained.

"Oh, I see," I said as I made a painful face.

"If they will give Me time," He said, "I will gently clean them. Oh you should see their faces as the dirt, muck, and pollutants are removed and the beautiful colors of their scales are revealed. They reflect in the crystal water. It is such a sight to behold. I can see them splashing and jumping around now."

"What else, what else?" I asked, excited to hear more.

"As the story goes, they live happily ever after," He said, smiling.

"And the scales You mentioned, what about those?" I asked.

"As the scales are removed from their eyes, they begin to see clearer; brighter. But they also see their own sins and others. Hmmm," He said as if taking a breath, "this can breed competition and judgment. And that jealousy you mention as the ugly green monster...it can show up too. This is not how it was supposed to be. It was for them to share what they have learned about themselves by what I teach them. Not to hold over another's head or even worse—cast them out. The doors to My church should never close. If My church is filled with My light, those who desire to live in darkness will not be able to stay. Isn't that your next question?" He asked.

"Yes, my next question was what about the ones who leave?"

"The Holy Spirit bobs for a bite. But some remember and run, and worse, tell others. It frustrates Me because they don't know. They didn't give Me a chance," He said, dropping His head.

"But you keep giving them chances," I said sympathetically.

"Yes, a true friend gives second chances," He said.

"Lord," I asked, "what about the ones who seek to harm the church? Surely You can't say, 'Let everyone in' and hope they change. What about the ones who come in to wreak havoc on the Body?" I asked.

"Have not all wreaked some havoc?" He asked.

"Yes, Lord," I began, "but not premeditated," I explained.

"Wait with that thought, for I know where you are going," He stated. "You want to know about the controllers and the Pharisees," He said.

"Yes," I said, shaking my head in agreement.

"I have a pool for them," He said.

"Lord, You do not show favoritism," I pointed out.

"I know, child, but even though I love each child with no special treatment, some need additional care. Do you understand?" He asked.

"Yes, I guess if I had one child who needed help in math, like myself, I would get them additional help where none would be necessary for the child who does well in math class." I found myself wanting to sway the conversation. "I want so badly for Him to say they would be of here," I admitted. "But I know it was due to their hurts that He wouldn't."

"Very good," He said sincerely. "You are growing in your process. You have learned to recognize and retreat."

"I also know that retreating to You is not a sign of weakness," I said.

"Child, I am impressed," He said. "There was a day when your temper sent you reeling and before you knew it there were more messes to clean up than originally started. I am grateful that even though you want to retaliate, you allow Me the chance to heal your pains. I promise that when you heal, your view is clearer. This is why I can make fair calls on the actions of My children. I do not have the emotions of a broken heart leading the way.

"I am broken for the Church because the Church is broken," He continued. "We have One sent who specializes in broken things. When He repairs it, you are made better. He checks everything that affected the original broken piece. The world's way of fixing is a Band-Aid. Rig the broken piece, hoping it will work, but not sure for how long—at least for now. This process that I speak of is not easy. I know that; but I am here to hold, nurture, and yes, hear you scream if need be. It requires heavenly strength to stay," He said.

"Stay?" I questioned.

"Yes," He said, "to commit to the process. But this too breeds jealousy," He said.

"Wow, that sure seems to be rampant in the Body," I said.

"You don't know the half of it," He said. "Now, ask your question," He said.

He knew my concern, so I might as well throw it out there. "Lord," I began, "what about the ones who seek to control and place law upon Your people?"

"You ask because you have been hurt," He said.

"Yes, that's true," I admitted.

"Then where do you go?" He asked.

"To our Secret Place," I answered. It appeared that another layer was about to be peeled from the tears my personal onion was creating.

"My Church keeps others out because they are afraid, not because I cast them out," He said.

"Do we just let them in and let them destroy Your temple?" I asked with concern. "Didn't Your Son get angry in the market?" I could tell I was getting a little heated under the collar.

"Is it the hurt or protection of My Church that the heat comes from?" He asked.

"I want them gone," I screamed. *There, I said it. They hurt me, and I want them gone. So, if You could just tell them to go away and don't let them back, I will be happy,* I thought, knowing He would not say that.

"You are right, My dear, I will not say that, but I will help you see through that anger so you can move on your path free of the need to shut the Church doors."

"Very well," I said, stomping over to Him. "Do what You need to do!" I said, frustrated like a child who wasn't getting her own way. As I sat down beside Him and looked into His eyes, my demeanor changed. He looked so loving and concerned for my heart. "Lord," I said, "I am tired of the hurting. What else can we do?"

"Let's get back to My pond," He said.

"What happens in Your pond?" I asked.

"First, may I tell you what happens in the other pond?" He asked.

"Yes," I said, "please."

"It is filthy, nasty. It is left to the elements of the world. Whatever or whomever desires to enter can do so. Sharks feed on the smaller," He added.

"But My pond is kept clean. It has the right amount of nutrients necessary to sustain all life. There is a balance and no hierarchy. Everyone is equally cared for."

I heard thunder crack and saw fire in His eyes that appeared to shoot flames. He spoke in an echo, saying, "At times a shark has shown up in my pond." His words made the earth tremble.

"How?" I said, shaking. "I mean, You bring them in, right?" I questioned.

"They are imposters, wolves in sheep's clothing," He explained in the same echoing voice. "They come two ways: hard, ready to devour or innocently. They came with all the right intentions, but once they were in the pond, they seized what they viewed as a golden opportunity to pull rank, to exercise authority that was not given. Oh this makes Me so angry," He said, slamming His fist down. "No pride in My pond!" The earth shook, and thunder cracked.

I envisioned the pool in our neighborhood with a sign that says "No Diving," but this pond's sign said "No Pride."

"My pool is a safe place, and I will keep it that way," He assured me. "There is a process to follow. The producer, which is Me, and My people, if they will do their part, will produce a product for my Kingdom or in this case, the pond."

"What is our part?" I asked.

"To participate," He answered. "No side-line watchers here," He said.

"What do You do with those who wish to make it an unsafe place?" I asked.

"I deal with them harshly and quickly. They can humble themselves or I will. The choice is theirs," He replied.

I waited for thunder, but there was none.

"No, no more thunder," He said. "I am quick to forgive and overcome anger."

He was back to His pleasant Self. Whoosh, I motioned my hand over my brow. *Note to self; stay humble.*

"See," He said, "I handle those who desire to mess with My children. I am a very protective Parent; but as you saw, I am also quick to forgive. I wish this for My children. Do not be quick to anger, but to forgive. Let Me handle the doors of the Church. If you believe I speak and are willing to listen, I will tell you when an imposter desires to cry wolf."

"Thank You, Lord, for spending time with me. I really appreciate it," I said.

"Me, too," He replied.

-CHAPTER 16-

Good Day

We demolish arguments and every pretension that sets itself up against the knowledge of God, and we take captive every thought to make it obedient to Christ (2 Corinthians 10:5).

"I think I want to start saying, 'Good day,'" I announced. "It seems more appropriate with the viewpoint we discussed the other day. I mean, if my perspective is good morning, I have left out a large chunk of the day. So, good day, Lord," I said.

"Well, well, well, what has you in such a good mood?" He asked.

"I tried what You suggested," I answered. "In my moment of panic last night, I talked myself down into a calm, rational state, and didn't allow my emotions to run the show. In doing that, I didn't get way out into left field. I kept contained and slowly drifted back to sleep," I said with a smile.

"Well, I am very impressed and proud of you," He said. "Well done, My child."

What? What did He just tell me? I asked myself. Well done? I have waited so long to hear those words, but I thought it would be once I reached Heaven.

"Why would you think such a thing?" He asked. "My children do things every day that make Me proud. Why would I wait until they are done in this earth realm to praise them? Oh no, I won't have that. I, too, want to be a light for them. Heck, I am *the* Light. Where do you think Barnabas learned to encourage?" He asked.

"I really like Your parenting style," I said. "You are a great Father."

"See, you just did it," He said. "You didn't wait until you met Me at the pearly gates, you praised Me now. And I thank you."

A question came to mind as He spoke. "We were made to praise You, I have heard. What does that mean exactly?" I asked.

"Praise means to worship, think highly of; and worship is a way of showing love," He explained. "I am love and you are made to love. Hmmm," He said, scratching His chin. "Let Me put it this way. Love is like water is to a glass. The glass needs something to hold and the water needs to be held. I am the glass. I want to hold you. If you will pour yourself out to Me, that is the position of worship; then I can wrap My arms around you. Worship is for both of us. You show love, and I get to give it back. It is not an idol or a chore."

There went His tone again. *He was getting fired up.* I laughed to myself. I wasn't intimidated; I was alert, as if to pay attention.

"Religious groups and cults are out there making praise and worship a regimen. It is not," He said sternly. "I want you to come because you want to, not because it is three o'clock and it is on the schedule." He took a deep breath and continued, "I want, just like any parent, My children to love and admire Me. That is praise and worship; one-on-one time, exchanging love and admiration for each other. You come saying, 'You are my only Father, and I exalt You.' It is a beautiful thing. Does that answer your question?" He asked.

"I think so," I said.

"You don't sound sure," He said.

"I think I thought it was more complex than that. Almost like I am not doing enough or reverencing You enough," I added.

"Child," He began, "please do not allow the world or even My Body to make it difficult. When you come it shows reverence. It is that simple. If you want to raise your hands, raise them; if you want to lay prostrate, then lay; I just want you to come."

I stood reflecting on what He had said. I realize that the position, the place, or even the time was not as important as being with Him. It was as simple as that.

Ting. I heard it again, Ting. "What is that?" I asked.

"You are getting lighter," He said smiling. "Pennies are falling from Heaven."

"What?" I asked.

"More coins are coming," He said. "As you learn the ways of My heart and pass it on, others benefit. They become coins making each of your loads a little lighter. Like pennies falling from Heaven."

"I don't understand the pennies part," I admitted.

"They are in reference to my angels," He stated. "They come down to help, to match change," He said, laughing at His own joke.

"To help what?" I asked while joining in His humor.

"My coins, Precious One," He said proudly.

"Oh, I want an angel to help me," I said excitedly.

"Oh, Daughter, you have one," He said with excitement. "Her name is Sara."

"May I meet her?" I asked.

"Yes, you may," He answered. "But come have a seat with Me first," He said as He motioned me to a couch.

THE COUCH

This couch is very uncomfortable, I thought as I sat down on the very firm, yellow cushion. I wasn't even sure if cushion was a fair assessment as hard as it was. "This is new," I said. I had not realized that we had been standing for so long. "Why the change?" I asked.

"To keep you on your toes," He said letting out a big laugh. "Get it," He said. "We are sitting, and it keeps you off your feet, but I said it on your toes."

I joined in the laughter as I rolled my eyes. *It was funny,* I thought, a little silly, but I liked it.

Just as quickly as He had joked, His tone turned serious.

"What is it?" I asked, concerned. "And why is this couch so stiff?" I said as I squirmed, trying to get comfortable.

"I want to talk to you about a pattern I am seeing," He said. "One that I have seen in the lives of many of My children."

"What is it, Lord?" I asked, concerned about His words and not so much about the couch.

"I have looked back over our conversations from the past couple of days, and I see your day is contingent on what happens—be it either good or bad. See, there is no bad in the heavenlies."

"But Lord, we are not in the heavenlies yet," I pointed out.

"There is where you are wrong," He stated. "The Kingdom is within you. You have the keys to all the treasures that are available as My children. It troubles Me that My Body is swayed by what day of the week it is or who they meet that day. Contentment comes from within," He said, "therefore whatever comes or doesn't come won't shake your day."

"I believe you are saying that You are enough," I said.

"You are getting ahead of Me," He said politely. "I am saying who and what you have been given are enough."

"Like my angel," I asked.

"Yes, to name just one," He replied. "Your happiness is not subject to your circumstances. Trials happen, things are sad; but if you are satisfied inside, you are able to walk steady when those come along. It worried Me because if a night's sleep is the determining factor of a good day, then what happens when a big mountain presents itself?"

Ouch, that stung. He was right but it still bit. As I sat there, I asked, "What is the answer?"

"Knowing who you are, not by what the world *says* but by what My Son, Jesus *did*," He said proudly. "Just like with My children, I had a specific plan for His selfless act. There were things I knew it would accomplish. I noticed you like to decorate," He added.

"Yes, I do," I said, smiling.

"I remember a Beautiful Women Night you and your friends put together," He said. "I believe it was a Cinderella theme."

Yes, it was beautiful, I thought. *Pink and glitter; it was perfect.*

"Yes, it was," He agreed. "Speaking of pink, you and a friend hung pink fabric from the ceiling, and it draped to the floor. You used it for decoration, and it also covered the black wall of the room."

"Yes," I agreed. I was remembering the night as if I were there again.

"As beautiful as the pink sheer fabric was, at the end of the night, it had to come down," He said. "There were things to be done in that room and the fabric was hindering those things even though it had served a great purpose just hours previous," He explained. "Your pink fabric is like a veil that once hung. It was beautiful, of the finest threads. It had the most exquisite beading and the stitching. Oh my, it was impeccable. But as beautiful as this fabric, this veil was, it had to come down. It kept My children from entering into My presence; and I could not have that. My heart couldn't take it. Through Jesus, that veil was torn; it no longer separated us. See, things have a purpose, but when that purpose is completed, it is time to move on, and moving on means change," He said.

I sensed we were not talking about the veil or even the couch anymore. I could now see the firm, uncomfortable couch represented how we often feel about change—uncomfortable.

"Very good," He said. I waited to see His next move.

"Then where do we go from here?" I asked.

"To know who you are, you may have to leave those things that no longer serve a purpose and allow yourself, and often your environment, to change," He explained.

This sounded deep, I thought.

"Yes it is," He confirmed. "We are leaving the surface of the well and entering the deep. Will you go?" He asked.

I knew I would, so I didn't hesitate. "Let's go," I said boldly. *Wow, where did that boldness come from?* I wondered.

"You are beginning to see who you are, what was done for you, and who loves you," He answered with a big smile.

Who loves me. That sounded sweet.

"Sara does, I do, Jesus, the Holy Spirit, the list goes on," He replied.

It made me think of the saying, *If you can count the number of people who love you on one hand, you are doing well. I must really be doing well,* I thought.

"You don't even know the half of it," He added.

-CHAPTER 17-

Sleep

In the second year of his reign, Nebuchadnezzar had dreams; his mind was troubled and he could not sleep (Daniel 2:1).

"Let me tell you about a playground," He said.

The mood was somber, yet thick. He didn't miss a beat as He went right into His story.

He began, "When you are asleep, you are caught off guard. That is his tactic. You wake, get your bearings, and hit the secret, red button that activates your defenses and BAM, the walls go up. All is well again. That is until bedtime. The sun goes down, the guards start to quiver as you tell yourself, 'Hold yourself together.' But *yourself* is already in motion.

"Panic lurks around the corner waiting for your eyelids to close. It wants to come out and play, and your conscience is the perfect playground. It has a swing of guilt, or a seesaw of loneliness, and a slide of disappointment. You are trapped within your own hell; and it laughs. It knows you won't let it out. You are more scared of what is out there than what is in here. It has you right where it wants you.

"That wall has now turned on you. You built it to keep others out, and it now keeps them in. You are a strong city crumbling from the inside out. If only you could see the light of day, you'd be fine. But you are kidding yourself. They'll be back unless you do differently today. Choose life," He said, finishing the story.

I sat there speechless, but had so much to say. That had been me. And worst of all, that was so many loved ones I knew. This had to stop. "Let Your people go," I cried out. "Let them go."

He looked at me with a half-hearted smile and then said, "My people need to let go. They have trapped themselves by the very devices they have clung to hoping to be freed. But it has backfired on them. They now are addicted to those very things and still imprisoned. It isn't just the addictions the world likes to point out."

"Like alcohol and drugs?" I asked.

"Yes," He replied. "That brings us to your dream."

THE DREAM

"I opened the door to find a little girl crying," I said. "She handed me a bottle of half-opened vodka and said with tears streaming down her face, 'Little girls aren't supposed to drink this.' I looked behind her and down in what looked like a parking garage. I saw what must have been her parents letting another little girl out of the car. I think it was her sister. I knew she was crying too, but there were no tears. I took the girl's hand and remember holding it as she came into the house. I also remember I knew she was coming. Am I forgetting anything?" I asked.

"What about the demeanor of the father?" He asked me.

"He wouldn't look up. He walked around the car, opened the door, and walked back to the driver's side; but he never looked up," I repeated.

"What about the mother?" the Lord then asked.

"She didn't get out of the car," I replied. "The car was a muddy, golden color, a long, older model. It looked familiar to me."

"How did this sight make you feel?" He asked.

"Surprised and confused that this poor little girl knew she wasn't supposed to drink the alcohol and that she was so sad," I stated.

"Her tears were from having to be an adult, but she didn't understand what was going on. This starts her confusion of not knowing what others wanted or were asking of her. She was a very smart little girl. She knew that you were not supposed to drink, yet she saw drinking over and over. She wanted someone to take the bottle away."

"Why did she come to me?" I asked.

"Her heart always wanted to grow up and get out," He replied.

I remembered I always wanted to do that. I would say, "I can't wait to get out of here." Then I would vow that I would never come back. I was surprised to realize such a thing.

"That is the reason the little girl was so far ahead of the rest of the family as far as location. The dad, mom, and sister were barely getting out of the car and she was already at the door. She wanted to separate from them," He said.

All He was saying was true. *But what about that vow*, I wondered. *How did it affect my life?*

"To be in control, your thoughts were driven by 'How and when can I get out of here?'"

"Wow, that makes sense. Lord, I ask Your forgiveness for that vow. I pray that You would take it and do with it what You desire with me never taking it up again. I am sorry for thinking and attempting to do what is Your job. I am sorry."

"I know you are," He began. "But are you truly ready to stop trying to grow up?" He asked.

I was confused.

"Be honest with yourself," He started. "Do you get up every morning with a sick feeling in your stomach?"

"Yes, I do. It almost feels like dread."

"That is the little girl getting up, trying to orient herself into a grown up to make it through the day. Making it through the day is dread. You can blame it on math or a doctor's appointment, but dread is having to do something you do not want to do. In the best terms, it is not having control," He said. "You feel you have no control over this math, so you dread it."

"Why, Lord?" I asked. "It's just math."

"Let's go back to the dream to see why," He said. "A child of an alcoholic rarely knows which way is up. Things in that type of household are unpredictable. The children often have to fend for themselves, and therefore become adults way too early. My children need to be children," He said in a stern voice. "If that would happen, My children would not be floundering around when they are adults trying to figure things out as a child. There is a reason you did not come out as an adult. There are things that you need that can only be given as a child. Love, nurture, respect," He paused for a minute, then continued, "Comfort, safety, and laughter.

"Children need joy. Children need to have fun. If they don't get it, they grow to be the size of adults trying to joke, but having no idea how. Oh!" He let out a scream. "It is so frustrating. Let them be kids—run, jump, play, and then worry about the grown-up stuff. You wanted to get to the grown-up stuff too soon," He said.

"Lord, but circumstances…" I interjected.

"Yes, My children are being raised by parents who did not have a healthy childhood either," He stated.

"Where does it end?" I asked.

"I can end the cycle every time there is a willing heart," He said. "With that, I can do miracles."

"Lord, I want to be willing," I said.

"That is the center of the onion," He said.

"Wow," I said.

"When My babies are born, they have a heart that is willing to be taught. It is fresh and clean," He added.

"Sounds like cleaning products," I said smiling.

"Funny you should say that," He said. "A willing heart is similar. It has the capability to clean and de-stink an entire polluted family. Where there is sin, there is stench. But too often that heart gets tainted by the very sins that it could have cleaned."

"What next?" I asked.

"I have to wait for the baby to grow up," He said. "Sadly, it is usually too fast because not only do we now have the sin to deal with, but the repercussions of growing up too quickly. Layers of the onion grow and cover the center. If they are still willing, we can do magic," He grinned. "It is when the onion begins to smell and lose the juices; then it begins to harden. Not impossible, but more difficult to peel."

"Lord, why was the father in the dream so downcast?" I asked.

"He didn't want to be that way," He said.

"The drinking?" I questioned.

"Yes," He said, "but there is always a reason someone drinks. He had his too."

"The child thing?" I asked.

"Yes, the child thing," He said sadly.

"What about the mother?" I asked. "She didn't even get out of the car to help her children," I said.

"She is drying up," He answered. "The flowing juice of Me is running dry. She is a shell of herself. Empty inside," He added.

I saw an image of people walking in a shopping center parking lot. The people were going through their day as if nothing was different from the day before. As my eyes saw their faces, some had no skin, only a bare skull sitting upon their bodies, while others appeared normal. "What is this?" I asked, startled and a little scared.

DRY BONES

"Dry bones," He replied. "Dry bones are a heart condition. This is why the church needs to take time to sit with Me. They don't have life, but they are trying to live. Life only comes after giving their life to Me. They don't see that I am the only way to quench what they need. Those bones will only become more brittle until they realize I am the only way.

"How can this be?" I squealed. "Why do people get more excited about the release of a Harry Potter book than You and Your Word?" I asked.

"I am dead to them," He answered.

"How can I help them want to come alive?" I asked. "What should I be asking? I want to stop this madness." *People needed their faces back,* I thought.

"Live," He began. "Show them Me. Continue to be My coins—the dry bones scare Me."

"I didn't know You got scared," I commented.

"I do when it comes to My children," He admitted.

"Where then do we start?" I asked.

"Let children be children," He answered. "And My adults need to come to Me to learn what they were not taught—how to be children."

"I think they are afraid," I stated. I knew this because I was.

"Why would they be afraid?" He asked.

"They are afraid that if they allow themselves to be children, they will go through what they did as a child," I answered. I began to cry. I don't want to be a *baby* anymore. I couldn't do it again. I am tired of putting on a brave face; I want a brave heart. "What is a brave heart to You, Lord?" I asked.

"Oh," He said as He put His arm around me. "Being a child is not being a baby; and Dear One, it is supposed to be a great time in My people's lives. Let Me, trust Me. A brave heart to Me is a child who desires to be free."

"Just *desires?* How can desire help?" I questioned.

"A desirable heart is open to be taught," He explained. "I just want the opportunity to teach My children the better way; My way."

I saw myself as a little girl running through a meadow. I was laughing. That was nothing like I had remembered my childhood to be like. I was scared to go back. It would hurt too much.

"Exactly," He said. "I am talking about the hidden secrets that no one thinks or in some of My children's lives, knows about. It's the husband who silently cries in his car before he enters his job because he can't seem to be enough for the bosses. Or the school teacher who fears for her job because the principal won't get off her back. It is the teenagers whose parents fight so loudly that they think no one hears them. It is the grandmother who sits alone in her retirement home hoping someone will remember she is alive. I could go on and on, but I believe you get the picture," He said.

"You mentioned addictions before we started discussing the dream. But I'm not sure where the addictions come in," I questioned.

"Each one of them has figured out some way to try and cope with their pain, their insecurity. Maybe it is shopping with money they really don't have or pornography if only in their minds," He said. "Whatever it is, if it isn't Me, it is an addiction."

I could understand if He meant idol, but how was He getting addiction? I wondered.

"Compulsively occupied," He said. "They run to their false need and it occupies their time away from Me."

That seemed complex, so I said, "Please tell me more."

"Let Me explain it this way because I think idol is confusing you," He said. "An idol is something you worship. Remember what worship meant?"

Yes, but I had to think hard. "A way to show love," I asked.

"Yes," He said. "If the truth be known, they do not love their addiction. They just cannot live without it, or so they think. That is the lie they have been told and they took it to heart. Your hearts were made to absorb. However, it was supposed to absorb love. But like a sponge, it will absorb what it is given. It is so sad," He said.

"So what do we do?" I asked.

"It isn't as much what you can *do,* as it is what you can *say,*" He stated.

"Excuse me?" I asked inquisitively.

"Be My mouthpiece," He said.

MEN OF THE WORD

"Lord, you mentioned earlier about a man who cries in his car before work. That haunts me," I said. "I feel badly because I have been so focused on hurting women that I have neglected the men who are in pain. I'm so sorry. They are just as important. Please forgive me."

"I forgive you, but you have done nothing wrong," He said. "Your heart is expanding. Its compassion capacity is growing."

"Oooh, I like that *compassion capacity,*" I said. "That sounds cool."

"It *is* cool, as you say. It is like a pregnant woman's mid-section. Gradually as the baby grows within her womb, her body expands to accommodate the new growth. You have a new growth growing within your heart, and it is expanding to accommodate," He explained.

"That is really an awesome concept, but what about the men?" I asked. I had previously asked God in one of our quiet times to tell me about Himself. I didn't like always being the one talking or being talked about. I sensed He wanted to reflect on that conversation we had begun several days ago, so I asked Him again. "Lord, I would love to hear about You."

"I am a Man of My Word," He started. "I wish more of My sons would be, but it goes generation to generation. One man steps out of the line and the next suffers. It trickles like a faucet that won't shut off, or it can be devastating, creating a domino effect. Those left in this suffering state try to pretend they are OK, but they really aren't."

"This makes me cry, Lord. What can I do?" I asked.

"Women can encourage," He said.

"How?" I asked, wanting to know.

"By supporting," He answered.

"How?" I asked again.

"I will show you," He assured me.

"Please do, my heart aches for them," I said.

"I know, Love," He said. "Do you feel that ache you mentioned?"

"Yes," I remarked.

"I feel it too! I walk around with this hope that they will let Me help them," He said. "Just like your first reaction is to want to help, to do something...I want to and can, but they have to let Me."

As His words filled the air, I saw a vision of men roaming around as if in the dark trying to find their way.

"They are clueless to what a man is because no one was there to teach them," He explained.

"Will You show them?" I asked.

"Yes," He answered.

"How?"

"My heart," He replied.

"How can we do this?" I questioned.

"Come to Me and I will show you what they need," He said. "Each one is different, but all of them have fragile hearts. They need the one I created as the *Helper*. They need the women in their lives to uplift and champion their efforts, not tear down and belittle."

"Those seem like such harsh words," I said.

"They are," He agreed, "but I see it all the time. The most valuable gift I have given to My women—encouragement—and they do not take it serious or deem it important."

"I had to ask, "What about the gift of childbirth?"

The woman gives the actual birth, but the man complements her," He explained.

That was a beautiful thought, *he complements her.* My husband complements me. I thought about a well put together outfit. It all flows, making sense—not like a clashing, mismatched outfit.

"That is it," He said. "When they are not working together, they clash like a mismatched outfit." We both laughed because as the words left His lips, I saw the Holy Spirit run into the room with a Pippy Longstocking outfit on—striped socks, a red blazer, and pink and green polka dot pants. And to top it off, He was wearing no shoes.

"Like this?" He asked, twirling around in His odd, to be polite, outfit. He could tell we agreed by the fact we could not stop laughing.

The Holy Spirit knows just how to lighten a mood, I thought. I was grateful for His sense of humor. He made me smile.

"That is a heavenly strength," the Lord said, "the ability to bring a smile to another's face."

I want to do that, I thought, *bring joy to others.*

HELP OR HINDER?

"I am amazed at how panic can be brought to calm," I declared. "Thank You for that wisdom, Lord."

"Oh you haven't seen anything yet," He remarked.

"Yeah! I look forward to it, whatever it is," I said smiling.

"I wasn't finished with our conversation about marriage yesterday," He stated. "Would you please come sit again?" He asked.

"Yes, Lord," I replied. "I am eager because I have something I want to ask," I said as I sat down. The couch was so comfortable. It was white, faux leather, the soft kind with just the right amount of cushioning. It was like falling into a cloud. Yes, that is what it was like, a cloud. "But to the question, Lord," I asked, "why did You call us to help?"

"I knew men would not ask for help, but My women naturally would offer," He answered. "Even in the case of Eve...she thought she was helping, but she was deceived by her lack of knowledge. They needed someone to bounce off ideas with the hope of bringing them closer together, not spreading them apart. It was meant to be a way to share experiences. The responsibilities are way too much for one person. Besides, My men won't even ask for directions," He said, laughing.

"I smiled with Him, because I knew He was joking due to the fact His sons meant so much to Him. But, I didn't want to know why some women did not help...if it was natural?"

"Eve and many of My women do not know they were created to help. Or they are unaware, or like Eve, they think they *are* helping. They help in a harmful manner instead of a helpful one. Then there are the ones who are misled into believing that helping is below them. Finally, the group that can be part of all of the others—the ones who haven't received what they need—to be loved, admired, and cherished. This is why I called the men to love their wives like Christ does the Church. But many do not realize how much Jesus loves the Church," He said.

"That is so sad," I said. Not that I began to fully know that amount of love, but I was on my way, like I hoped for everyone else.

"*Help* does not mean less than," He began to explain. "It actually is the opposite. It is a very honored position in My eyes," He stated. "She may have a more effective way of doing something, yet he may be more equipped to handle the task. Would she let her pride keep them from fulfilling the calling? It can be an exhausting position, but it is great value and reverence to Me. I have put My men in the care of My women. But I am worried," He added.

"Why, Lord?" I asked.

"Because they have become distracted," He answered. "I sent My Son Jesus to Mary and Martha's home expecting and hoping they would take care of Him. He needed them as much as they needed Him. Martha was distracted," He said.

I saw a vision of women doing laundry. They were frantically folding clothes while rushing from one end of the laundry to the other. Neither helping each other but instead running into each other. I heard the Lord holler, "STOP!" Then the voice in the room; a representative for the women began, "We as women are tugged between who made us and what we were made to do. From the Garden we were given the responsibility of the family, yet we are called to help too."

"Does not the help of your husband fall into the same family to which you are given?" the Lord asked the spokeswoman. "When My daughters treat the men unkindly, it breaks My heart. Jesus had a lot on Him—so do My sons today. They need a friendly face to come home to, to sit with. Do not fight these responsibilities," He concluded.

"Are you not aware that the men are not fulfilling their responsibilities?" the spokeswoman said as she turned with fire in her eyes toward the Lord.

"Yes," He said boldly in her direction. "How dare you think you will question Me in such a manner," He exclaimed. "Get behind Me, satan," the Lord demanded.

I watched the spokeswoman stand as if a statue.

"Ladies," the Lord said in a soft voice, "you have allowed the enemy in. He has deceived you into believing things like, 'If my husband does not try, why should I?' and 'When he gives me a smile, I will smile back.' These attitudes breed divorce, and the enemy knows it. Please do not limit Me or the lies he will tell. You have covered your ears to Me, hearing only his voice. Come to Me, and allow Me to heal the hurts that stir within your broken hearts. When you allow Me to help you, then you will desire to help others," He stated.

"But we barely have time for the chores we are given," the spokeswoman said. Her body was stone now, but her mouth still worked. I saw the women in the laundry room beginning to fall apart. The hard plaster that had surrounded their bodies was beginning to drop to the ground.

"Your hearts are opening," He said, completely ignoring the statue. "You feel you have more to do because someone has told you that you need to do these things. Someone has filled your thoughts with fears and insecurities of not being enough or keeping with up with others," He explained.

"STOP," I heard the statue yell at the Lord. "You are ruining years of manipulation and lies that I have fed into the hearts of these women."

The room was silent until a soft, sweet voice from the back corner spoke up, "I want to try. I want to give you a chance."

The tears began to roll down my face and the Lord's face. All He ever wanted was a chance.

One by one, women throughout the room began to profess they wanted to give Him a chance. As they spoke, parts of the statue began to dissolve right before my eyes. First an arm, then chest, until all that was left was her mouth and an ear.

"Why those parts?" I asked the Lord.

"Do you see that woman in the far left corner over there?" He asked me.

"Yes," I answered. She was wearing a beautiful, yellow and white dress with daisies on it.

"She looks happy on the outside, but inside she has been burnt. She keeps the enemy's mouth here. As long as there is one, he will have a voice to speak and an ear to hear," He said.

"Lady, lady," I said running up to her. "Let him go, give the Lord a chance."

"It is no use," He said. "She has closed her ears to Me," the Lord explained.

"No, no…," I screamed. "There is always hope," I blurted out trying to shake her. She was numb, with no reaction even to my shaking.

"Why?" I asked, turning to the Lord with hurt in my eyes.

"The Body has hurt her, the world has deserted her, and the enemy comforts her…or so she thinks," He explained.

Sitting on the floor, I began to kick and stomp in a temper tantrum. "I refuse to believe there is no hope," I said bluntly. I sat in silence for what seemed like hours, every few minutes looking up at the woman hoping she had changed her mind.

The Lord said, "It is her choice whether she will change her mind or not. She has the decision to make."

"So…" I said, still staring at the lady.

"So, it is not your responsibility to make her change her mind. My women and men take on responsibilities that are not theirs. Tend to your own house first," He said.

As His words began to sink in, I felt lighter, like it was OK to stand up. I had felt like I had to stay there and wait. That someone should, or we would be deserting her.

"No, no," Jesus said, stepping into the room. "It is not your job to stay with her. If she will not budge, you must go or you will miss your path."

"I will stay," the Lord said. "It is *My* responsibility. There are three houses," the Lord began, "the one that is your tent, which is your heart, the actual tent you reside in, and then the house of David and all of his descendents. If you do not tend to *your* tent first, all of the other homes suffer. That is the example of Mary and Martha. Mary knew her tent needed tending, so she sat with the One who could mend, while Martha tended to her home," He explained.

We were back on the couch again. I loved our time tending my tent. I loved Him.

-CHAPTER 18-

Love

We love because He first loved us (1 John 4:19).

"Jesus loves each of you to the point of death. He would have died for just one if necessary. If My children could just conceive this," He said with a sigh.

"Lord, please tell me what His love for us looks like," I asked.

"Hmmm…it is an action," He began. "His love has movement, yet can be still. He doesn't tell you one thing and then not do it or tell you and do another. He covets no one above His Church."

"Wait, Lord," I replied. "I know You are supposed to be first. I want *You* to be first."

"Dear one," He began, "by Him exalting the Body above all else, that naturally puts Me first."

"Oh Lord, that is the most romantic thing I have ever heard. Please go on," I said.

"My Son is romantic. He has a glow for His bride that only love brings. He talks about you all the time," He said excitely.

My heart stopped. I could feel the anticipation rising up in my chest. I started to hyperventilate. Could I possibly meet Him? I stopped myself. *Stop thinking that way.* Then I felt a presence from behind. *Don't look, don't look,* I told myself. The warmth of His presence moved in, it was over the back of my neck. I was stiff. *What do I do?* I asked myself.

"Wait for Me," I heard. "I am building you the most extravagant home you could possibly imagine.

"I listened without breathing, head still facing forward. I didn't want to turn around, I couldn't. I mean this was Jesus...My Knight in shining armor. If I looked, He might go away...and I couldn't bear that. So I stayed turned forward, at times forgetting to breathe.

He said, "You take my breath away, too."

That was it, I began to sob. Hands over my mouth and eyes tightly closed, I cried. "He was romantic," I said.

"No," I heard the Lord say, "He *is* romantic. My Son is alive and well and still pining over His Church."

As the Lord spoke, I could still feel His presence on the back of my neck. I sat there feeling His breath and hearing Him breathe. What I would give to have that sound on my noise machine I listen to at night. It supersedes any other sound.

"Beloved," He said, "I must go, but I will return. Wait for Me, and love the others."

Love the others. I thought that odd after such romance. Why would He say that?

"Because you are family," the Lord said. "Do you not have romance with your husband, but love your family and friends?"

"Yes, Father, you are right." I noticed the difference between my Father's voice and Jesus' voice. My Father's was mature, wise, and smart sounding. Jesus' was all of these plus a voice of pure seduction. The words flowed off His lips like the sticky off a lollipop. His words made the air taste good. They captivated my attention. I felt my heart hanging on every word. It was like a cool glass of water on a hot summer day or the steam off a hot tub tucked deep into a mountainside. I do not think my heart could have taken seeing Him, too. But I wasn't going to miss an opportunity to ask before He left. "Can I see You?" I asked softly.

With words that could melt a glacier, He said softly, "Wait for Me. I want your eyes to behold Me as I behold you on our wedding day."

I thought about the special night away that couples spend apart to create the heightened romance of seeing each other on their special day. *Could I wait?* I wondered. *Oh, He is worth it. I can. I will.*

"Very good," the Lord said. "Very good."

"Son, You must be on Your way," the Lord said.

I began to cry, "No, please don't."

"I must," He said, "your palace is not ready and nothing less than the best will do. I have the finest silks, plush pillows, and...."

I was sorry to interrupt, but He must know. "I just want You, just You," I said. "All of that other stuff is nice and I appreciate it, but I just want You."

The Lord began to smile and giggle. "Hang on to that thought, My dear. The things of this world are fleeting, but the love you can gain while He is away will never leave you."

But I don't want Him to leave, I thought.

"Sweetheart," Jesus said.

He called me sweetheart. I feel like a school girl with a crush, I thought.

"A good friend says goodbye, but does not walk away without letting the other know He is leaving," Jesus explained. "I said I was leaving, but that I would be back. It wasn't goodbye."

"Wait, but I'm Your beloved. What do You mean *friend?*" I said in an offended voice.

"Whoa," I heard the Lord say, "that is no way to talk to your Groom. That is exactly what I meant about my women helping. A sharp tone does not help."

"Yes, Father, I'm sorry," I agreed. "And Jesus, I apologize."

"Forgiven," they both said at the same time.

I could sense His presence fading. His back was to me as He slowly, poetically stepped away. "I will miss You," I said softy.

"I will miss you, too," He said as He totally drifted away.

"Then take Him with you," the Lord said.

"What?" I said, as I snapped out of the cloud my head was in. I was still hearing His voice and now mourning the sound of His footsteps walking away. "Why did He have to go?"

"Because there are family members missing," the Lord answered.

I understood. They deserved Him too. Everyone did.

"Now, to answer," He spoke and once again startled me out of deep concentration.

"Yes, Sir," I said.

"To answer your friend question, are you not a friend to your husband as well as his beloved?"

Yes, I would hope to be. I noticed He answered a lot of my questions with questions. "Why is that?" I asked.

"Because I want you to think for yourself," He replied. "But we will talk more on that later," He said. "I too want each couple to be friends and lovers, not one or the other."

I was shocked, *He said lovers.*

"Now, now, Little One, I created love *and* sex," He said.

Oh, my, He said sex!

"OK, calm it down," he said as He chuckled. "They are both important pieces of the tapestry called marriage. The man and the woman are one, but within the one are many different strains that, as we discussed, complement each other. When it is complete, others see an illustration, a picture of who they are together. When they look closer, there will be My face. Woven into each of them is Me, so I am bound to show up in the picture."

"It sounds beautiful, Lord, a true masterpiece," I replied.

"Yes, but if there is a breakdown, if the man does not love the woman like My Son loves the Church, or the woman doesn't embrace her role as his helper, the tapestry suffers. It is yet another lineage that suffers," He said. "Have you heard of an art collection?" He asked.

"Yes," I replied.

"That is what a lineage is," He said. "One tapestry is the inspiration of the next piece and so on. Within the weaving is a blood line and a marriage line. The lineage that suffers is not by blood but by vow, the marriage vow."

THE MARRIAGE VOW

"Do you know what a vow is?" He asked.

Before I could answer, He continued, "It is a decision you make and decide you won't break it, or change your mind about. It is not up for discussion."

I knew I had made vows before, and they turned out to be bad news for me.

"Those are not the vows I am talking about," He replied. "Vows that are made to take the place of My reign are nothing but pride. A vow made in agreement with Me and when I am the Decision Maker is blessed. It is all about who has the authority to make and execute the vow. If My people make the ruling, then they have taken on My authority and become the judge. This is not good. It is saying, 'I am better equipped to handle this area of my life.' I don't take kindly to self-appointed judges, either to their own lives or over others," He said.

I could see what He was saying. I knew in the past that acknowledgment and repentance were the ways to rid myself of such trouble. I can say with complete confidence, once I gave Him the reins back, the area I had attempted to rule over was much better, much better.

"I believe that is enough for today," He said. "I have so much more to talk to you about this subject...but all in due time."

"Thank You for today, Lord...and please tell Jesus I am waiting."

BALANCE

"What would you desire out of the time you have set before Me today?" the Lord asked.

"I feel behind," I replied.

"You are not behind," He stated.

"Lord, I feel very anxious this morning. It feels like I am already behind, and I haven't even started. I don't like this feeling at all. It makes me feel nervous. Things that I need to do are bouncing around in my head like ping pong balls. I can't catch them, and all I seem to be able to do is chase them. I feel overwhelmed. You can jump in here any time," I finally said, "because I could go on and on."

"I was just waiting for you to take a breath so I could get a word in edgewise," He said, grinning.

I inhaled a deep breath and listened—still racing through thoughts of things to do and hoping He would give me a quick answer so I could accomplish what was on my mind.

"Uh hum," He said. "Do you see that?"

"No," I replied, a little curious but more agitated.

"You want a quick answer so you can do what you feel is pressing and move on," He pointed out.

"Yes, so?" I asked.

"When you move from this situation, there will be something else," He stated. "Wouldn't you rather learn how to be calm instead of rushing through one thing to the next hoping not to miss anything or become overwhelmed and give up?"

I stopped for a minute and thought about what He had proposed. *Of course,* I thought, *I would like to be calm; but really, was that possible with all of the things I have to do? And how did He know I had to fight the urge to give up and call it a day sometimes?*

"Now you know how I know," He interjected. "I don't have to know your thoughts to know that; I have seen your and others of My children's actions. They usually fall into two patterns. Those who run until they give out so they give up and believe they can't get it all done so why keep trying—or the ones, like you, who go, go, and go. They try to outrun the pile of things to do. Both get tired, and these reactions actually affect their sleep."

"How does it affect our sleep?" I asked.

"Because you go to bed overwhelmed from the chores of the day, carrying them over to the next. Worrying about what you didn't get done that day adds onto the things for tomorrow. Do you see what I mean?" He asked.

"Yes," I agreed.

"It is just like when you wake up in a panic," He continued. "If you follow that panic, it is leading. If you follow this panic through your day, it is leading again. You have to ask yourself, 'Who is in charge?' So Dena," He said, "Who *is* in charge?"

"Well, not the panic," I replied, "so I guess me. But I think a better question would be who is *leading?*" I realized.

"Yes, and *I* would be a better answer, because I know what *really* needs to be done today and what can wait until another day," He explained.

I remembered a speaking event that I had been invited to this past summer. When I went to the Lord about what He would like me to speak about, He said that the event would not transpire. This was great to know because I didn't have to spend time on an event that would not occur. Upon remembering this, I shouted, "I get it! I should come to You and allow you to plot out my day," I said, rejoicing.

"Yes, come to Me," He said, clapping.

"Lord, what about when it is believed we don't have time to come to You?" I asked.

"I would ask one question, 'How is it working for those who don't come?' If they feel they are getting by OK, then I would say, 'Why just get by?' If they are stubborn and want to do it on their own, then I am sorry to hear that, because that will lead down a path different from what I have planned. And as you know, the path I have is greater than anyone can imagine," He said.

"Let Me give you some pointers," He said. "First *evaluate*, take inventory of what is on your plate. I can guarantee you, if I put it there, you can handle it. Then, *coordinate* by doing things in clumps. If you have three errands near each other, do them at the same time."

"You can save a lot of time that way," I heard the sweet voice of the Holy Spirit. He was dressed as a *Leave it to Beaver* house-wife. With flour on His face and a dish rag in His hand, He said, "I know how grueling that carpool line can be."

Not only did He know our troubles, but He knew how to make me laugh at them.

"That brings Me to the next point; *stimulate* by making the most of each activity," He added. "Even grocery shopping can be fun. Now comes the one that some of My children won't like—*don't procrastinate*; don't put things off," He said, chuckling. Without missing a beat He continued, "Then there is *eliminate*. Some things just don't need to be done, so scratch them off your list. And a big one, *appropriate*—is it really something you should be doing?"

"Goodness," I said, "how many do you have?"

Laughing, He replied, "I could go on and on but only two left. *Mediate*, spend time with Me. And finally, *recalculate* by stopping and retaking an inventory. Ask yourself questions like, 'What do I have left? What is no longer necessary?' If you don't know where you have been, you won't know where you are going," He proposed. "So how do you feel now?" He asked.

"Pretty good now that we have discussed our day," I replied. "So, Lord, light my path!"

I spent time with my Savior, which brought direction but more importantly friendship. He cares about the time He has given me and wants not only for me to enjoy it, but to live it to the fullest. This is the day that He has made, and while I go about the things that are asked of me this day, I will rejoice and be glad in it.

"Amen," I said.

"Now that we have some pointers to guide us into not rushing or becoming overwhelmed, let Me introduce you to someone who is a great example," He said with excitement.

THE RESIDENT BUILDER

"I think now would be a good time to finally get to Noah," He said.

I could see Him off in the distance. I thought this strange since all the others had come to greet me.

Then suddenly I heard him holler, "Hello over there."

"Hi," I said.

"Why doesn't he come over?" I asked.

"He is a man of little words. He has a lot to do," the Lord answered. "He has gotten so good at building that he has become our resident builder."

"Yes," I heard him holler again politely, "the animals keep coming, so I keep building."

"What, Lord, the animals come to Heaven?" I asked surprised.

He chuckled, "Oh yes, my dear. A righteous man cares for his animals."

I remember reading about Noah and so many others called righteous.

"Are they not still righteous when they greet Me in Heaven?" the Lord asked.

"Yes, I suppose so," I said.

"Then why would I ask them to forsake their loved ones? Are their animals not their loved ones?" He asked.

I thought about my kitty, Annabelle. She was set in her ways, but I did love her.

"I don't flop on My children," He added. "As they say, 'What you see is what you get.' But the more you unwrap, the better I get," He said, smiling.

"Father." I laughed with a surprised look on my face. I could see the Holy Spirit dancing behind Him covered in gift wrapping and a big, shiny yellow bow.

"What?" the Lord replied happily. "This surprise coming from a woman who wants her grandchildren to call her Grammy?"

"Touché," I said, "You got me there." I had chosen Grammy because it represented a prize. No, not in a prideful way but in an I am a child of God way, therefore we are all considered a prize because we are His. We laughed. What a sense of humor He had. Put us together and we could bring down the house. "We have done it again, gotten off track," I said.

"Oh no, I always know where we are. It just may appear to you we are off track. You know that My thoughts are not your thoughts." He laughed.

"Noah did not rush," He said as a matter of fact. "He was given specific details and a deadline. He was excellent with his time management skills.

"He took his time, read the directions, asked Me questions, and waited on Me to answer. He was faithful. When others thought he was out of his mind, he let it roll off his back and kept looking forward," He said.

"Not to be ugly, but he sounds perfect," I stated.

"Watch yourself, Dear," He said. "No need for that green-eyed monster."

"Sorry, I didn't mean it hatefully. I just don't see how he did it all right," I explained.

"Well, it's because he kept coming back to Me. I never said he did it right the first or second time. I see the end result, the transformation completed," He said.

"Boy do I have egg on my face," I said.

"Yes, you do, but I will be happy to help you wipe it off," the Lord said as He reached over and pretended to wipe my chin. "Now, why I brought up Noah," He said, "is because we were discussing marriages. Ones where one is helping but received no love, or vice versa. Things are rough. And before the flour has sifted through the colander, they rush into a divorce."

"God, please help," I pleaded.

"They rush through that too," He added. "No one waits anymore. Stop! You want things to stop. You have certain things you are tired of. Me too," He admitted. "I want My people to give Me time to clean up the messes they find themselves in."

Wow, He was speaking a mile a minute with such force. He meant what He was saying.

"Dena," He said in a calmer voice, "I just want them to be happy…and they want the same thing. But they are going about it all wrong."

I thought He was going to cry as He said, "If they would just come to Me and wait—no rushing. Just like I did for Noah, I will walk them through it."

The mood was heavy, when all of a sudden I heard Noah, who I had forgotten was still hammering away. He hollered, "Do you know how hard it is to get so many animals on a boat? You can't rush them." He laughed as he went back to hammering.

Yes, I thought. *I guess you'd have to be patient.*

"Honey," God said, "*patient,* now there is a good word to explore."

I would have normally laughed hysterically at such a funny comment, but I had just heard the cry of my Lord's heart. I was in a state of mourning, but yes…

"Want to know about patience?" I heard from across the room. "Try waiting on a couple of ducks waddling across the deck of a boat. They had a mind of their own," he said, chuckling as he turned the saw back on.

I looked at God with sympathetic eyes. "I love You. I'm sorry."

"Sometimes that is all a person needs to hear," He said.

"Hey Noah," He yelled, "put that stuff down and come on over here."

Noah yelled back over the noise of the saw and asked, "What?"

"Come on over here, please," God said louder.

He put down the saw and took his safety glasses off. As he came closer, I could make out his appearance clearer. He was a tall, stocky man wearing overalls and a beard. Not like Santa, his face wasn't rosy, but he had friendly eyes. Yes, the eyes stood out.

He walked over and said, "Yes, Sir," to the Lord.

"Son," the Lord said, "I want to talk about your patience."

I could tell Noah was blushing under his beard.

"Father," he said, obviously embarrassed. He had a boyish quality to his voice I noticed.

"If Noah had rushed, many animals would have been in jeopardy. But by taking his time, all were safe, a little sea sick," He laughed, "but fine."

"Yeah," I heard Noah holler. "You would have loved that smell and the clean up. Whew, it was no fun, but I loved those critters."

I could tell he meant it.

"I knew if I rushed," he said in all seriousness, "lives could suffer, and I did not want that.

"Look how grand that ark was," He said. "How it is still talked about today. I need lives that out-live their physical time on earth. Ones that leave an impact on families, communities, and the world," He said, raising His arms for emphasis.

"Lord, I want that," I said. *That,* I thought, *is the ultimate way for me to matter. To matter enough to endure and what you endure stays behind.*

"Then, dear, don't rush," He advised. "Flow with My current; neither against it nor resisting it."

"OK, I will try," I said.

"You are already doing better," the Holy Spirit jumped in and said.

I could always count on His encouragement. I had asked earlier that day where we would start, and the Lord laughingly replied that we had already begun. I was prone to want to hurry up and be ready, rush through each day. Noah had shown me the importance of not rushing through his patience in building the ark and loading the animals.

"Noah enjoyed the creative process because it was with Me," He said. "The end result was a very large boat, but every nail was hammered while spending time with Me. Knowing the importance of not rushing is a heavenly strength."

I could see now how my impatience was causing my days to fly by, but most of all I realized that I was cheating myself out of precious time with the Lord.

"I can't stand for that any longer," I said taking a deep breath. "Let's build."

CHAPTER 19

A New Perspective

See, I am doing a new thing!... (Isaiah 43:19)

"I come this morning with some apprehension," I began. "I am not sure what this sadness I am feeling is all about. My emotions are bubbling up, and my heart feels funny."

"Child, that is compassion," He said. "Your heart is softening to those I asked you to pray for."

"Last night after we spoke, I thought you might be up to something because when I would think of them as a child being harmed, I felt a new perspective. I wasn't happy about it, but to view them as small, I found I had no choice. It wasn't their fault either." Whoa, the tears are harder to hold back now. "It wasn't my fault either."

"No, dear, so many of My children are harmed, and it is never their fault," He agreed. "That does not dismiss what they do with it later, though. Like, Jezebel who was misled and mistreated, it was not her fault; but it was her responsibility to accept help when I sent helpers her way. I send My children helpers, but some are stubborn and will not accept help," He said.

"Some, Lord, like me, don't trust others, so they don't let them help," I admitted.

"You are right, My child," He agreed.

I sat in disbelief that I could possibly have even an ounce of concern for those He had called me to pray for. I had spent so many years building a steel, bolted wall so they could not penetrate my soul again. The hurt was so deep that I didn't know if I could withstand the flood that was going to surface. I knew it was a time of choice; I was facing a sort of crossroads. Do I run with this new perspective, or do I just run? I contemplated. Running was not an option. I had made a promise to God early on to see this through.

"I am going to hold onto that promise, no matter what. Lord," I said, finding it difficult to swallow. "What's next?" I asked.

"We take it slow," He said. "I want you to get used to the idea that they were children. Continue to pray and allow yourself to feel."

Interesting...allow myself to feel, I pondered. *I guess that's what I had done, stopped myself from feeling.*

"No, you were feeling; but it just was a mask to the real feelings you held," He explained. "Once you see them as I do, I want you to feel what is really there. It is going to be painful, but the path of avoidance is worse. It causes you to miss out on great people I send your way. Dena, I have never lied to you. Trust Me," He asked.

"No Father, you haven't," I replied. "OK, Lord," I answered, "I will trust You."

I could almost feel my heart quivering. It was as if the walls were starting to quake. I had to let go of those that had hurt me in order to let them out. In my attempt to protect myself I had hung on to each one tighter. I wanted a day when they were merely people from my past. Like the apostle Paul said, let go of the past. I want to let them go. I had way too much luggage, and God had said to pack light. I needed to put some things down. I might as well start with the heaviest piece of baggage.

"This revelation had been tiring. The energy I had expanded over the years to contain my hurt had taken a toll. My body could use the break," I admitted.

"Speaking of your body..." He said.

"Yes, Lord," I replied. I had known this one was coming, but honestly had tried to avoid it.

He laughed, as He said, "You know what it says in My Word, *'Your body is a temple.'*"

"Yes, of course," I answered.

A TEMPLE

"Describe a temple to Me," He asked.

"Grand," was the first word that came to me. "A building that is well-maintained and treated with kit gloves because of what it represents and houses," I said, quite proud of my answer.

"Now tell me what it looks like," He asked.

"Plush, with the finest silks and the most precious stones," I said. "The details are magnificent and the decoration is trimmed in gold," I said, smiling.

"One more," He said. "What does it smell like?" He asked.

"Roses," came out of my mouth, "but I don't like roses," I confessed. "Why would I say that?" I asked.

"One person ruined roses for you," He said.

I knew what He was talking about. A person who had set out to harm me had given me roses years ago. Since then, I have not been able to get past the association. "What do I do? What is this all about?" I asked.

"Deep down you really like roses, but the hurt from another won't let you like them anymore," He explained.

So far it was making sense.

"That is the way you really feel about these people," He stated. "Deep down you really love them, but the hurt that is associated with them will not let you love them."

"Lord, You are brilliant, but that really hurts," I replied.

"Stick with Me," He said.

"OK, I'm right here."

"One bad memory of a rose keeps you from ever enjoying roses again. That is sad, don't you think?" He asked. "Association of someone or something that is painful can cause a good thing or person to be prejudged and labeled. Think of someone you are not fond of," He said.

"I can do that," I replied. A person's face popped into my mind. She had not treated me fairly as a child.

"Now," He continued, "do you remember recently when you met a woman who reminded you of this woman from your past? The association of the two women's similar features could have ruined the new relationship you now enjoy."

He was so right. When I met my new friend, she did make me think of the woman from my past. But He had shown me the comparison. Then she and I discussed it and now she is one I would call a mentor. I would have hated to miss out on all she means to me.

"Yes," He said, clapping, "but so many do miss out. One because they don't know they are doing it; and two, they don't know what to do about it," He explained.

"What *should* they do about it?" I asked.

"Just like you did," He stated, "they should let Me show them why, be willing to go there, and give the new person a chance. It is so sad to punish someone for another's sin. Let's try My way and I believe you will see that it works," He said. "Are you up for it?" He asked.

"Yes, but somehow I don't think I would enjoy answering that way," I replied.

"Think about a time you liked roses," He said.

I knew the time to which He was referring. My grandmother loved roses. She had perfume that smelled like them. When I let myself think about it, it brought me to the temple that I had described. It smelled like my grandmother; full of fragrant flowers. I found myself sitting in the middle of the temple. There were plush pillows and the aroma of roses. Then my stomach began to hurt as if I needed to throw up.

"Lord, what is this?" I asked.

"That is the bitterness and anger you have harbored in the bottom of your stomach toward the woman with the rose. For your temple to be pure," He said, "all unclean emotions must be vomited out."

"Lord, I want to be clean," I shouted.

"Let it surface and hand it to me. As Jonah was vomited from the whale and returned to Me, I will receive you, too. Let it go, My child," He said with concern.

I felt this putrid taste rise in my mouth. I did not want this ill-will toward her anymore. No offense, but she was not worth my temple being defiled.

"Stop a minute," I heard. "Let's take responsibility where it lies—you let her in," He pointed out. "It was *you* who allowed this vile to enter your temple. And it is with My help you can remove it."

"Lord," I said, "I ask Your forgiveness for the hatred I have harbored in my temple toward your child. Please help me remove all negative feelings and replace them with compassion." The very thought of feeling compassion toward someone like her caused a flaring in my belly.

"Think of her as a child; add her to your prayer list," He said.

"Lord, this one is going to be more difficult," I admitted.

"I know. But do you know why?" He asked.

"No," I said.

"The others you deep down love, but she is not that important to you. But she *is* important to me," He said.

Darn, I didn't want to hear that. So many emotions rose with that statement. *I am jealous and downright angry that He likes her,* I admitted to myself.

"Why would you not want Me to like her?" He asked.

"Because of what she did," I said.

"OK, what if I stopped liking you when you did something that someone else didn't like?" He asked.

That calmed me a little, but I knew it wasn't over.

"I am a fair judge. Right?" He asked

"Yes, of course," I said.

"If I condemn one and not another, I show favoritism, making Myself a liar. My Son did not come to condemn, and I love all of My children the same, plus I do not lie. Please remember the ultimate goal; My Will is that all have eternal life. I want all children who want to come, to know they are invited. If I am hateful, why would they want to come? But if I am just, they will respect and grow to rely on Me.

"For Me, please try to add her to your list. We will take one step at a time. Now back to those for whom you prayed last night: I want you to, like the rose, think of good experiences you had with them. Focus on those times. This will make feelings of compassion easier," He stated.

"But what about what they did?" I asked.

"Seriously, we are all aware of their mistakes," He said.

"Mistakes?" I yelled. "They were far more than that," I said as I gritted my teeth.

"Hmmm." He stood there with His hand on His chin. "This is going to be tougher than I thought, but all things are possible," He said. "Dena, I want to speak candidly with you. You may think that the only one you are hurting is yourself by hanging onto this resentment, but you are also taking your family with you," He added.

That was harsh, and I was not happy to hear it.

"You have a choice similar to the one Jezebel had to make," He said. "Will you succumb to the help I am offering, or will you allow your heart to travel a path that will end in bitterness?"

I sat there a few minutes, steaming over what He had said. I didn't know if I was angrier about dragging my family along or the Jezebel reference. I was suddenly back in my temple. I noticed a spot of rust on the wall that I had not seen before. I walked over to it. As I touched the burnt-red color of the steel, it began to crumble and fall to the floor. I looked where the steel had been. There was a large hole where sunlight was shining through. I turned to look for God, but He wasn't behind me. "Where are You?" I asked.

"Right here," He answered. I felt He was motioning me to look through the hole.

"I am the Light," He explained.

"But, Lord, did You see my temple crumble?" I asked. "Can it be fixed? Can we repair it?" I asked, concerned.

"Are you asking Me for My help?" He questioned.

"Yes, yes, of course," I said, almost panicking.

"Pick up those pieces that fell to the floor," He advised.

I bent down and scooped them up into my hand.

"Now hand them to Me," He directed.

I reached through the hole, but before I could get all the way, He met me in the middle.

"I will never ask you to do something that I would not do myself," He explained with a smile.

I love that, I thought. *He truly never is ceasing to amaze me.*

"Now, do not be afraid, but you will not see Me for a moment," He said calmly.

Before I could question, the specks of rust came together and I heard a loud slurp sound as it sealed the hole. The light was gone but the hole was fixed. "Oh, no," I yelled. "I did not want to trade the repair for the Light." I had started to panic, and then I heard footsteps approaching from behind me.

"Here I am. I told you not to be afraid," He said.

I ran to Him and hugged Him tightly. "Lord, Lord, I thought You had gone," I said.

"No, I never go, you just can't always see Me," He explained.

"What happened?" I asked.

"That rust was the effects of sin," He said.

"The hatred and anger I had felt toward the rose lady?" I asked.

"Yes," He replied. "It had caused that place to erode over time until it created a hole. But you asked for help. That opened the door for Me to assist you in forgiveness," He said happily.

"But what about the Light?" I asked. "You were outside and I could not see you."

"I cannot be in the presence of sin. I had to turn; but once the hole was sealed, I could look again," He explained.

"That explains why You were outside, but now You are in here," I said.

"I could return to you closer than I was before because as sin is removed and layers peeled away, we grow closer," He said.

I liked that thought. "I don't want to ever lose sight of You again," I said.

"That is a great theory, but we have many other rust spots to detect. For now, though, let us enjoy our time," He said.

I didn't feel anxious or worried. I had seen His gentle way and heard His step-by-step instruction. I knew there were the others for whom I had begun to pray, and there would be more rust... but all in due time.

Hey, I thought, *my Father says that.*

He replied, "With every hole that is patched, you reflect more of Me. Stick with me, Kid, and we will go places."

We sat in the temple on two beautifully made pillows, drank tea, and shared stories. I liked my temple. It was all I had described, but best of all was the company I kept.

Suddenly, the presence in the room was righteous. I lifted my head because I knew royalty was in the air. I could not explain it, I just knew someone of great importance was about to enter. I looked up, but had to cover my eyes. The light was so bright it stung my eyes. Not, in a painful, but helpless way. I wanted to look, but my eyes could not withstand the intensity. I turned my head toward my Father. There was something different about Him; He had a glow about Him. From the ring of light that now outlined Him, He handed me a pair of sunglasses. "Here, take these," He said.

Are you sure? I thought, but I took them. I noticed they were hot pink and louvered. Placing them on, I felt a little silly, but He had given them to me. Once they were on, I tried to look again at the reverenced presence that had entered the room. I could see a light that was not as intense, but still strong; there was a pale pink glow coming from the form.

"Dena," I heard it say, "do not be afraid. I am here to be whomever you need."

WHOMEVER YOU NEED

"Who exactly are you?" I asked.

"I am your Mother," she replied.

"No you're not," I yelled, "no you are not," as I cried into my hands. "No!" I cried again as I began to pray in tongues. I felt Her wrap Her arms around me like I had seen when mother birds completely surround their babies. Her arms were like wings, and

I could feel the pink. It made Her a mother. She wanted to be my Mother.

I collapsed in Her embrace. I had wanted to be held for so long. I wanted to be a child whose only worry was to stay put in her mother's arms. The harder I cried, the tighter She embraced me. I cried until there wasn't a tear left in my body. All I could say was, "I love You" over and over. I was tired, but I wasn't going to move. I had waited so long to be held; no way was I letting go. She held me for what seemed like hours. Slowly She peeled away. All three of us sat on the pillows without a word between us. I was trying to clear my head and soak in all that was before me. I didn't want it to end.

In a soft voice, I heard the Lord say, "Dena, this is the Holy Spirit."

My mouth hit the floor. No way, this could not be.

"She has come today to comfort you. You have seen Her before, but maybe in Her teacher role or as you will see, your Daddy. Whatever you need, She will be. There is no job or call that She cannot make."

Still speechless, I sat looking at Him. "Why the louvered glasses?" I said, finally able to mutter a few words.

"Your eyes could not take Her direct light," He answered. "It had to be broken into sections for you to bear the intensity."

"And the pink?" I questioned.

"Well, she is a woman today," He stated.

He and I laughed. But I noticed She did not grin. "Why is that?" I asked.

"She takes Her job seriously, as do We all," He explained. "She is full of emotion, but not controlled by those emotions. She takes nothing personally; therefore, She always has the best interests for Our children."

This was more than I could take in. I wasn't sure what was next or even if it was right to assume a what next. *It feels odd to sit here while She is being silent,* I thought.

"Allow Me to explain," He said, "She has been with you ever since you loved on My Son Jesus. She waits silently until you ask, or until She needs to prompt you about a situation. She will not step over boundaries or force Herself on you, but the minute you ask, She is immediately beside you. She has been here all along, you are just now able to see Her."

I felt honored, relaxed, and uncomfortable all at the same time. *Why uncomfortable?* I wondered.

"Because you are very aware of Her presence now," He said. "It makes you uncomfortable because you feel you are being watched, like the show *Big Brother* I hear you kids watch."

I didn't want to admit it, but He was right. It felt like I was being watched.

"Do you plan on doing something wrong?" He asked suddenly.

"No," I said.

"Then why worry?" He asked.

Because what if I do something wrong? I wondered.

"She has no ruler to slap over the back of your hand," He stated. "She tells me, and I handle it."

Oh, I didn't like that at all. It made me think of a tattletale.

"You have the wrong idea," the Lord said. "She is here to help you, not to get you into trouble. And if you do, She doesn't run to tattle, She calls Me to step in. Kind of like sending in the 'big guns.' Our hope is that you will stay on the right path. Instead of just *hoping,* We try to help. But you have to want it," He advised.

"You say that a lot," I said, "the *help* word."

"I say it in hopes it sticks," He said.

This had been a very overwhelming morning. I was ready for a rest, but as I had learned, I wanted to ask Him first.

"Lord, I'm tired," I said.

"You have done well, but I believe you are rushing off," He pointed out.

He was right, again. "I have one thing left I want to tell you," I admitted. I knew that if I rushed, I would miss Him. This was another reminder because He had told me exactly that before.

"The reason I keep referring to *help* is that is the reason Jesus asked Me to send the Holy Spirit in the first place," He explained.

This was unusual; He normally asked me a question, He didn't just give me the answer.

He continued, "So if you don't know that you can ask or if you won't ask, She is wasted."

That hit me hard. I didn't want to waste Her or make Her feel that way.

"Just like it is good to allow others to do their parts in the Kingdom, it is good to let the Holy Spirit. All of us working together supply the power needed to see My Will come to pass," He said.

I felt like I had a new friend. The Holy Spirit was not *big brother*, she was a friend. Or in this case, my Mother. One who had my back and would hang out with me. It felt good.

"Now, My sweet one, you may rest," the Lord said.

But, Lord, I thought, *with that revelation, I have a burst of energy.*

He laughed. "You kids."

I joined in the laughter and then turned to the Holy Spirit and asked, "Where would You like to go?"

"You have done it now..." the Lord said with a grin, "...She loves to travel."

I was excited about the journey we were going to take. I suddenly thought I'd better get that rest.

"Yes, dear, you should," the Lord said, "She loves adventures."

-CHAPTER 20-

The Journey

The king said to Daniel, "Surely your God is the God of gods and the Lord of kings and a Revealer of mysteries, for you were able to reveal this mystery" (Daniel 2:47).

I woke to someone shaking my arm saying in a whisper, "Dena, wake up, it's time."

"Time for what?" I asked.

"To go on our journey," the Holy Spirit said.

With eyes half open, I noticed He was dressed in a safari outfit, including the all-terrain boots. Not sure I was seeing or hearing Him correctly, I asked again, "Time for what?"

"You heard Me," He whispered, "a journey."

"Where to?" I asked. "What do I need?" I realized I was doing it again, asking another question before giving time for the answer.

"We are going to a castle," He replied. "Grab your ice skates."

I hurried to get bundled up and grabbed my skates.

"Oh, you won't be cold there," He said.

"But what about the ice?" I asked.

"Warm ice," He said.

Starting to get my bearings, I asked, "Like the warm snow and the mountain climber?"

"Similar, but different," He said. "Now come on, we have many miles ahead of us."

"OK," I said, still unsure what this was all about.

"I told you to watch out," the Lord said. "He likes to go on adventures."

"Actually," I said politely, "You said *She* did."

"Yes," He replied, "but I also said She would be whatever you needed, and today you will see."

We hiked for what seemed like miles. My legs began to wobble, and my throat was dry. "Can we take a break?" I asked.

"Sure," He said, "this looks like a great spot." He cleared some fallen leaves off two large rocks for us to sit on.

"How much farther do we have to go?" I asked. I remembered as a child asking if we were there yet.

"We have all day to get there. My hope," He continued, "is to enjoy our time together along the way."

Sitting in the woods brought back childhood memories of camping trips.

"It makes me think of My children," the Lord said as He caught up with us. "You know the story...we're headed on a three-day trip that ends up taking forty years."

Wow, that is a big time difference, I thought; but I knew that was not for me to judge.

"No," He added, "but it is for all to learn from."

"Do we have time for a story?" I asked.

"Oh, yes," He said, "there is always time for a story. Those children of mine got sidetracked by their own distractions. They complained and fussed when they could have been rejoicing and praising. I sent them coins to lead the way—My way—but they couldn't be pleased."

"Why all the fuss?" I asked.

"I'm loving this story," the Holy Spirit said, "but it is going to get dark soon so we'd better get on our way."

As we grabbed our skates, the Lord continued. "They could not be patient. I take care of My children. Period! Manna today, shelter, whatever they needed. But they wanted it all right away. This world…" He said, shaking His head. "If they trusted Me, they wouldn't need it all right now."

"Ooh, ooh," the Holy Spirit added, "live in the moment."

"Very good point," the Lord said, "living in the moment."

His point made me think of the Pilates class I had taken earlier in the week. I had a list of things to do after the class. My focus was on the to-do's to the point I was not enjoying the Pilates class. That was the first time I had heard Him mention, *in the moment.*

"Yes," He said as He held back a tree limb so I could safely walk by. "I want My children to know I have them to the point that they can live in the moment."

"How can we do that?" I asked. "Wait," I said, "let me try." His presence gives me confidence to attempt things I wouldn't normally. Plus not fearing being rejected if I wasn't right made me bold. "Come to You," I said, trying to think of things I had learned along with what He had said to me as I lay on my Pilates mat that morning.

"Yes, the first one is right," He said smiling. "What is next?" He asked.

Hmmm, I thought. "Keep coming?" I half replied. I drew a blank.

"Yes," He replied. "It is in building our relationship that you learn you can trust Me. But what about in your class?" He questioned. I was still drawing a blank.

"That is OK, it relays a good point," He said. "My children need to remember. It is when you forget, you do not know what to do, or you become complacent—then look out, wrong things we have learned can creep back in. So keep coming to Me, build our relationship, and meditate on what we talk about."

"But how does that help us live in the moment?" I asked.

"Look out," the Holy Spirit said, "there are some thick weeds up ahead. I am going to go up there ahead and clean them away for you. See you at the castle," He said as He sped up and waved.

"Be safe," we both said, continuing our conversation.

"It is in Our time and knowing My Word that can take you on a three-day trip in three days," He explained. "You will begin to know that I will provide, and then you can be in the moment."

I remember with excitement. "While I was in my class, every time my mind wondered about events that would take place later in the day, You would remind me that they were taken care of, that I was to focus on my current surroundings. I then focused on my breathing, the music, and You."

"Yes, yes. It is different, so it takes practice," He said. "Many will not put in the time to practice because they are like My children heading out of Egypt; they are impatient. They want it now," He repeated.

"Boy, are they going to miss out," I said.

"Yes, dear, they will," He agreed.

"Lord," I began, "I don't want to miss out on a thing You have for me because it means I am closer to You. Show me ways that I do not know so that I can know You more."

He smiled as I noticed a white castle with a beautiful solid sheet of ice large enough to skate on in front of it. I could see someone on the ice.

"Go ahead, dear," the Lord said, giving me a gentle push.

I walked with skates in hand and butterflies in my stomach. As I got closer, I could see myself. It was me as a young girl holding the hand of a man. *Oh,* I gasped, *that man is the Holy Spirit.* He wore a t-shirt that read, *Daddy*. I knew now why He was here today. The tears began to roll down my cheeks as I felt a warm hand touch my shoulder. I turned to see the Lord standing there.

"What is this?" I asked.

"Did you not pretend when you were small that Flash Gordon was your father?" He asked.

"Yes, I did."

"Why was that?" He asked.

"I don't know for sure. I just remember in the movies he always came in and saved the day. I wanted someone to come in and save me that day," I said, beginning to get choked up.

"I know, My daughter," He said, holding my hand. "Will you help Me today?" He asked.

"Yes," I said.

"Watch with Me as He skates with you," He said. We sat in the grass just in view of the two.

"What is it we are looking for?" I asked.

"How a father should be," He said. "Tell me what you see."

"I see Him listening and helping her learn to skate," I said.

"What else?" He asked.

"He is patient," I said, crying.

As the tears rolled, I heard Him say, "Jesus loves you."

I turned toward the Lord.

"A good father points his children to Me and doesn't try to *be* Me," He said softly.

"Why are You showing me this?" I asked.

"Because it is never too late to have a Father," He answered.

With tears flowing, I jumped up and ran onto the ice. It was warm, and therefore I didn't slip. "Father," I cried as I ran into His arms.

"I have been waiting for you," He said with a tear in His eye.

"This had been one of the best journeys I had ever been on. I love You both so much." They had come in and saved me and my days. "I love You," I repeated as we skated in the moonlight. I realized it was I whom had been helped that day.

Downpours and Showers Bring Faith and Endurance

"I'm angry," I began. "I'm not sure why, I just know I had a dream. In that dream I was angry about a situation that is irrelevant to anything going on in my life, but I was mad in the dream. So I woke up mad and now I'm awake and mad. What is that all about? How can I transfer an emotion I feel in the dream to reality? It isn't fair to my husband...I was mad at him in the dream.

"He didn't do anything," I blurted out. "It all makes me think of the question You asked Jonah, 'Do you have a right to be angry?' I feel like I am about to devour something. Can this be productive?"

"Stop for just a minute," He interjected, "one question at a time."

I knew I had a history of asking questions before I gave Him a chance to answer, and then asking more questions. "I really have to stop that," I acknowledged.

"As far as the situation with Jonah, He couldn't be pleased. I wanted him to realize what he had and where I had brought him. There was no pleasing him. He needed to stop pouting and inventory his life. It was a wake-up call," the Lord explained.

"Oh, I see," I said. "But I'm still haunted by the words, 'Do I have a right to be angry?'"

"As a whole, probably not," He said.

"Why?" I asked, perturbed.

"Your life is good, yet you tend to focus on the negative instead of the positive," He pointed out.

"The half-empty instead of the half-full," I stated.

"Yes," He answered, "often it is all in how you look at things. You can look for the rainbow or focus on the downpour. I leave that up to you. Me, it is all about what I can learn in the downpour so that the rainbow appears brighter."

"I like that," I said. "The saying...not necessarily the downpours."

"Let Me propose it to you this way," He said. "Do you like the sound of rain?"

"Oh, yes, I listen to it every night as I fall asleep." As I thought about it, I enjoy a good heavy rain. It is refreshing and has such a soothing sound.

"Refreshing, that is the result. Do you remember the story I told you about the rain drops?" He asked.

"Yes, I loved that one," I answered.

"On, we'll say normal days, the rain falls in a calm, reasonable manner," He began. "But there are times in a raindrop's life that the clouds rumble and light flashes, causing the path they are on to accelerate, and down they come. This can cause a panic. But remember, the goal is to reach the ground. So, would it make sense to want to speed up the journey because it gets you to your goal sooner?"

Logically it would, I thought. "But what about the panic?" I asked.

"That seems to be the area most concentrated on. If somehow they would recognize that it is a good thing wrapped in what appears to be bad," He explained.

"Hmmm, I don't know about that," I commented.

"Wait before you decide. I have more," He said.

"OK," I agreed.

"Let's say the raindrop is going through the day cascading downward like the day before, when a strong wind blows and knocks it—you—off course. This is followed by what feels like a rocket propelled at you; then you are headed faster, faster toward the ground." He stopped and shook His head. "Oh, I want them to get this," He added. "The rocketed force can be an advantage instead of a hindrance. If they recognize what is happening, get their bearings, and flow with it instead of fighting it, several things will occur: they move faster toward the goal, and they build up endurance."

Wow, I hadn't heard that in a while, *endurance.* "And remind me why endurance again?" I asked.

"It is the key to faith and belief," He stated. "Remember My children of Hebrews 11? They were commended for their faith. Do you know how they grew to be faithful? By their willingness to endure," He answered. "Over time, faith is built by the downpours and showers. If they had stopped mid-stream and said, 'That is enough for me,' they stop their path to the ground. Stay on those roads when it is smooth and when things get bumpy. Ride that downpour. Strap on your floaties, and let it take you where you need to go...because remember, I let it take you," He said.

I saw a vision of the Lord's hand under a faucet. His fingers were slightly spread as the water flowed between them. "Child," He said, "it all passes through My fingers. I know when the storms are brewing and when the sun will shine. Have faith that I know what is best. I will never harm you nor leave you. No drop falls without My knowledge. I have you," He said. "Did you get all of that?" He asked as I came to from my vision.

"Yes, it is beautiful," I answered. I felt such calmness. Yes, even a peace. There was no anger. I liked it.

"To answer your anger question, you have a right to choose whatever you would like. Do I think anger is best? Absolutely not," He said.

"You know I'm going to ask, Lord," I stated. "But what if someone really hurts me?"

"In that moment you may choose to be angry, I can see that. But if you carry it like luggage, it will only weigh you down," He said. "Do you see how you brought it to Me this morning?" He asked.

"Yes," I answered.

"Well done. That is the right way—the way I hope you will always choose to handle your anger," He said.

ANGER

The next thing I knew, I was back in the temple. We were seated in the same circle on the same pillows: the Lord, the Holy Spirit, and myself. I looked around the circle waiting for someone to begin. Begin what? I did not know, but I could sense something was coming. I thought to myself, *Remember the rain. If a downpour is coming, prepare to flow. How do I flow?* I wondered.

"Yesterday," the Lord began, "you asked to travel with the Holy Spirit."

"Yes, I did," I replied. I could tell I was a little excited with a side of nerves.

"To travel, there are requirements," He stated. "Ones that will benefit you and make the journey more enjoyable."

"I'm all for that," I replied. "What are they?"

"First, you have to rid yourself of all that luggage," He stated.

I had not seen any luggage on our trip to the castle where we ice skated.

"No, but when we realize what we have missed or believe we have missed, luggage begins to reveal itself," He said.

I looked to my right and there sat what appeared to be a mountain of mismatched bags. Big ones, small ones, and some so stuffed they were bursting at the seams. Shocked, I looked back at Him and said, "This could take awhile." But then a light bulb went on. What if we had a downpour? I heard the most excited clapping I had ever heard. It was like we were at a Mets game and the crowd was going wild. "But wait, I don't even know the Mets," I thought.

"No, but I do," said the Lord.

"Can't we pull for the Indianapolis Colts? You know how I like Peyton Manning," I said, smiling.

"Whose story is this?" the Lord asked with a chuckle.

"OK, but my turn next time," I said smiling. "Wait," I said as I noticed there was clapping coming from not only around the circumference of the room, but there are people in the background as well. I could not see them, but I could hear the claps and cheers. "Who are they?" I asked.

"They are the people who will benefit from your willingness to ride the rush from the storm," He stated.

That sounded cool, but why would they cheer for me to have a downpour? "Was it a mean cheer?" I wondered.

"No," He replied, "not at all. Loved ones who want the best for you will cheer because they know you will be closer to Me when the rain stops. They will support and encourage you," He explained.

"I love that they are so supportive, but how will they benefit?" I asked.

"What you do or don't do affects their lives," He said. "Too often My Body looks at their own gain, but in the setup of how the Church is supposed to run, all areas win or lose. They are a team made up of individuals. Not individuals made up to use the team."

"Well, for them and for me, give me my floaties. I have a stream of water to catch," I said, ready to jump in.

"Whoa there, little beaver," He laughed.

Beaver? What's that about?

"They are very cute and love to flop around in the water, but most of all they are crafty. They know which sticks to swim with and how many at a time," He explained.

"Cool," I said as I jumped in.

"I love your excitement. That is the second step in flowing with the downpour," He said.

It shouldn't surprise me that He knew I had asked the question in my mind. But it just never seems to get old. I laughed as I asked, "What's the first step? Did I miss it?"

"No, dear, you passed it with flying colors—you agreed to take the journey," He said, smiling, while others clapped again.

I stopped and thought a minute about the possible magnitude of that decision, but He had not let me down yet, and I believed today would be no different. An overwhelming sense of gratitude came over me for my Lord. I remembered all of the people in the background clapping, but I just realized His clap was the loudest. He has always been there to support me even when those behind the scenes had bailed.

I began to tear up as I realized His faithfulness. He had not abandoned me when others had. I was truly never alone. But how could I have thought such a thing? I had dismissed His presence, yet He stayed. My heart was heavy. I was sorry. I sensed Him move closer. His hands from behind took my forearms in a gentle grasp.

"I have been your hands when you could not write," He said. "I helped you function when you felt you had no life left to breathe. I knew the investment would pay great returns," He said, tearing up. "You, like all My children, are worth it."

I began to cry. No one could touch my heart with sweeter words than my Lord.

"You will make it, I know you will. I have been your sideline cheerleader all along." As the words came out of His mouth, I saw the Holy Spirit jump up from His pillow in the biggest jump I had ever seen. He had on a cheerleading suit with pompoms to boot. "Go, Dena," I heard Him say. Then from the background the crowd began cheering, give me a "D," give me an "E," and so on until the grand finale when they shouted, "Go, Dena!"

I was laughing and crying at the same time to the point I was choked up. As I cleared my throat, I heard a faint voice coming from the crowd. It was soft but clear. "Go, Dena," it repeated over and over, never seeming to tire of the words.

I turned to God with a puzzled look.

"It is My Son," He explained. "He cheers on every one of My children."

I was in awe of the love in His voice and the concern in His commitment. He didn't have to, but it was apparent He wanted to.

"He is the Church's biggest fan. He roots them on as He prepares His return. He is committed to His Bride," He told me.

I stood there not knowing what to say to what the Lord had just shared with me.

"How about thank You?" the Lord suggested.

I felt horrible that I didn't think of that. Maybe I was trying to make it something huge?

"Thank You will suffice," the Lord said. "No need for flowery words and grand gestures. A sincere thank You is all He'd ask."

I started walking toward the wall from where I heard His voice coming.

"That is far enough," the Lord said. "He can hear you. Remember, He wants it to be a surprise," the Lord reminded me.

My desire to see Him grew leaps and bounds that moment. The anticipation was building. I needed to see my Groom. I knew what the answer would be, *in due time*. I laughed to myself. I stopped a few feet shy of the wall. "Jesus," I whispered, "if You can hear me…"

I heard His cheer stop and He replied, "I can hear you just fine, My Bride."

My knees began to melt. I thought they might buckle, causing me to fall to the floor. I managed to hold myself together and continue, "I love You, and I cannot thank You enough for Your continual support." It seemed not to be enough, but it was sincere. I really meant it.

"Dena," He started, "you are very welcome. Anything for My bride," He said with passion. Just as He had stopped cheering, He went right back. I could hear the names of His Church come off His lips, "John, Mary, Dan, Scott, Casey…"

The list seemed endless. "He is reading the names out of the Lamb's Book of Life," I hollered. I turned and ran to the Lord, "Is it true, is it true? Is He reading the Book?" I asked.

"I cannot tell you that. That is private between My heart and theirs," He answered.

I understood, but I was going to choose to believe He was. *But wait a minute,* I thought, *what about those who are not listed yet. Is it not fair that He call them too? What if His cheer is the straw that breaks the camel's back and softened their hearts to come? Oh, I had to rethink my choice. I had best leave it to Him. He knows best.*

"Look," I heard the Lord say as He pointed to the pile of luggage. Some had disappeared. I felt lighter.

Still in His cheerleading outfit, the Holy Spirit sat back down on His pillow, and then we joined Him. It had been a great day. I was closer to the end of the journey, but there were more bags to contend with. For now, though, I was going to enjoy the new, lighter feeling. We sat and smiled.

CHAPTER 21

The Hall

If you keep on biting and devouring each other, watch out or you will be destroyed by each other (Galatians 5:15).

I woke to a room with pictures hanging on the walls. I noticed I felt bloated, like I had eaten too much salt and puffed up to a very uncomfortable size. With a closer look, this room became a long hallway. Down the walls of this hallway were portraits of people. Some I recognized, but others I did not remember. I could hardly look at them, for their faces where bruised and mangled. Although they were obviously in great pain, they all wore smiles. The hallway began to spin and turn as if caught in a time warp. Slowly I became dizzy from the movement of the room. "Lord," I cried out, "what is this place?"

"It is the Hall," He said.

There was no emotion to His tone. He was one dimensional. I knew I was in trouble, but I wasn't sure what I was supposed to do. The room continued to spin as I began to get very sick to my stomach. Faster and faster the walls were spinning; so fast they were now a slur of lines blurring by my face. Faster and faster.

It stopped. I looked to my right and saw the luggage. I was in the temple, but I could still see the faces. I looked for God. Where was He? I could sense His presence, but had lost Him visually.

"Child, you know some of these faces," He told me.

"No," I cried. "No, it can't be."

"Yes, child, it is true," He confirmed.

"Please tell me I didn't do that to them," I begged.

"It wasn't just you," He replied.

I could hear faint crying from my right. I didn't want to look, but I had to see what was there. It was coming from the luggage. I turned my head to confirm the crying was from the luggage. It was getting louder and louder. There were no more cheering voices coming from the background. It was a cry of pain and what must have been excruciating pain. It got louder until I thought my ear drums would burst. My knees buckled, and I fell to the floor, grabbing my ears to try and block out the screams. My head hit the floor and I yelled, "Make it stop, make it stop."

In the same tone, He replied, "They want it to stop, too. Everyone wants it to stop, but they continue to scream," He stated.

For what felt like an eternity, the room was filled with my screams and their pleas. Until suddenly, I felt my back give way. I now laid flat on my stomach with intense pressure above my face. From the corner of my eye I could see an elephant's foot inches from the side of my face. I didn't dare move—or did I try to make a run for it? *I could roll away, jump up and run*, I thought.

"Where are you going to go?" the Lord asked.

"Out of this trouble," I said.

"How do you know it is trouble?" He asked.

"Because I don't like it," I said bluntly.

"It will only follow you," He informed me.

"What? What is this?" I asked.

"You brought it with you, and it will go with you unless you take care of that luggage," He said.

I noticed that the screaming had become whimpers now.

I was angry now. I could feel the pressure fill up inside my head. "I was hurt, too," I said.

"Yes," He acknowledged, "you were, and as long as you keep that attitude to justify the screams, it keeps the elephant balanced. But what if you allow *Me* to justify the hurt? What do you think will happen?" He asked.

"The foot will drop?" I guessed.

"You are right," He said.

"What good will that do me? That would crush me," I said.

"Are you afraid of that foot?" He asked.

Why so many questions? I thought. "Yes, it is heavy and will hurt me," I answered. It seemed so obvious.

"What if I tell you that I can take what you did, too?" He asked.

"I would say, 'take it,'" I replied.

"Are you sure?" He asked. "There is responsibility for what was done and what you did," He said.

It was all I could stand. I swung around toward the bags and screamed at the top of my lungs, "Stop your whining. Cry if you're going to cry," I screamed. "Cry, baby, cry! Where did that come from?" I began to sob. "What was happening? Make it stop," I pleaded one more time.

"Honey, let yourself out of the suitcases," He said. "It is OK to cry."

My heart stopped. I was so confused, yet I understood, or at least I thought I did.

"You are one of the bags," He stated. He pointed to a nice-sized pink suitcase with white polka dots. It had a very pretty black trim and from what I could tell a beautiful, pink, silk lining. My mind flashed backward as I remembered I had seen that lining before. It was in the casket my grandmother was buried in. It was more than I could stand. I fell to the ground holding my stomach, praying the elephant would crush my head.

"He won't," He said. "Your will to live is greater than his ability to move."

Somehow what He said was supposed to be comforting. Did He not just see my grandma lying there?

"Go over to the suitcase," He motioned.

I got up and slowly drug myself to the pile.

"Step in," He directed.

I looked at Him with crocodile tears and a face that resembled a lost puppy. *What do I have to lose?* I thought. *My heart is lost anyway.* I picked up one foot and placed it in. Before I could lift my other foot, I was standing over the casket as my grandmother lay before me peacefully. She was absolutely beautiful. Her gown was as pretty on her as I remembered. She was the most beautiful woman I had ever seen. I hung onto the side of the casket, and then fell to the floor. With what strength I had left, I sat with my back pressed against the casket, arms limp and sobbing. I just wanted to sit with her and cry. Floods of memories bombarded my head. "I wanted to cry," I said out loud. "I really wanted to cry."

"Why didn't you?" He asked as He sat down beside me.

"They said not to. A man said not to ask for her to come back because it wouldn't be fair to her. I didn't want to hurt her, so I didn't. I remember being in the big room where all of the family met; they were talking, but no tears," I said.

"Are you sure?" He asked.

I looked around the room closer. Wait, in the corner, there was someone I had not seen before. I walked closer. Could it really be? Was it Jesus?

"Yes, dear," He replied.

"What is He holding?" I asked

"It is the heart of everyone in the room. They were crying," He said.

I could see the pictures in the Hall again. The faces were changing. I could see portions of each person's face more prominently now.

"What you are seeing are the areas that represent the pain they felt that day. They did cry. But like you, they put on brave faces," He said.

I had been watching television. I felt a rush of guilt come over me. I had not cried. I watched television instead. "How could I? What was wrong with me? Was I that cold?" I cried.

"Stop," I heard Him insist. "I want that!"

"No, you can't have it." I stood there with my head down, as I said, "I need it. I deserve it."

"Don't you think you have punished yourself enough?" He asked.

I had not seen it that way, but He was right. If I held on to that guilt, I could swat myself over and over at will.

"It is my will that you not live under condemnation, be it from others—or yourself," He said.

I cupped my hands together and lifted my head. Slowly I placed my hands over my heart and then moved them toward His hands. I wanted Him to have it. Not because I didn't want responsibility, but because I had taken responsibly. It was over. I had cried.

As I stood there motionless, I saw a vision of John sitting at the table with Jesus as they broke bread. John was very comfortable with Him; I could tell because he had rested his head on His shoulder. I followed. I rested my head on Jesus' shoulder.

"I am here," He whispered. "Cry if you need to. I won't think you are a baby."

"Why is it You now, Jesus?" I whispered.

"This is a matter of the heart; it is My territory," He stated.

For whatever reason He was there, for now I just was grateful for the comfort. I had held that pain in for a long time. I had cried here and there. And the mention of her name would stir up a tear, but I had not faced myself before. I had not let myself miss her. I had taken what that man had said to me and allowed it to keep me locked in my own luggage. *I was glad to be out, but now what?* I wondered.

"You are exhausted," Jesus shared. "Get some rest. I will be here in the morning when you awake."

For now, that was good with me. I knew there were many bags...and still the faces in the Hall.

I heard the Lord whisper from above, "In due time, Child."

FAITHFUL

Hours later, I awoke to find He had kept His promise. My head was still resting on His shoulder and drool from my sleep was puddled on His shirt. He did not seem to mind. I don't remember the sleep, but it was needed. I had tossed and turned with visions of the portraits replaying in my head all night. Still half drowsy, I lifted my head. Trying to get my swollen eyes focused, He looked at me.

Was I dreaming or still asleep? Why was He allowing me to see His face?

"It is I," the Lord spoke. "I have returned to take you on the next part of the journey."

I began to cry, "Lord, I'm tired and weak. I can't think straight, and I'm troubled."

"All of these are true My child, but if the trouble is not dealt with, the other symptoms will not fade," He said.

It made sense, but I didn't know if I could stomach the Hall again. Those hurt faces grabbed my soul and wouldn't let go. "Will You help me?" I asked.

"I can do better than that; I will carry you," He offered. He bent down with such care and scooped me up in His arms. I rested my head on His chest and hung on with my arms wrapped around His neck. They were like spaghetti, but I did not fear. He had me. As He stood up, I noticed my grandmother was gone. Her beautiful body no longer lay in the casket where I had last seen her. There were those darn tears again. They floated down my face as I asked Him, "Where is she?"

"She is with me," He answered.

"But Lord, I saw her leading the choir." I was confused.

"Yes, that is where she is, but you did not let her go from this room. Now your tears have released her. You no longer see her here," He said tenderly.

I knew this was an onion moment, but I was too tired to bring it up. The night had been an emotional rollercoaster, and I sensed the ride had not come to a stop yet. I closed my eyes and drifted to sleep as He carried me to our next destination. Too beat to resist, I nodded off.

I woke to a crowd cheering, "You did it!" We were in the temple again. Much different from last night. I quickly looked to my right. They were still there, but no screaming. The bags were silent.

Oh, there was the Holy Spirit. The sight of Him was refreshing. The Lord placed me gently on the pillow where I had sat many times before. I took a deep breath and waited.

"Dena," the Lord began, "you did well. Good job, My faithful servant," He said. I had dreamed of the day I would hear those words from my Lord.

Tears again. *Really?* I thought. It seems all the tears I had held back had cracked the dam and I had no control when or how fast they flowed.

"That is the next step to the process," He said proudly. "Feel the emotion."

It sounded so simple, yet I had spent my entire life trying to hold it back. "Feel the emotion," I repeated. "Honestly, I am exhausted," I stated. As much as I was happy to see the Holy Spirit and to hear the cheering, I could not get the faces out of my mind. *Am I ready?* I wondered. *I know where He is going to take me. Can I do this?*

"Excuse Me," I heard.

It was a different voice from the ones I had heard before. Pleasant would describe it.

Again, I heard, "Excuse Me."

"Yes," I said, not knowing where it came from.

"It is I, the Holy Spirit," He said.

I turned to Him, but His mouth was not moving. "How can this be?" I asked.

"I am speaking from inside your heart. It seems you think you will go on this next phase on your own, when in fact that is far from the truth. Look around you," He directed.

I turned my neck so I could get a view of the circumference of the entire room. Faces were peering from the perimeter of the room. They were smiling and had an eager look about them. I could see my daughter; there was my son-in-law; and friends I hadn't seen in years. It was overwhelming the love I felt from their smiles. It was support. I noticed a presence that I had not before.

I turned to the left, and there sat my husband. He took my hand and began to tell me how much he loved me and that he knew I could do it all alone. I had wanted him to be proud of me, but didn't know how or when. Everything I had tried, I had hoped would be the thing that did it. My husband said, "I have always been proud of you. It was you who wasn't proud of you."

Where had he gotten such insight and wisdom? He was beautiful. I reached over and hugged him like I had never before. I needed him.

"Yes, you have, dear," the Lord interrupted. "But you won't let yourself fully engulf yourself in all he has to offer you."

I knew he had provided financial support and a hug when I had a bad day, but this was deeper. I had not allowed myself to fall into his arms. How could we be a complete one if I kept us separate? I wanted to let go.

I knew what I had to do. I kissed my husband as I got up and walked toward the suitcases. There was a black, hard case in the far left of the pile. That was the one. Without hesitation, I un-latched it and began to step in when I heard, "NO!" The Lord ran over to me as to stop me before I could enter.

"You cannot go there alone. Wait, I will go with you," He offered.

This scared me. What could be waiting that was so horrible? Did I really want to go now? Was I ready? I remembered what the Holy Spirit had said earlier; how I must have thought I was going on the next phase alone. I turned to the Holy Spirit and said, "Will You go, too?"

Without a word, He walked over. I looked at my husband sitting on his pillow all alone. "What about him?" I asked the Lord with great concern.

"He must wait here, but what you experience will affect him, too," the Lord advised me.

"Then why can't he go and help me do it right?" I asked again.

"There are some things you need to take care of alone; he must wait," He explained.

"No, no that doesn't make sense. If we are one, then why can't he go?" I asked with a raised voice.

Calmly the Lord asked, "Well isn't that the way you have been doing it?"

Wow, that one hit me right between the eyes. I looked at my dear, sweet, supportive husband and mouthed, "I'm sorry." Then I turned to my Father, asking again, "Can he please come?"

"Yes, he may," the Lord said gladly.

I ran over to my husband to jump in his arms, but as I got to the pillow, he was gone. Vanished into thin air. I was puzzled. "Lord, where did he go?" I asked.

"Honey, take a look inside," He said.

I looked down toward my chest. I could see his smiling face. He had been with me all the time; I just had not included him.

"You can do it," I heard him say as he blew me a kiss.

My emotions had overtaken me again. All I could do was blow a kiss in return.

"Now, this is new for you," the Lord began, "the way this works is communication. Why is communication key?" I asked.

"Communication is how we get to know each other. It is the same with a married couple. It is how you build and maintain a relationship," He said. "Tell your husband what happens as we go along. A marriage breaks down when communication slows up. He wants to be included, so share your adventures with him. He is a bridge to your success. There are many, but he is your strongest ally."

"I love you," I said as I looked at my husband's face again. "I love you!" I looked down to the floor and saw the hard casing on the suitcase had softened. *Wow, it's working,* I thought.

"Did you question Me?" the Lord asked with a chuckle.

Oh, how I had missed that laughter. "Lord," I asked, "please don't ever stop making me laugh."

"Oh I will remember you said that. You haven't seen the half of it." He grinned as the Holy Spirit began to shake His head.

"You have done it now," He added.

I don't care, I thought. I loved His laugh, and I prayed to hear it more. We all stood there laughing. I found myself glancing down often just to check on my husband. It was nice having him so close. I remembered how we had often told each other how we wished we could put each other in our pockets so we could carry each other around all day. I had something better than a pocket; he was in my heart.

BETRAYAL

It was like a steaming, hot volcano that would erupt in a matter of seconds—but which second was unclear. It hurts from the pit of a rumbling stomach and burns as the molten lava of hatred made its way up my esophagus. Don't blame or held me accountable when the bubbling liquid spews out of my mouth. It burns. It's bitter and unbearable. It is betrayal.

"I am angry, Lord," I said as if it was perfectly clear. "How could someone who is supposed to love you hurt you so badly? Why would they? Why so mean? Where do I go from here?" I asked as I began to sob.

Hurt doesn't touch the knife wound in my side. The blood springs out of the hole left behind by the hands of a family member. I loved them, and I thought it was mutual. Was I naive to think they were supposed to love me too? What about protection? Are not the ones who care for you supposed to watch over and guard you from predators? How can that be when the one stalking you is that one? I hold back the tears until it felt like my head was going to explode. This was raw, and nothing can stop the intensity of the cut I now see.

"Hey, Little One," I heard a voice say.

I knew it was the Lord, but my patience was thin.

"Don't run, My child," He said. "I know you are hurt, and understandably so, but please, there is a line here; please be aware of where you put your feet."

"Daddy," I cried out. "Abba Father, it hurts so badly. Please make it better." I felt like a little girl as I ran to His side. As my hand racked across His waist, I felt something raised and bumpy on His left side. It was protruding from underneath His shirt. "Oh my," I gasped as I looked up. It was Jesus. I began to cry and yell, "No!" I had touched His scar. "Did I hurt you? I'm sorry I did not mean to touch it. I was only trying to hug..." I explained.

He stopped me in mid-sentence, "Child, child, do not worry, it is healed. I am OK." He grabbed me tightly and held me. "I am OK," He repeated.

I stood in His arms crying. I knew all the stories about the day of His crucifixion. He had been cut, He had been flogged, and He had been betrayed. How could I be so insensitive? I stood there limp. The volcano had subsided. I was numb. As I looked up into His eyes, I saw sympathy. They were blue like the sky, but clear like a crystal brook. There was warmth. As most living in Jesus' time would have had brown eyes, I asked God what should I make of the blue eyes. He explained, "that I see them in blue because blue brings peace and comfort. Those in heaven are not subject to our earthly eye colors. They are pure now and it is reflected in the eyes." I had wanted someone to sympathize, to tell me it was horrible and they were sorry that it had happened. I gazed longingly into His eyes, hoping the pain would somehow seep from my body and be received by His own. I whispered, "Please help me."

"I began that help 2,000 years ago," He replied to my plea. "The pain that you are feeling, I felt on the cross."

I have stepped into His body, I thought. "What do we do now?" I asked.

"First, let Me lead," He said. "Don't be the leader; don't try to handle this alone. You did the first thing when you didn't run. Dad and I lose more of Our children because they run away from Us in their emergencies instead of coming to Us. It makes it harder to heal when they leave an open wound unattended. It needs attention as soon as possible. The longer it is left, the more chance of infection. Some are eaten up with infection." His head dropped.

I could tell that saddened Him greatly. I swallowed hard as He continued.

"I am proud of you. You took Our Father's advice."

"What was that?" I asked.

"You included your husband," He answered.

I knew what He was referring to. When the news of the betrayal had been revealed, I remember the time in the temple. I looked at my chest to show Jesus what it had done. I saw my husband there. I wanted to talk to him about what I had learned. It had gone well. "Yes," I heard. "It had."

"That was the second step, talk to someone who cares," He said. "If the Body of Christ would communicate with those who are safe, it makes the pain more bearable. I bore that pain; you don't have to keep it."

"Jesus," I asked, "You mentioned *safe.*"

"I believe that Abba told you about how He created the Garden with the intention of it being a safe place for His children to play," He asked.

"Yes, He did," I replied.

"Sadly, just like danger found its way in there, it has found itself into My Church. I am not implying you need to be afraid; they are only human. But you do need to be aware," He stated.

"How do we be aware?" I asked.

"The fact that you know it is happening is a start," He said. "Knowing what My Lord says and His character allows you to compare the tendencies. Let Him explain."

"But what about those who sneak in?" I asked.

"Dear," I heard a deeper voice. It was God.

"Where did Jesus go?" I asked.

"He will be back. Your heart has many layers of hurt. He handles that, as you know. He will be back," He repeated. "Right now, we need to deal with the *logos* of the matter. Those in sheep's clothing will tell you what you want to hear and do what they think will trick you. You must be aware of their tactics."

"Lord, You keep saying *aware*," I pointed out. "That could drive a person crazy just trying to stay one step ahead. That doesn't seem like You," I said.

"You are correct, it isn't," He agreed. "My people cannot stay one step ahead all of the time because they do not have the capability to know everything that is coming. Only I do."

"So, they must stay with You."

"You got it!" He cheered. "If they are out there winging it on their own, they are bound to get blindsided, not to mention becoming paranoid. They will begin to think there is evil behind every door," He said.

"That seems like a lot to add to the already overwhelming pain," I said.

"You got it. They try to bear the unbearable and add more weight to an already heavy load. It is safe under My wing. Come there," He advised.

I knew as I stood there I was under His wing. I could feel the calmness. The rumbling was still in the pit of my stomach, though.

"Child," He began, "that pressure of pain must come out. The questions are when and how? Each one will be accountable for the answers to both questions."

I knew He was referring to my comment earlier about not holding me accountable. I knew I would be when I said it, I was just angry.

"Yes, I know that, and I understand being angry, but what you say in the heat of an explosion is still your responsibility. Once the words leave the mouth, there is no suction device to retrieve them. The damage is done," He said.

"What if I don't care if it hurts the other person?" I was shocked I had said that out loud.

"You are not going to like this, but it is the truth: when you hurt one of My children, you have Me to contend with."

He was right; I didn't like it. *But,* I thought, *on the other hand, what about when I am hurt by another?*

"The same rules apply to you too. The one who hurts you will have to face Me too. I show no favoritism. That is why I warn so many times about judging. Be careful, I say, because the plank in your eye is noticeable to Me too," He advised.

I knew this was far from over. I was calm at the moment, but as He has said, the volcano eventually has to erupt or it will implode.

"I am trying to stop as many casualties as possible," He continued.

I saw a vision of Jesus in a room. There were hearts lying all over the floor. Some were pumping slowly, as if on their last breath, while others were beating incredibly fast as if gasping for more breath, and some were not pumping at all. I looked into His eyes as tears cascaded down His checks. He was walking around the room trying to pick up each heart from the floor. But just as He would get a few picked up someone would come by and knock them out of His hands.

"Before He can mend one, someone knocks it down again. He won't give up," the Lord said. "He is diligent about saving as many hearts as possible before it is too late."

"Too late?" I asked.

"Yes, I won't put Him through this forever," He said. "He will return." It was so quiet I could have heard a pin drop.

Finally, the Lord looked at me. "Look," He said, as He pointed toward Jesus again. "See those hearts in His hand now?"

Yes, I nodded.

"Do you notice anything different?" He asked.

"Yes," I said with amazement, "they have feet and hands."

"Their experience with hurt grew feet and hands," the Lord replied. "Feet to walk back to Him if knocked off again and hands to grab on tighter to His hand if someone tried to knock them off."

"That is incredible," I said.

"Yes, it is. Look at your chest," He said.

I looked down. "Oh my," I said with amazement. Right before my eyes, I saw a hand evolve from my heart. It was like the sweet, gentle small hand of a baby.

"Yes, is it precious," He said. "You are a baby at this, but over time if you keep holding on to My Son's hand, your hand will grow strong."

I stood there trying to take in all I had seen and heard.

"Look quickly," He said.

I turned back to Jesus and saw a heart with what appeared to have smooth, yet larger hands protruding from it.

"That is one of My children who have matured," He said with a proud voice. "No matter what life threw, no trial or tribulation kept him from holding on."

"I want to be one that holds on," I said excitedly. Something that came to me while I watched was that the focus had been on *my* healing not the person who had betrayed me.

"Very observant," He said. "Too many times in the midst of hurt, My children want Me to rush in and decapitate the betrayer, when My main concern at first is to stop the bleeding. That is what we have done today. There will be many surgeries to heal the cut, but there needs to be healing between each. Meanwhile, allow Me to do My job and handle the betrayer. I am a just and fair God," He reminded me.

I am comfortable with that, for now, I thought. Coming to Him has drawn the lava back again, for now. But somehow I knew that when the volcano started to blow again, if I would come to Him, He would know what to do.

"I love You, Lord," I said as I saw Jesus continue to scoop up hearts off the floor. "I wish He could rest."

"He will, but not until every heart has a chance," the Lord spoke. "Help Him," He said.

Wow, I had always been the one who asked Them for help. "Yes, Father, what can I do?"

"Try not to knock any hearts out of His hands. If My children would help pick them up instead of knocking them off," He said, "many more would come to know Me and be healed."

Oh, my heart sank. I was now in the Hall. The room began to spin. "Lord," I cried out, "I'm so sorry." I knew the portraits were reflections of the aftermath of hearts knocked off. I fell to the floor and began to cry. "I'm sorry," I repeated. Names of the victims started spewing from my mouth—Stephanie, Lisa, Jamie—the list went on and on. Finally the last, Sarah. I fell prostrate from exhaustion. "I'm sorry," I whispered with what felt like my last breath.

I woke in what seemed like hours to find I was in the temple. Still exhausted, I slowly pulled myself up. There was no one in the temple. I looked around and noticed the luggage was smaller. A blue one stood out. I walked over to it. "What about this one?" I asked myself out loud.

"It is healing," I heard a voice from behind me say. I turned to see the Lord walking toward me. "You have sought forgiveness for those in the Hall that you contributed to their hurt. The blue bag represented the sadness they have carried. It is getting smaller," He explained.

"That is good, right?" I asked.

"Yes. Oh, yes," He said.

"Lord, what about going to those I have wronged?" I asked with fear in my heart.

"Do not fear, Child," He began. "I will tell you when and if you are to go. That fear tells me you need your own healing first. We will work on that, then whether to send you out," He said.

I knew a particular person on that wall I had hurt multiple times. Honestly, I was afraid to confront the person, and more, I was afraid He would ask me to.

"I will never ask you to do something that I don't go with you and have prepared you for. There is a prep time," He continued. "You know the saying, 'Where I send you I will go.' If I send you out before you are ready, then it is on Me. You have to remember that I am trying to save a world here. There is enough disaster without putting My own out there prematurely.

"I often delay, or that is how My Church sees it, but it is for your own good. I know the timeline. That is not of your concern, but know that approaching another who has been hurt will be sensitive. It has to be done at the opportune time. It is not only you I am preparing. Let Me make that call."

Gladly, I thought. *But what about those who will take that as an opportunity to never apologize?* I wondered.

"Do not worry about them. I don't miss a thing," He said.

We both laughed. Not out of disrespect, but because we knew I needed to mind my own business.

"Before you go today, I want to ask you one last favor," He said.

"Sure, Lord," I replied gladly.

"Let Me handle the one responsible," He asked.

I thought hard before I answered. This would be a big leap of trust.

"Trust is a heavenly strength," He added.

"I needed some exercise," I chuckled.

"Well, the gym is open," He laughed.

"Well, given the weight, I'm coming in," I replied.

"Thank you," He replied. "I won't let you down."

-CHAPTER 22-

In Need of
Promises Kept

Therefore, if anyone is in Christ, he is a new creation; The old has gone, the new has come! (2 Cor 5:17).

"I'm so frustrated, but honestly I know it is truly hurt. My husband and I had been on a trip and God had promised an open heaven experience while we were gone. It had not happened; and I was hurt. Lord, You can't be like the others who have let me down," I said. "You just can't."

"What if I am?" He answered.

"Then You are no better than the humans I have put my trust into and they let me down," I answered.

"How did they let you down?" He asked.

"Promised things then never delivered. I cannot go through that again. It will crush me," I announced.

"Dena," He said.

"Yes, Sir," I answered.

"It is going to be OK," He said with an assuring tone.

"Don't tell me that because You don't know that." There was a pause because I knew He knew everything.

"Tell Me what you are thinking. I can take it," He said.

"If You don't do what You said You would do, then You don't care for me anymore than they did," I said.

"What had been promised to you, they could not afford," He said.

"I hate this! It hurts, and yes, I want it to stop."

"Then let's peel away," He said.

My thoughts went to my daughter. I knew that I had done the same thing with her. I wanted her to have everything, so I would promise and then could not deliver. Honestly, I couldn't imagine it was that they loved me and wanted me to have everything.

"About your assumption," He started, "you think that if I or anyone doesn't come through that we do not care for you. This is not the case. You start to panic and basically freak out because those emotions you felt when others have let you down bubble up. Then to protect yourself you make a mess."

"What do you mean *make a mess?*" I asked.

"You leave, or say something that hurts them," He explained. "It is a tit for tat. You hurt, so they end up hurting."

"Like I did this morning with You," I asked.

"Yes, like you did with Me," He said.

"I'm sorry," I said.

"I know you didn't want to hurt Me, but you meant it all the time," He stated.

"What do I do?" I asked. I sat there waiting for the answer as the intense pain in my chest pounded. I could hear the hurt screaming from my chest. I flashed backed to the suitcases of screaming people. I didn't want to go there, I needed help now.

"That is the problem," He began. "You want help *now* when it often takes a moment. I watch My people run around from person to person, place to place, thing to thing trying to stop it now.

A big heavenly strength is to breathe. Take a breath, and come to Me," He said.

"I'm here, Lord. What now?" I asked.

"Let us finish what we started this morning," He said.

"OK," I agreed.

"You have assumed they don't care and the thought of Me doing the same terrifies you. Why do you think this is true?" He asked.

"Because I have put all of my eggs in one basket," I answered.

"It is not who you think I am, as much as confusion about who you think I *should* be. You can do nothing without Me. So to try is futile. Of course, you are going to be tired. Fear won't measure up," He concluded.

"What about the baskets?" I asked.

"Who asked you to put everything into one basket? I just said make Me the most important egg! I like others in our basket with us. Why don't you climb in the basket, too?"

I had never viewed it that way. I guess I was on the outside looking in. "How do I get in the basket?" I asked. I started to cry.

"I will show you," He said sympathetically.

"Promise?" I asked.

"Honey, I haven't abandoned you," He reminded me.

"I am afraid You will," I said.

"Why?" He asked.

"Because it keeps happening," I admitted. "What do I do or not do that makes people leave me? Do I have to promise them things so they won't go."

"No you don't," He said. "We will get to the bottom of this," He promised.

"God, please be big. I need You to be big. Why do I need You to be big so badly?" I asked.

"I am your last hope," He said. "If I don't or won't come through, then you are lost."

What You are saying is true. "How can You help me?" I asked. I waited. Should I think of Him like so many, to be God doing His thing as they go about doing their thing? *Stop,* I thought, *if He is not big then...*

"Then what?" He asked.

I lost my thought. I needed to decide where in my life He fit. How big was He? My mind knew that He was bigger than I could imagine. No eye had seen. Wait; maybe it wasn't how big He was, but how big He would lift me.

"Now you are thinking rightly," He said.

"But why do I need You to make me big?" I asked.

"Think about it," He said, smiling. "You say so many have left. How does that feel?"

"Painful," I answered.

"Now, think about yourself."

"I need to be big so that I have value," I said. "We are at the value again."

"Yes, you struggle with worth; self-worth," He stated.

"What do we do?" I asked.

We both looked at each other with a grin and said, "Peel."

As over that word as I was becoming, I knew it was the key. I wasn't frustrated now, still hurt, but I could go about the day until we could meet again. "One last thing, Lord," I said, "I pray to know I am valuable."

He said, "First, we will have to address what *value* means to you. I have a feeling that it is incorrect in your mind."

"Why does that matter?" I asked.

"If I explain value to you, but you believe it is something else, then the truth won't help you," He explained.

"Thank You, Lord," I said.

"For what?" He asked.

"Taking the time to help me," I answered.

"Honey, you are worth it," He said lovingly.

"One day I pray to know that," I said.

"You will," He said.

Just those words "you will" sent a sharp pain through my stomach. Too many had strung me along never to pull through.

"What about the ones who did?" He asked. "You are in the very house of some that did. Focus on them, and we'll talk more later," He suggested.

I went on with the day, but honestly I was just waiting to see Him be big. *This is deep,* I thought.

"Then stay," He said.

I knew He was talking about not skimming across the top of the well, but to be one who stayed. Stick it out. It will be worth it.

"But what if it isn't?" I questioned.

I didn't want to play this *what if* game. I wanted to stop hurting.

From what seemed out of nowhere, a man's name that I knew came to mind. "I am angry at him," I announced.

GOING DEEP

"Why?" the Lord asked.

"Let's just cut to the chase," I said angrily. "I'm mad…no I hate men because they take things from me. Yes," I screamed, "I am blaming all for the sin of one." I screamed as loud as I could force my vocal cords to work. "Someone has to fix this!" I yelled.

"Or what?" He asked.

"There will be heck to pay," I said forcefully. I knew I said it and so be it. "What can You do with that, Lord?" I said, full of rage. I turned to find Jesus standing there.

"Oh, it must be a heart matter," I said sarcastically. I figured if They were going to bail on me, I might as well speak my mind.

Jesus said, "You are speaking your heart. And honestly, Dena, it isn't pretty."

"Don't You think I know that? Don't You think I want to look beautiful? A perfectly wrapped package with a handmade bow and streamers flowing from the top, yes that would be nice," I continued. I sensed I had calmed down, but I was not sure why.

"Dena," He started.

That was strange, only God said my name.

"That is because this is so deep that it takes us all working at the same time," He explained.

"You would do that? All three take the time to help me?" I asked surprised.

"Of course, you are Our Bride. The one with the utmost value to us," Jesus answered.

That was the calm I was feeling—the warmth of a perfect Trinity.

"You mentioned a package," He said.

"Yes," I said.

"That is what you are pretending to have, but you know differently so you strive to make it happen. You can't, My beloved," He said.

There was the tender voice I loved. I could listen to Him talk all day. As He continued, I saw the Holy Spirit in the corner of my eye. I could not believe my eyes. He was wearing a package.

"What in the world?" I blurted out.

Jesus turned toward Him and began to laugh. "He is serious about His role," He said, laughing.

He had dressed up in a present costume. I had to laugh. The sentiment was so touching, and the need for a good laugh meant as much.

He came closer to Jesus and me and said, "I heard someone in the house needed a gift."

"Holy Spirit," I said, "You *are* a gift Yourself." I took a deep breath. I was going to make it. I was surrounded by ones who loved me. Now, if I could just get my thick skull to believe it.

They laughed. "Dear," I heard the Lord say, "We have dealt with tougher."

I stood there gazing at the three of Them. Here They were with the world falling apart, but taking time with me. I wanted to focus on those who had been there for me and stop punishing others for the ones who hadn't. How that would happen I could only imagine. As the words passed through my mind, I felt something in my hand. I looked down to see a ladle. I looked up to the three of Them and grinned. I knew where we were going—deep.

SINS OF OTHERS

"I'm so upset. I was expecting this big something and it didn't happen. I waited all night and You didn't show. I'm so sad and disappointed. Why? You knew how much I needed this. Why?" I repeated. "Can't You see how hurt I am? I have failed."

"Why do you say you have failed?" He asked.

"No, that's not the answer I want. I want to know why You let me down. You said You wouldn't."

"Honey, what did You expect?" He asked.

"No, don't make this my fault again," I said. "The others did that, too. They said if I had done this or hadn't done that they would have done what they had promised. Not You, too," I said, almost hysterically.

"I am not like them," He replied calmly.

"But You did the same thing," I said.

"OK, we can go around this mountain over and over, or you can listen for just a minute," He said sternly.

"I'm listening." I thought, *I don't think there is anything He can say to make this better.*

"Do you remember when I said you were going to write a book?" He asked.

"Yes," I said.

"Well, you are," He pointed out.

"Yes," I answered. "What does that have to do with what You promised me?" I questioned.

"Everything," He said.

I was tired of those short answers. I was getting frustrated and tired of the whole thing. Really, I just wanted to crawl under the covers and cry myself to sleep.

"I'm still listening," I said.

"I know, I am just giving you a minute to calm down," He said.

"I don't want to calm down; I want You to do what You said You would do," I insisted.

"Again," He asked me, "what is it that you think I was going to do?"

"Take me to the heavenlies. You knew that was specifically what I had asked."

"No, what you had implied," He said.

"No, what You kept saying, was, 'just wait.' I felt strung along."

"I want you to know that I did not string you along," He said. "Let's talk about the situation that you are referring to. When you were to be given an item from someone you felt you could rely on."

"Yes, I knew it well. What about it?" I asked, frustrated because we had already discussed that fact.

"Did you get that item?" He asked.

"Yes, but not when they promised it," I said.

"What happened when you got it?" He asked.

"I didn't care for the style," I admitted.

"So, you got what you were promised and still weren't happy, am I correct?" He asked.

"Yes, but it didn't come when they said," I insisted.

"That I know. Do you remember our conversation when you admitted you often promised things that you couldn't deliver?" He asked.

"Yes, but I didn't blame the person I had promised," I stated.

"Are you sure?" He asked.

I hate when He asked that question because it usually means I did what I just said that I didn't. "OK, I remember vaguely something," I admitted.

"Child, before this was brought into the light, you too would blame others for items you could not or honestly did not want to come through with," He said.

I knew He was right; but darn, I wish He hadn't been.

"Now, back to this frustration, I believe you called it, about what I promised you," He said.

"Yes," I said as I sat there with a look of aggravation.

"You have been in the heavenlies for weeks now. Every time you spoke to one of My children, you were there. The problem you have is that it wasn't the same as what others have experienced," He explained. "Just like item you wanted and were so upset over, you got what you asked for, but when you got it, it wasn't how you wanted it."

If I could have crawled under the table, I would have. I felt my face turn red and my body clothed in humility. "You are right, Lord," I admitted. "I cannot say I'm sorry enough."

"Once is all I ask," He stated.

"I'm sorry I got so angry," I said. As the word *angry* came out of my mouth, I remembered Elijah. Did I have a right to be angry? He had blessed me with so much and given me so many chances, yet I still had a temper tantrum. "Lord," I cried out, "I pray to be more grateful."

"Very good, My child, we shall work on that," He said, smiling.

BE BIG

"Lord, where did I get misunderstood?" I asked. "When I would ask, You would reply how grand and big this was going to be. I'm confused."

"You ran with the idea," He stated. "You needed Me to be big."

"Yes, but how did I miss You?" I asked.

"You didn't miss Me," He said.

"Yes," I answered.

"You are basing your worth on how big I show up. I am going to be Me. I change for no one. And I will help you be you. But if I ran to do huge things to prove to you or for you to prove to others, I would be jumping through hoops for all My children. And dear, I don't run a circus," He said.

I understood what He was telling me, yet I didn't know what to do now. I needed to tell others what He did because I had told them how big He was going to show up.

"Do you believe I showed up big?" He asked.

"Honestly, Lord, no," I said. "I know You show up, but not what I would call big. I remembered the weekend, it had been great...but big, I wasn't sure.

"Exactly—you are not sure," He agreed. "You have no idea what was planted while you were here. There is the process of planting. There was good soil to work with. I expect great fruit to come in your life and the lives of all the others. Dear, you don't need to prove to others that I am big," He said. "I will take care of that. And as far as your need for Me to be big, we will work on that too."

I sat wishing it was all taken care of, but we know the onion. "Lord," I said, "I'm sorry that I continually compare You to others. And more than that, I really do not like to group everyone in a group because one did wrong."

"It is OK, I understand," He said. "Remember, I can see your heart. We are going to get there. Just hang tight," He asked.

I needed time to process what He had said and I had felt. I wasn't angry, just a little shaken.

"Dear, know that you can come to Me when you are angry, sad, frustrated, or happy. Come however you are," He instructed.

"Thank You," I whispered. I really wanted something big. I was still disappointed. "What do I do?" I asked.

"Come to Me," He said.

"Lord, I'm right here," I said.

"Yes, I see that. We exposed many issues today. It is not a magic wand. We will deal with each one as I see fit," He assured me.

I hate when others have the final say, I thought. *I want to do what I want to do when I want to do it!*

"Are you ready?" I heard Him ask.

I knew where we were going because I had felt Him prepare me for a while now.

"Yes," I blurted out, "I hate me. There, I said it, are You happy?" I said.

"Hmmm, young lady, I am fine with anger, but I do not tolerate disrespect," He replied.

OK, I thought. *I just admitted this horrible thing and You are worried about my attitude?* "Now what should I do?" I asked.

"Well, you check your tone, and then I will ask you a question. What about your husband or other men in your life that you love?" He asked.

"I don't know," I replied. I know that I love my husband with all my heart, and yet another great man came to mind. Why did I get so defensive with some men while a few I adored?

"Why?" I asked.

"Let's go in through the back," He suggested. "What about the ones who get your blood boiling?" He asked. "What about them makes the hair on the back of your neck stand up?" He asked.

I knew right off the bat. "They try to make me do something I don't want to do. They try to tell me what to do," I admitted.

"Do you know why that bothers you so much?" He asked.

I had an idea, but I wanted to hear what He had to say.

"The incident that caused you such traumatic pain," He stated.

The incident when I was a child involved a man who forced me to be in a circumstance I did not want to be in. Where we were going to go with this I wasn't sure, but I was scared. It would be painful, but it would be worth it—I hoped.

I was in the room with this man. I see him holding me down. "I don't want to do this," I scream. But he does it anyway. "Please," I cry out, "please. Somebody make it stop. Please. It's never going to stop." I drifted off. I felt a tap on my left shoulder. I turned as tears ran down my face. It was Jesus. I could not see His face, but I heard His voice. I fell to the floor at His feet and held on tight to His ankles, "Please make it stop," I cried.

I felt rough grit under my body. Not sure where I was, I looked around. It was the adulterous woman. She was lying on the ground at His feet. Arms locked tight, she held on to His ankle as if her life depended on it. She had been thrown there by the men who sought to embarrass her. Her eyes filled with tears, she looked up at Him as if she knew He was her last resort. I knew how she felt. Men had abused and used her; she had given in.

"You are right, My daughter," He said softly, but full of authority.

He had never called me that before. I had needed my heavenly Father that horrible night. *Where was He?* I wondered. I laid there watching this beautiful woman with long, brown hair and brown eyes the size of well-polished coins hang on to this Man until her hands were white. Her grip must have impressed Him. Their eyes met, and He extended His hand. He was going to help her up. Would she let Him? Yes, she placed her dirt-covered hand in His rugged palm. Gently He motioned her to stand as He softly helped her up.

I want to be lifted up, too, I cried to myself. I want out from under this man I have fought to get out from for so long. Jesus stood in front of all the accusers and proudly displayed His love for this woman, her face hidden by her tousled hair and tear-stained face.

I heard Him say, "I have made her beautiful. She is My Bride. No man shall come between her and Me." The place was silent. I could have heard a pin drop.

"I wanted a Savior, one who would softly lift me from the accusers and be proud of His Bride," I said softly. It is Him and me again. We are no longer in the arena circled by those who sought to harm her. I must have drifted off hanging on to His leg. Then I heard him say, "Wake, My child, it is your turn."

Startled, I looked up as He handed me His hand. It was the same one I saw Him hand to the woman. My hair tousled and faced stained with my tears, He gently lifted me from the dirty ground.

Our eyes met as He began to speak, "Beloved, I am sorry a man chose to harm you. Rest assured he will be dealt with. But My concern is with you. You did not ask nor deserve the harm that was placed upon you. I have dressed you in white. You are pure in My eyes."

Not fully grasping what He was saying, I stood there numb. "What about the men I hate?" I asked.

"All men should not suffer for one man's evil," He said. "If Our Father had punished us for the sin of His fallen son, we would all have been doomed to an eternal life of hell."

"Jesus," I said, "You said in hell. But sometimes I have felt I was living hell on earth; my own living hell."

"I understand that you felt that way," He said. "It is true God did not mean it to be that way," He said.

"Then what can I do?" I asked.

"Go to the mountain. When I went to Gethsemane, I was at the lowest point in My life. I knew what was ahead, and I wanted out," He said.

"You Jesus? You can do anything," I said.

"Yes, I wanted another way. I was flesh, and flesh wants what it wants. Just like you want to do what you want to do. Can I tell you a secret?" He asked.

"Yes, of course," I answered.

"That is your flesh talking," He said.

I had never thought about it that way. I just didn't want anyone else to keep me from leaving if I wanted to go. I remembered countless jobs I had worked at that I would panic when it neared five o'clock. I was afraid they wouldn't let me go.

"What else?" I asked.

"I went to the mountain alone, but I asked My Body to pray. To tackle some hurts, you need a prayer warrior and to dig your heels into the mountain," He advised.

I knew I needed time with the very One I had disrespected earlier. I was drained.

"Go talk to Him. I will be here praying," Jesus said. He slowly let go of my hand and turned to walk away. "I am here praying," He repeated.

I stood there at a loss of what to do next. Then I saw my Lord coming in the distance. I ran and jumped into His arms. My arms wrapped around His neck. I cried, "I need You, Father, I need You."

"I am here, child, I am here," He assured me.

Without knowing I was going to say the words, I heard myself ask, "Why weren't You there?" I buried my head in His shoulder and cried. I noticed something wet falling upon the top of my head. I looked up to see tears falling from His face. The look of anguish broke my heart.

Barely able to speak, He said, "It broke Me to witness your torment. I had no choice."

I wanted that to be enough, but it wasn't. I was grateful He sympathized, but I wanted a reason.

"Child, I have given you a reason, and like the big event that you didn't get the way you wanted, I do not believe this is what you want either," He said.

He was right. I wanted something to justify why He had not stepped in. I wasn't sure I was going to get that answer.

"Hold on a minute, I have an answer for everything," He said. "To be honest, I have the only real answer. I cannot go against free will," He answered.

"But what about orchestrating something like the whale with Jonah?" I asked.

"You are grabbing at straws," He said.

"No, I want proof," I said.

"Proof of what?" He asked.

"Proof that this man did regret what he did," I admitted.

"OK, what does that have to do with My not sending a whale?" He questioned.

"Lord, I'm flustered. I'm not sure what I want."

"I do," He said. "You want it to have never happened, but it did. So, now you want someone to pay. It is common for Me to be the first one blamed. I didn't stop it or send a whale when the real answer is that I didn't create evil. Pride did," He said.

"But You created pride," I said.

"Pride of a good job, not in oneself over another," He corrected me. "Allow Me to continue. If they overcome blaming Me, the next is revenge toward the one who harmed them. This I completely understand. The only answer to this is Me. That is not what they want to hear. They want some form of vengeance placed upon that person. I won't do that, and what I decide to do is justice. All want to be fair when it is them who causes a face to appear on the Hall wall, but few want to be fair when the face hung down the hall is their own. I promised you I take care of My business. But like My Son, I am concerned about you right now," He concluded.

His words strangely were comforting, at least enough that I had calmed down. "Help me, Lord, I need Your truth," I said. In one blink of my eyelids, we were walking toward a park bench in the most beautiful field I had ever seen. There were flowers swaying in the light breeze. The long grass kissed against my ankles as we slowly made our way to the bench.

"After you," He said, motioning me to sit. "Do you remember this place?" He asked.

"It seems familiar, but not in a definite way," I said.

"This is our spot," He said, smiling.

With emotion, I asked "Our spot?"

"Yes," He answered happily "When you drifted off during the incident, this is where I took you. Sweetheart, this place is your whale."

Crushed by the enormity of His words, I sat frozen. Then the tears flowed. "Oh, You cared," I cried out as I hugged Him tightly. "You cared."

"Oh, dear, more than you will ever know," He responded. "Well, maybe close when your grandchildren come along." He chuckled at the thought. "I brought you here to play."

I looked around the field and saw a swing set.

He pointed to the swing hanging from the beautiful red bar. "I pushed you as you swung back and forth. Oh," He said leaning back deeper into the bench, "we laughed and laughed. It was a beautiful time."

I must have looked foolish as I sat with my mouth wide open. As I did, I saw the most elegant butterfly fly by as if in slow motion. "My whale," I cried in a soft voice.

"Yes, dear, I love My animals. They represent meaningful things to me. This butterfly," He said as it landed on His thumb, "symbolizes the new creation you were becoming out of that horrific night. I have had My eyes on you all along. You want Me to be grand, you said? I am grand when My children are. Dear, therefore I am *very big.*"

I stared at the pink and purple with a hint of yellow butterfly. Her wings were more beautiful than stained glass, transparent with color.

"Her colors are like a mosaic. You were fragile; that's why you broke. When I transform you, I build in confidence. Each piece I hand-polish, because some pieces are sharp, jaded, shaping you. The difference in colors is your individual personality, the reflection of your human spirit. Remove the dirt, polish the edges, and temper the glass. I have a beautiful handiwork that My light reflects from within for everyone to see," He said.

I knew I still had anger toward men in general, but I knew one Man I loved. God had sent my own whale in the shape of a butterfly. Today, I wanted to look toward being that new creation letting go of the things of the past that were holding me back. I heard singing as I sat there on that bench.

The Lord was singing, "You are My sunshine, My only sunshine; you make Me happy when skies are gray…We have a song too," He said with a *big* smile.

A place and a song, how romantic, I thought. I sat nuzzled up to my Savior and watched the trees sway and the birds fly against the blue sky. Peace; I needed it. And He had given it.

He is big.

-CHAPTER 23-

The Room of Men

So God created man in His own image...
(Genesis 1:27).

I woke in a panic. I envisioned myself picking apples. They were all over the ground. I turned my shirt up at the bottom to hold the ones I was gathering. Faster and faster, I gathered them. The more I collected, the more I would lose out the side of my make-shift shirt bucket. I became frustrated because I couldn't keep them in.

I'm not at the beach, but there is sand as far as I can see. I try to gather the sand as I cup my arms and rake the sand toward me. The sand spills over the top of my arms. I cannot control it. It is escaping. Over it goes. I try harder with no more success. It appears the more I fight it, the more I lose. "Stay," I yell, "didn't you hear me...stay!"

I'm in a room with men now. They are bobbing around the room. The walls are red—blood red, somewhat like I'm feeling. I said, "Stop!" and I meant it. I yell across the room. None of them appear to be listening. I go up to one man in particular, *I'm going to make you listen if it kills me,* I thought.

Then I hear the Lord say, "It may very well do that."

I stop, with fire in my eyes, to see where His voice is coming from. Violently, I spin around; He sticks His hand out to catch my arm. I stop suddenly. We are face-to-face. I'm not like I have ever seen myself before. We are in a staring match. *I won't budge,* I say to myself. The look in my face reflects determination and stubbornness. I will stand here until the end of time if necessary. *I've had it. They won't listen, and they think they know everything. Well, I'll show them.*

"Show who?" He asks with a stern voice.

"Those men," I replied coldly.

"Do you know where you were?" the Lord asked.

"Don't need to," I answered sharply.

"I believe I would be concerned," He said as sharply as I had replied.

"Doesn't matter," I said, standing my ground.

"Listen, little lady, I am here to tell you that if we do not address this matter, you may find yourself on the same path as many of My daughters before you," He insisted.

Still focused on my stance, I asked with a *who cares* attitude. "Who?" I asked.

"Michel, Rebekah, and…" then He stopped.

"And who?" I insisted.

"OK then," He said, "Jezebel."

With my face puckered like I could spit nails, I replied, "So?"

"Oh, Child, you do not know the ground you are treading. There is no good that can come of what you are setting yourself up for," He warned.

"But You can make good of anything," I said sarcastically.

"I will not be mocked," He replied. "I am here for My children to cry, have a temper tantrum, and laugh. But in no way will I allow you or anyone to disrespect Me. Do I make Myself clear?" He asked.

My shoulders dropped, still angry at the world, my face relaxed. Still too stubborn to apologize, I sat in the middle of the floor. Before I could get comfortable, I jumped up from the floor. "Oh no," I yelled, "I'm not sitting down here!"

"Why?" He asked.

"I will not have them looking down at me," I yelled. "No way!"

"Why?" He asked calmly.

"Don't know, but it's not happening," I said as I stomped my foot.

"Why then will you sit at the feet of My Son?" He asked.

"He is safe; I feel comfortable and wanted," I answered as I began to cry. Through the tears I said in a whisper, "I am afraid of them." My whole body gave way. It took all my strength to hold my composure and not fall to the ground.

"Oh, child," He said, "Thank you."

"Thank you for what?" I asked, still sobbing.

"For admitting your fear," He said. "We can work with that," He added.

The crying had stopped now as I was frozen. Emotionless, I stood there before the Creator of the universe and Heaven, feeling vulnerable and lost.

"Honey, you are not lost, I have always known where you are," He reassured me.

"Then why do I..." I started to say, but stopped mid-sentence because I was too weak to finish.

"Come with Me," I heard Him say.

"Lord, I can't, I'm overwhelmed," I replied.

"Yes, you can, lean on Me," He replied as He walked over to my left side and wrapped His arm around my back.

I leaned into Him and placed my head on His shoulder. He was careful and slow in stride as we walked into the crowd of men.

I saw faces I knew and some I didn't remember. They had blank faces. Like robots, they walked here and there, never running into each other, but some seemed stuck. They were walking into the wall, but could not seem to figure out how to turn around. Some had paper bags over their heads while some were sitting on the floor rocking back and forth.

The Mind of a Man

"Lord," I asked softly, "what is this place?"

"The mind of a man," He answered.

"What?" I asked insecurely as if I had heard Him incorrectly.

"This is how My men feel," He stated.

"Surely not all of them," I wondered.

"Dear, that question is to make you feel better," He pointed out to me. "Remember the elephant's foot?" He asked.

"Yes," I answered.

"It doesn't crush if you continue to justify what you do by the fact that others do it too. The same thing applies here; if there are a few men about whom this does not apply, then you can justify this room," He explained.

In a sick sense, if it is not all of them, then it is OK, I thought.

"Well," He continued, "it is not OK, not if it is one or all. It is not OK," He said louder this time. "One man hurt you, and the whole room pays," He asked.

"No, I never meant it to be that way," I said as I began to cry. "I'm sorry," I said.

"Come with Me," He said as He took my arm.

"Where are we going?" I asked.

"I want you to see what I see," He replied.

"No, Lord," I begged.

"Haven't you prayed to have eyes like Mine?" He asked, still walking.

"Yes, I have, but I'm afraid," I admitted.

"Fear, no; but brokenness, yes," He said, still walking.

We stopped, and He said, "Look there," as He pointed to a man sitting in the corner.

"What is he doing?" I asked.

"Playing with rocks," the Lord answered.

"Why?" I asked.

"He is smarter than a box of rocks, but he has been told he isn't—until he isn't sure anymore," He answered.

My mouth dropped, and my head followed.

"No, look up," He demanded. "Look over here," He said as He pointed to one of the men with a paper bag over his head.

"What, Lord?" I said with humility.

"He doesn't know to come out of the rain. My men have been beaten down by the very ones I created to help," He stated.

That was all I could stand. I began to cry.

"No, we are not done. I brought you here so you would stop. Yes, I have things I want My children to stop, too," He revealed. "My women are killing My men," He said.

"What?" I gasped at the thought. "No, we can't possibly be," I remarked.

"I don't mean physically, but spirituality. They are crushing the life out of their human spirits," He explained.

I saw a vineyard with lush purple grapes ripe for the picking. A beautiful maiden with a gorgeous, red and white checked, flowing dress was picking the best there is to be found. I can hear her sing and see her dancing. She seems so happy. I watched her gather the grapes and place them in a wooden barrel.

Then her face turned angry. Violently she rips off her shoes and steps in the barrel. With force, she stomps, pounding and pounding the grapes until she is exhausted. With a grin, she steps out of the barrel, gives a smirk, and leaves the vineyard.

I can hear crying. It appears to be coming from the barrel. Slowly I look into the barrel to see faces, many faces. It is full of men—but wait, some are not full grown. "What?" There are boys, maybe twelve, sixteen tops. "What in the world?" I cried out. "Lord, what is this?" I asked in horror.

"It is the heart of My men," He said. "A beautiful maiden comes along and lovingly picks them to be hers. They are happy dancing and singing until she believes another wants in her vineyard," He added.

"What? Another?" I asked.

"Yes, there are many vineyards and many maidens," He said.

"Jealousy?" I questioned.

"Far more than that...it is ownership," He replied. "She wants what she wants and she wants it when she wants it, and if the men do not jump through the appropriate hoops, she will crush their spirits," He said. "*You can't do anything right. Why did I marry you in the first place? I should have listened to my parents,*' and the list goes on and on until they are left smashed at the bottom of the barrel."

I just couldn't imagine this to be true. I had said some things in the heat of the moment...but crushed, I really didn't think so.

"Don't fool yourself," He said. "Here or there adds up and over time those remarks...well you have seen what happens. I called My daughters to help My sons, not hinder them," He said.

I thought how little fun I was having. Where was the laughing and joking we had done?

"This is serious," He replied.

"I know, Lord, but this seems so harsh," I said.

"Yes, very well. Then stop. Please," He asked.

"I want to, I want us to," I said.

"Do you remember seeing the bottom of the barrel?" He asked.

"Yes," I answered. "There were many faces there."

"Yes, she thinks one man does her wrong and the next pays," He said. "It is a continuing system."

"They haven't had what I knew they needed," He said.

"What is that?" I asked trying to understand.

"Love...to be admired and cherished," He stated. "Knowing this explains why I called the men to love their wives like Christ does the Church."

"God, it seems to be revenge," I noted.

"On a level, yes it is," He stated.

"Lord," I cried, "I can't stand anymore. We can't be that terrible."

"No, you are not...but your actions can be," He said.

I hated to hear this. I love my husband. "This is more than I want to hear," I admitted.

"It has to be addressed," He stated. "I created marriage to be fun and supportive. Not degrading and protective."

"Wait, Lord, you said protective," I pointed out. "Aren't we supposed to look out for each other?" I asked.

He stopped for a minute as to think before He spoke. "Dena," He said with a serious look on His face, "who are you really looking out for? In the name of protecting the other it is necessary to ask, 'Is it really myself I am protecting?' I created My men to be strong because they are made in My image. But when My women try to distort or dictate what that strength looks like, it confuses them. They are designed to love their wives and strive to love them. They will, in the name of love, do the best they know how to please their wives. Their wives must be aware of what they are asking of them," He explained.

I stood there as what He had said soaked in. This was serious, like He had said. Knowing that I was going to the elephant again, I had to say, "But Lord, there are plenty who do not take care of us like they are supposed to."

"Yes, you are right, but that does not justify treating them as personal objects," He answered.

I don't treat my husband that way, I thought.

"Have you ever told him he…"

"Stop. I don't want to hear the question," I blurted out quickly to stop Him from asking. "I will just take Your word for it and seek You to do better," I said humbly.

"Let Me show you something," He said.

THE REMOTE

I walked into a room. It had electric blue walls with light blue lightning bolts painted throughout the space. There were big bolts and small bolts, with one huge yellow bolt that ran down the wall and onto the floor to the middle of the room. These bolts were all on the right side of the room as I was looking in. The yellow bolt directed me to a girl, shall I say a woman. She was throwing up. Bent over with no one to hold her long, brown hair back, over and over she threw up. No bucket, just yesterday's meals hitting the floor. As soon as it hit, the bolt opened and the vomit slid in. Then BAM, the floor shut. Oh the smell. It was horrific. I wanted to help her; but as I walked toward her, a wall of chicken wire fell from the ceiling, almost hitting my toes. I looked up to see a snaggle-toothed, gray-haired, long-nosed woman laughing.

"She can't be helped," she said in a screechy voice. "You're next, little missy," she added.

"No, I am not," I yelled back. "You have no influence over me," I said with confidence and a *see there* attitude.

"I don't, you say?" she squawked back. "You will see, you will see." The Plexiglas window shut with a loud thud. Then she disappeared. I heard from behind the window, "You will see."

All of a sudden the bolts opened and flashing lights lit from the boxes behind the walls. On and off like strobe lights, flashing and flickering. Then the images appeared; girls eating toilet paper, or mounds and mounds of lettuce. One woman explaining how to mix a drink concoction that she assured would shed unwanted pounds. I spun around to find boxes all around the room: 42", 52", and even 82" television screens. There was nowhere to turn that my eyes did not meet the images. Girls in bikinis with men drooling at their feet. Women leading them around as if they were dogs to parade for show. I turned to find the door. This wasn't for me. I would just leave. As I turned, the double doors slammed shut.

"There is no way out," I heard the mean woman from before say.

"God," I hollered, "the woman won't let me out," as if I was tattling on her.

"*You* won't," I heard Him reply.

What? I thought, *Did I hear Him correctly? I must have.* I repeated, "No, the *mean woman* won't let me out."

"It is *you*," He said again.

I stood there unsure still if I had heard correctly. Looking around the room, I realized I was in a bigger version of the boxes that were on the walls I had originally seen. "I want out," I said calmly.

"No!" she yelled.

"Lord, she won't let me," I said, getting a little annoyed now.

"You have given her the power," He said. "Take it back."

I heard her yell again, "No!"

"Turn the knob," He said.

"You can't," she yelled.

"Yes, you can," He said. "Who are you going to listen to? You have to choose."

"Me," she hollered. "Me."

Now I was getting a little nervous. "You, Lord, You," I yelled. "Help me."

"I will, but you have to turn the knob," He directed.

"Where, Lord, where?" I asked. Now I was borderline panicked.

"On the remote," He replied.

"I turned from the doors to see a black vinyl captain's chair sitting in the middle of the room. *It had not been there before,* I thought.

"It was there all the time. You just didn't want to see it," He said. "You were too fixed on the televisions."

"Televisions?" I yelled. "What is it...the television's fault she throws up?"

"No," He answered. "She didn't turn them off."

"But Lord, they are everywhere," I said in her defense.

"So am I," He replied, "so am I."

I started toward the chair when the television screens changed. There was a little girl, heavy-set with pretty, short hair. She looked about ten years of age. I could not see her face, but I could hear her crying. My heart sank. "Little girl," I said to the screen, "what is it?"

"They said I was fat. I am fat," she said. She turned suddenly, with fire in her eyes and Ex-lax in her hand, she barked, "Never again."

I gasped; it was me.

"God, God, God," I screamed as I stumbled to move back from the screen. "God, help," I yelled as I fell backward onto the floor.

The window above me opened and the face of the hateful, scary woman from before stuck out. "See, I told you," she said proudly. "See."

"No," I screamed as I shielded my eyes to block her from my vision.

"They are already there," she said as she laughed at me. "The images are already there."

"No, no, no," I began to cry.

Suddenly the bolts shifted, and it was quiet. An eerie quiet. Still on the floor, I saw a girl in the opposite corner. Hesitantly, I got up and walked toward her. She was so thin, I thought. I could see her vertebrae and collar bone. With her back toward me, I tapped her on the shoulder. "Can I help you?" I asked.

Slowly her head turned over her shoulder.

"Oh my," I gasped. Her mouth was taped shut.

"She doesn't eat, leave her alone," the mean woman said.

Angry now, I turned toward the middle of the room. I was going to get to that remote if it killed me. Faster, I sped up, just before I jumped for the chair, a net fell from the ceiling. I jerked; upward I went. I was quickly tangled in a black and green cargo net suspended twelve feet above the room. Dangling.

All I could hear was her laughing. "See," she said again.

Furious that she thought she had me, I yelled, "Let me down!"

"Can't do," she said sarcastically.

"Can't or won't?" I replied hatefully.

"Doesn't matter, either way I've got you," she said as if proud of herself.

A light bulb went off in my head. "No," I shouted, "I am the Lord's!" Suddenly, the harness snapped, and down I fell into the hands of my Savior.

"I have been waiting for you," the Lord said.

I hugged His neck. "Thank You, Lord," I said.

"No…thank you," He replied.

A LESSON LEARNED

"What a beautiful day You have made," I said. "I have to thank You, thank You, and thank You again," I said. Yesterday I had the opportunity to take a *thirty* as my husband calls it. A thirty is a nap during the course of your day. The great thing was that I could. I thought about the time that I had been at the pool one evening and my husband was resting. I had hoped for a day when I could do the same.

"Well, Lord, yesterday was that day," I said. "I fell asleep. I actually took a nap," I rejoiced.

I heard Him clap and say, "It is only going to get better."

I let out a, "Yee ha!"

"But there is something else you wanted to bring up, isn't there?" He said.

"Yes, I do," I responded. "Last night I woke up for a brief mini-panic. When I woke, it was to the fact that I was worrying about my husband not getting enough time to work out. Once I processed the worry, I realized it wasn't mine. That I had taken on his worry. I was worrying for him." I laughed. "What do You make of that?" I asked.

"Very good deductive reasoning, but it happens all the time," He said. "Someone worrying about what another person is or isn't getting or is doing. That was wordy," He said. "Let me break it down by bringing in My son, Moses."

"What? Moses?" I said. "Can this day get any better?" Honestly, I was hoping for someone younger. I was in a playful mood, and I didn't want a stiff dictating to me what I should or shouldn't do. "What about a young guy like Timothy?" I asked.

"Excuse Me?" the Lord said.

"I just want someone fun," I admitted. *Maybe I should have kept my wish to myself,* I thought, *but He'd know anyway.*

"How do you know that Moses isn't fun?" He said sternly.

"Well, he's portrayed as up in age, very serious, and well, boring," I said.

"Hmmm," the Lord pondered a moment. "Come here please, Moses," I heard Him call.

Coming around the corner, I saw a man with a full beard and long hair. Both were white and grey and appeared to be soft with waves. But what struck me the most was his eyes, they matched his smile. He was grinning ear to ear.

"Yes, Sir," I heard him say in a very tender voice, a voice that I was not expecting. He seemed very genuine and dare I say it, fun. He had a walk that wasn't quite a bounce, but a smooth pace. He glided—that is what it was, he glided.

"Moses," the Lord said, "this is My daughter, Dena."

He has not introduced me as His daughter before. Why is that? I wondered.

"Hello, Dena, very nice to meet another family member," Moses replied.

"It's nice to meet you, too," I said.

"I apologize for being out of breath, I was playing ball with the children," he said.

Oh, how nice, I thought. "I hadn't noticed," I replied.

"Yes, Dena, Moses plays with the children often," the Lord stated. "He believes that the way to share his wisdom is to start when they are young."

"It keeps me young, too," he admitted.

Boy, do I have egg all over my face…again, I thought.

I saw the Lord smirk and wink at me; He knew I had opened my mouth and inserted my foot.

I know He knows, and I owe God an apology. Moses is a man of title. That must explain calling me His daughter, I thought to myself.

"But not as the world sees titles," the Lord said. "Moses had great responsibilities to a lot of people, but he knew those people contributed to his success in the mission I had laid before him."

"May I interject?" Moses asked.

"Yes, please," the Lord replied.

I could see their respect for each other. It was special to witness and beautiful to watch. I was now finding myself wanting to be like the one I had complained about meeting. Boy, I sure was wrong. I regret saying a word.

"Hold up," the Lord said. "Do you know how I feel about regrets?" He asked.

"No, Sir, I don't," I answered.

"They are a waste," He replied. "Did you learn something from what you just experienced?" He asked.

"Yes," I had.

"Then the so-called *regret* was a golden opportunity," He pointed out. "Now, Moses, you wanted to say something."

"Yes," he replied. "There was a time when I was running myself ragged, I believe that is how it is expressed today. But my father-in-law came to me one day out of grave concern and pointed out to me how many things were falling through the cracks. He was concerned for the project God had entrusted in my hands, but he was also concerned for my well-being. He noticed I was looking tired."

Hmmm, there sure seems to be a lot of tired going on, I thought.

"He posed a great solution, and it helped everyone," Moses added.

I remembered the story, but it sounded much more exciting coming from this dear man.

"Now tell her the rest," the Lord requested.

"Oh, yes," he said with blushed cheeks. "I was not very good at this delegation thing, as it is called. I had been used to doing things myself, and the thought of others doing it caused some sleepless nights."

The Lord said, "She is waking worried over what others are not doing."

"Taking on the worries of others," Moses stated.

"Yes," I answered.

"Dear," he said, "take it from someone who lived it, let people be responsible for themselves."

He was right; my husband had plenty of chances to work out. I was not stopping him, and in most cases, I would suggest good times.

"It is up to him and others if they do the things they want to and need to in their allotted time," the Lord said.

"That makes perfectly good sense," I said. "What about ones that you delegate and they do not meet the deadlines?" I asked.

"She is a tough one," Moses said to the Lord.

"Tough but fair," He replied. "Tough but fair."

I felt as if I needed to interject. "I love for others to step up and walk out their callings. I know that I cannot do what the Lord asks of me without others' help. I was curious about deadlines because I get that question a lot." There was a moment of hesitation after I finished speaking.

"First of all," Moses replied, "God's children must realize they are God's representatives, not the judge's."

Oh, this is big, I thought.

"Then select capable, trustworthy men and women who fear the Lord," He explained. "Make sure that you teach them the guidelines of their responsibilities and the laws. Then, as they say, the chips fall where they may. You will have some that seize their roles and shine, and some you will not invite back. But just as my Father has been patient in training me, I strive to return the favor," Moses said.

"Last, let them have the reins. We have all been given titles, or gifts as some may call them. There are prophets, intercessors, teachers, and many more. No gift is obtainable without the others. It is like a finely oiled machine. One piston moves smoothly if the grease is not only placed in the correct position, but maintained regularly. It is the same way with those sent to help. They need to be placed in the area of their gifting and supported. Check on them and help them when they run into trouble," Moses said.

"There is one thing I would like to add," the Lord said, "*receive help*. You were not meant to do this alone, so accept the support when it is offered. Be wise, but when it is good, let it happen. Others deserve the same opportunity to move within their roles… let them."

"I have to get back to the game. It has been very nice speaking to you. And Dena," he said as he jogged away, "God is always there to run things by. He won't leave you hanging. See ya," he said, jogging off until out of our view.

I stood there a minute awestruck. He was nothing like I thought he would be. He was cool, yet very smart. I was going to miss him.

"Young lady," I heard the Lord say with a correcting voice.

"Yes, Father, I was wrong," I admitted. "I completely misjudged him. He was fun and far from boring. I could have listened to him for hours."

"Very good, keep that misjudgment in mind," He suggested. "My family tends to do that too often. When you sleep, do you not have enough of your own worries to fill your time?" He said. "Let others have their roles and sleep with them."

He was right. Although I hoped to get to the point that I cast off my worries before I sleep. *Hey, I think I've just hit on something.* "Lord, Lord," I said excitedly. "What about casting my concerns *before* I go to bed?" I asked.

"Sheer genius, I say," He agreed.

"Well, I wouldn't say that, but maybe a good idea," I said.

"Yes, I love the idea of ending the day with you before you drift off to slumber," He agreed.

"Very poetic," I replied.

"Well, I love a good bedtime story," He said.

Maybe He would share some with me, I thought. I couldn't wait to see...or could I? All of a sudden I was a little worried.

"Why, child, are you worried?" He asked.

"I think of David running in the night, fearful for his life, and no one to help," I said.

"Oh, honey," He said, "I was running right beside him. How do you think he knew how to get to the cave? I wanted him safe so we could talk."

"So, the bedtime stories won't scare me?" I asked. I was thinking about a period of time when I would sleep over with my grandmother and she would turn on a radio station that played scary stories at night. She would fall asleep to the story. I hadn't thought about that in a long time. I felt like a little kid; I didn't want to listen, but I wanted to be with her.

"Why didn't you tell her?" He asked.

The answer didn't come quickly. "I just did what she said because I loved her," I finally answered.

"That is not good," He added. "Not the loving, but the following blindly."

I know that now, I thought. I was kicking myself for not speaking up. That was not the only time I didn't speak up, and I had paid dearly.

CHAPTER 24

A Voice

Train a child in the way he should go, and when he is old he will not turn from it (Proverbs 22:6).

Softly, He said, "Child, you have a voice, use it. Your words can heal or devastate. But one thing is for sure, if you are silent, they do no good when faced with a situation that needs a response."

"But aren't there times when silence is best?" I asked.

"Yes, hopefully that is a given." He said.

"If you can't say anything nice, don't say anything should be a rule. You know, one that is magnetized on the refrigerator or crocheted on a pillow." I replied.

"I am talking about following the crowd when the crowd is clueless to the trouble they are walking into," He said.

"What about those who know the trouble?" I asked.

"They are a different breed," He replied. "They are rebellious, and I will contend with that. I am focusing on the ones who do not know the voice of the Shepherd and are aimlessly following deceiving voices."

"Yes, I should have spoken up," I agreed. I swallowed hard. I knew where we were going with this, and to be honest, I had already began to cry. I did not tell what had happened when I lived through *my incident. Stop,* I thought, *I never said I lived through it. I did live through it, but why didn't I tell anyone?* I knew. It rose up in me like I was a child again.

"No one would have believed me!" I screamed at the top of my lungs. I had learned to keep my mouth shut because I believed no one would believe me anyway. I sat there in a coma, dead inside and glazed eyed. "I wish I had spoken up," I said faintly.

"Dear," He said, "you have been very brave."

"I didn't feel brave. In fact, I felt like a coward," I said, beginning to cry again. My thought moved forward to an extra bedroom of a condo that my husband and I had rented while waiting to move to our own condo. I would lie in the bed of that room and talk to God about the situation and pray that He would make it clear. "Wait," I said, startled at the revelation I had just received, "I didn't believe it myself."

"You are right," He said. "You had tried to pretend it was not there, but it would not stop nagging at you."

He was right; it would show its ugly head often. I had gotten to the point of just facing the truth, whatever that might be.

"You are ready," He had said. "It surfaced, and we have been dealing with the repercussions ever since. Something like that is what an onion is made from. It is like pulling a log out of your eye, it is bound to leave splinters behind. The wet, moist environment of your heart is perfect for the log to soften, then when removed it splinters. But it is nothing I cannot tweeze out," He added.

That made me smile.

"So, come to Me," He asked.

I stopped Him and said, "Please no scary stories." It felt good to use my voice.

"No scary stories," He promised.

I have to admit, I was still a little worried. Would He believe me? I knew I loved Him during the day, but if the truth be known, I would have to see about the night. I felt a little badly for not being sure.

"Levels of faith," I heard Him say as He joined Moses and the kids in a game of kickball.

I stood and watched the red ball pitched to the boy at home base. He drew back and whopped it. Kids scurried as Moses flagged him to first base. I wanted to play.

I heard the Lord, yell, "We need a player on third... interested?"

Yes I was, but something was holding me back. "No thanks," I yelled back, "I'm just going to watch." I tried to go on about my day, but the thought of not taking this golden opportunity to play with God, Moses, and those adorable kids was troubling me inside. I ran back to the ball field hoping they would still be there.

"Lord, Lord," I said as I came running, "please come here."

He came running, "What is it, child, are you OK?"

I hated to drag Him away from the game, but I needed Him. "Lord," I started to cry as I fell into His arms, "I wanted to play." I began to sob uncontrollably, and I fell deeper into His arms.

"Then why didn't you, child?" He asked looking me in the eyes.

"Lord, I don't know, I just froze; I was scared," I admitted.

"Of what?" He asked.

"I don't know," I said, crying even harder.

"Yes, you do," He said reassuringly.

"Can You just tell me this time, instead of making me answer Your question with a question, please?" I begged.

"Now, Sweetie, you know begging doesn't work, and I will direct the conversation in the best dialogue to free you," He said. "You want to play, but you are scared. Think about what you think would happen," He said.

"I might have fun," I said under my breath.

"OK, what is bad about having fun?" He questioned.

"I might miss something," I said.

"Well, aren't you missing something anyway?" He asked.

I had never thought about it that way.

"You are assuming that because you had a bad experience when you let your guard down, it will happen again—this is basically what playing is. You are not alert to your surroundings because your focus is on the game, it *will* happen again," He explained.

"What You are saying is true, but what do I do?" I asked, raising my head.

"The way I see it, you have two choices: play and take a chance, or stay frozen on the sidelines," He stated. "I can tell you without a doubt, the sideline is not where all the excitement is."

"So You are saying it is basically a decision, a choice," I replied.

"Yes, it is that simple," He said.

"That seems too simple," I noted.

"What is the need in making it hard?" He asked.

"I don't know, but I'm sure I have done it before," I said. *Actually often*, I thought. OK, then, I decided to play. We both looked toward the field. I could hear the laughter; I wanted in. We began to run, but about ten strides in, I stopped dead. "What in the world?" I asked, stunned. "My feet won't move."

"Another layer," we both said at the same time.

I was OK with that because I knew I was closer to the playground than I had been only moments ago. I looked back to where I had once stood and smiled. As I turned to face forward, I heard Him quote what Paul had penned, "Forgetting what is behind."

"But Lord, forgetting?" I questioned.

"Dear, dear one, can we enjoy watching the game and answer more questions later? Too many questions makes Tom a dull boy," He said, laughing.

Then it hit me. I had not been talking about Moses being boring, I was talking about me. I was worried about being boring. It hit me like a ton of bricks.

I could tell He knew the revelation I had just gotten by the comforting yet *see* grin on His face. I could learn a thing or two from Moses and not just how not to be serious.

The Lord placed His arm around my shoulder and said, "In due time, in due time, you will play...in due time."

I stood there soaking in His presence. Playing would come, but I was enjoying this moment on the sideline. I remembered His words, "The best is yet to come." If out there was better than right here, I was in for some kind of fun.

"I love You," I whispered as I tilted my head toward His.

"Me too," He replied.

STOP THE SUN

"Lord, I am so baffled and overwhelmed," I said. "I have so much to do and very little time to do it. I toss and turn and plan through what should be my sleeping hours. I look around and see all the things left to do and things I missed the day before. Often I lay in bed thinking I should get up and start now if I ever want to get it all done. However, I have tried that before, and it gets me in worse shape than I started because I am dead to the world by noon."

"What is it that you are so worried about, child?" He asked.

"Lord," I replied, "managing my family and my job." See, I love the work that the Lord has blessed me to do, but I equally love the family He has surrounded me with. I seem to always be torn between how to balance them so no one gets left out and so I don't feel stretched so thin. Like so many nights, I lie in bed trying to play out the next day's demands. Like a day planner in my head, I rearrange the meetings, people, and miscellaneous events in an attempt to juggle them fairly. It can become overwhelming—like last night. I want to do it all, but seem to fall short too often.

"By whose standards?" I heard Him ask.

"Mine, I guess," I replied. "I feel in a panic. That panic only makes my attempts harder."

"Do you feel like a slave to the clock?" He asked.

"Yes," I replied almost in tears. "You hit the nail on the head." I had heard and read so many *how to organize* your day books. Some had been very helpful, but I knew I was an organized person. I had calendars, post-its, and multicolored file folders labeled with what to do next. Yes, unorganized I wasn't—in a tizzy I was.

"Lord, I truly believe this is not how You planned us to spend our time. This energy I spend spinning my wheels surely could be of more benefit in other areas," I commented. Somewhat comforting, I knew many women who suffered from the same evil word *balance*. We fit the clock, and actually each other, into our days to justify how we spent that time. But that is another subject. I felt it acceptable to cry out for many of us who are career-yet-want-to-be-at-home women when I asked, "God, help us, please?"

"Hang on," He said, "let Me get someone for you."

Moments later He returned with a man of average height, balding, and with a wonderful smile.

I don't have time for this, I thought. I have too much to do already to add meeting someone new today. Anxious and tapping my foot, I smiled back as he walked toward us.

"Dena, I'd like you to meet Joshua," the Lord said introducing us.

"Hi," he said.

"Hello, nice to meet you," I responded. I meant it, but I couldn't help but think, *How is he going to help me calm down and get my stuff done today?* Then it hit me. God had stopped the sun for Joshua one day. "Lord, excuse me," they were talking. "I hate to interrupt, but I believe I have the solution to the problem."

They both turned to hear what I had to say.

"Yes, dear, what would that be?" He asked.

"Stop the sun," I said as if I had solved world hunger.

They turned to each other and grinned.

Not sure what was funny, I repeated myself, "Stop the sun."

"Child," the Lord said, "that is great and at that time things appeared to stop, but as a solution for your problem, it is not the answer. Can you imagine if at everyone's request I, zap…" He motioned as if He had a magical wand toward the sky, "…stopped the sun?"

Not amused, I understood His point, but was aggravated that I still had no solution.

"Time is not your enemy," He said boldly. "How does *time* sound to you?" He asked me.

"Like a gun going off," I answered. "The race has started, and I am already three legs behind."

"What about Joshua?" I asked curiously.

"Now you want to hear from me?" Joshua said, smiling. He had been quietly standing nearby the entire time.

"Would you say *patient?*" God asked, joining Joshua in smiling.

Yes, I'm not wild about that word either, I thought to myself.

Joshua said with an average voice, not panicked or excited, calm, yes I would call it calm, "First, I loved your slow-down-stop-the-sun proposal. I would have loved that too." He grinned. "But what God showed me was He has given us plenty of time to do what He asks us to do."

"Then I must be way off base," I said, "because I'm about to pull my hair out."

We all laughed as Joshua was bald.

"No," Joshua said while laughing, "it is genetics, not time restraints."

"It was nice to laugh," I said. It seemed those times were too few and far between—but back to business at hand. They both were staring at me. "What? What is it?" I asked.

"Too much business and not enough pleasure," they said at the same time.

"I can't get all my business done to get to pleasure," I replied.

"Hmmm, she is a tough one," Joshua said.

"You said it, son," God said.

"What shall we do?" Joshua asked.

"Tell her about your trip with the men up the mountain to check out the village," He suggested.

"Oh yeah, good one," Joshua agreed.

"See, me and about twelve other men were headed to this town to check it out for our camp," he began. "It was quite a journey, so we loaded up all the necessary supplies, food, extra gear, and water balloons.

"No way," I said, like he was crazy.

"Oh, yes," he said, grinning ear to ear.

"Lord, are You sure?" I asked just to double check and make sure he wasn't pulling my leg.

"Let him finish," He said as He grinned at Joshua.

"OK," I agreed.

"Yes, water balloons," he said, continuing the story where he had left off. "Do you really think we lined up and marched face forward for hours on end? No way," he replied. "If I was going to travel, I was going to have fun. Or at least two of us were."

"Are you talking about Caleb?" I said with a spark of excitement in my voice and a sparkle in my eyes.

"Yes, he is a hoot," he replied. "The girls say cute too, but I don't know anything about that stuff."

I thought how I had looked forward to meeting Caleb. Before the words came out, a tall, blonde, curly headed, blue-eyed guy walked over toward us. "This must be Caleb?" I mouthed.

"Yes," Joshua replied. "And that is the reaction he gets every time he shows up. Do you know how hard it was for me to get a date with a best friend who looks like that?" he asked.

"Oh," I said as if to feel sorry for him.

"Don't," he said, "I've had the onion treatment."

I laughed again and said, "Joshua, you are funny."

"Thanks, it got me through my peeling," he said.

Again I laughed.

"Well, back to the trip," he said. "We loaded up whoopee cushions and hand buzzers."

"And remember the squirt gun," Caleb added.

"Oh yes," they said, laughing together.

"We had a blast on the way up," Caleb said.

"What about the others, how did they do?" I asked.

"There were a few sticklers, I'll call them," Joshua said.

"They were all business and no fun," Caleb added.

"That seems harsh," I said.

"Or was it because it hit home?" God asked.

I felt them all staring at me. "OK, I get it, go on with the story," I said, nodding.

"Yes, they didn't enjoy our pranks as much as others. But we had a serious job to do, so why not lighten the load on the way?" Joshua questioned.

"I guess, but what happened when you got there?" I asked.

"We did our job, headed back, and reported our findings," Joshua answered.

"Perspective," I heard Jesus interject.

"Hey," I said as I looked surprised to see Jesus. "I thought You only showed up when heart matters were concerned."

He smiled, "Don't ever think you have Me figured out...I just might surprise you. This *is* a heart matter," He said.

Just when I thought I had it figured out, I thought. "Not you, too," I said to Joshua.

"Oh yes, I love to have a good time," Jesus said smiling. "Remember the party where the host ran out of wine?" He reminded me.

Oh my, I thought. *I have been missing out. I really need to enjoy myself more.*

"All work, no play makes for a hectic life," we all said in unison.

"It is all about perspective," Jesus said. "If you think life is like a mule you are plowing through life with, life will appear grim; and yes, all you will do is push to get through it, get to the end."

"That is what the serious men on the trip did," Joshua interjected. "They moaned and groaned until we reached the destination, only to turn around and moan more as we headed back. It was their attitude that scared all of the people in our camp."

Jesus added, "When you see the world through pain-stained glasses, everything looks like a hurdle. I've carried a cross; I know what real hurdles are."

"It was not supposed to be this way," I heard the Lord say.

"How was it supposed to be, Lord?" I asked, desperate to know.

"Peace," He answered. "When you are doing what I call you to do, it is peaceful. There may be chaos around you, but peace is on the inside. Do you see those gutters?" He asked.

"Yes," I replied, surprised to see them in the distance. It appeared as if the raindrops were trying to hang on. But much to their dismay, they fell.

"That is My Church trying to hang on," He added. "Stop trying to hang on."

"Lord," my heart ached, "we are just trying to hold it together." Some days it was all I could do to maintain composure. Some forms of it are tiring. Yes, unnecessary, but still tiring. "If we let go, I believe there is fear we will fall apart—maybe to the point of being irretrievable."

"That slippery slope," He said as He shook his head. "Fear of catastrophe from one end of the spectrum to the other."

Yes, He was right. I had often held on so tightly for fear of falling.

"Look again at those raindrops," He said. "Once they let themselves fall from the gutter...well, you tell me. What do you see?"

"I see a cascade almost like a dance. There is such freedom as they fall," I said.

"Each drop has a specific place to drop. Just like My children have a specific role to live," He said. "Honey, just like Joshua, Caleb, and the others' duty that day was to report on the findings of that village. They had a choice to enjoy it or fight it," He said. "It is all in how you choose to look at it."

I watched as Joshua and Caleb walked away, waving and smiling. I wanted to remember the fun they had even as they—no, especially as they—fulfilled their duties of the day.

-CHAPTER 25-

About the Heart

Jesus turned and saw her. "Take heart, daughter," he said, "your faith has healed you." And the woman was healed from that moment (Matthew 9:22).

"Lord, I come with a heavy heart," I began. "There are good people out there who have given up. I don't mean they have given up on You completely, but they are hard. My heart is broken and my body aches for them. I don't have the answers," I cried out from my heart.

"Yes, you do, child; it is Me. I am the answer," He replied.

"Lord, how can I explain to them how wonderful You are?" I asked. "They are so sad and disappointed. I can't make them believe You are the answer."

"No, you can't...that is My job," He said.

I began to cry as I said, "The glass is half empty for them. I know, I was there. I had tried and tried and all it seemed to get me was tolerable. That's not right. I need you. *They* need You, yet they are not excited."

"Are you excited?" He asked.

"Yes, Lord, very much," I answered. "Do You get disappointed?" I asked.

"Yes, sometimes," He replied.

"Why?" I questioned.

"Because it is an emotion that you have," He began. "If you are looking for it to completely go away, then you will be disappointed again."

"Lord, please help," I asked.

"What is it you wish, My child?" He asked.

"I want my loved ones—and honestly everyone—to love You like I do," I shared.

"That is a little vain because even you have moments when you slip," He said.

"I know, but I want them to be excited about You. They have hurts that seem to have them blocked off. They have questions that seem to have them where they won't budge. Don't You have something that You can say to make them soft?" I asked. "What will it take to soften their hearts?"

"Why do you think it is their hearts that will make a difference?" He asked me.

"Because we love from our hearts, right?" I replied.

"Very good," He said, clapping. "I think it is time we talk about the heart."

"The thought of one's heart scares me," I said.

"Why is that?" He asked.

"I see people I love, and they are so hurt that they speak bitterness. I don't want to lose them to hell," I said bluntly.

"Oh, little one, we need to talk," He said with a sweet concern in His voice.

I began to cry harder. "There are very dear friends and family members of mine that the thought of them not loving You literally breaks my heart. I am scared for them. I want them to love You."

"Honey," He came over to me and held me as I sobbed into His shirt. "They are going to be OK," He said reassuringly.

"How can you say that?" I asked. "There are people all around the world who won't budge. I worry for them."

"I am touched that you are so concerned; but dear, that is not your burden to carry. Remember when we talked about burdens?" He said.

"Yes, Lord, I remember." Yet, I had never thought about taking on *God's* burdens. My tears overcame me as I placed my face in my hands crying harder. "I love Jesus so much. I hate to see Him hurting," I said.

"Oh," He said. "There it is."

"What?" I didn't understand.

"By the hardness of one's heart, another's heart is softened," He said. "Stand back a minute," He said as he placed His arm across my chest and slowly moved me back a few steps.

All of a sudden I heard loud neighing and galloping sounds. Then around the corner came a chariot pulled by a strong, brown horse. Standing atop the chariot was a man with great posture wearing a white tunic with gold tassels. Upon his head was a golden helmet and held firmly in his hand pressed upon his chest was a silver shield, not perfectly round. I thought, *How that gold and silver clashes...isn't that just like me to notice that.*

"Whoa! Whoa, Nelly!" I heard him say with a deep voice.

The horse came to a stop.

"Wait," I said, "I had only noticed one horse pulling the chariot, but now I was realizing there were two."

"Yes," the Lord replied. "It takes two to pull the chariot, just like it took two for Pharaoh's heart to harden."

"What?" I blurted out.

"First, allow me to introduce you to Pharaoh," the Lord said very professionally.

The man stepped down from the chariot with an air about him. Very confident and very royal, he knew he was a king and presented himself as one.

Shall I bow or kiss his hand? I wondered. That's what I had seen in the movies. No, I decided, I only worship one King, and this one is not Him.

Respectfully, I said, "Hello, very nice to meet your acquaintance."

"I am sure; and it is '*make* your acquaintance.' But I would expect no less," he remarked.

"Excuse me," I said with my hand on my hip.

"Now there will be none of that," the Lord said as He looked at us both.

I stood there with an attitude, but knew better than to call this man out, even if he deserved it.

"Does he?" I heard the Lord ask.

Darn, I thought, *I have to remember He knows what I'm thinking.*

"Well," I stumbled getting my words out, "he did have an attitude," I finally said.

"Hmmm," the Lord said with His thumb and first finger gripping His chin, "seems to Me not too many days ago, a little girl of Mine had an attitude herself."

"Caught," I said. "You are right, touché."

We both laughed.

Standing apparently restless, the Pharaoh remarked, "What is the meaning of this call?"

The Lord turned to him abruptly, and said, "When I call, it is for a reason...so rest in that."

It obviously wasn't what he wanted to hear by the way he rolled his eyes and shifted his weight.

Oh, I thought, *he's going to get in trouble.*

The Lord looked my way.

I knew I had better mind my p's and q's. I had grown to know my Father's moods. I liked His correction and enjoyed His jokes. He made me feel safe.

The Lord began, "Let's get started, I believe I was going to talk about hearts. Now, where was I?" He asked.

"Lord, You were about to talk to me about the ones we are so burdened for," I said.

"Yes, you are right," He said, "but if you recall, I asked you not to take on My burdens any more than you should another's. My people are Mine to carry. I only ask you to help point them to Me." As He took a breath to continue, I noticed what had been the scenic view of the outdoors was now surrounded by mirrors. Everywhere I turned I saw 12x12 perfectly square mirrors; floor to ceiling. Overhead was the bluest sky I had ever seen; beneath my feet was the same dirt that had rolled up with the chariot. This transformation did not seem to disturb the horses.

"Oh, we are used to it," Pharaoh said, "don't worry about it."

"Yes, do be concerned," the Lord corrected him. "This is a reflection. His arrogance and conceit brings forth any that indwells in the heart of who he visits," the Lord explained.

"What arrogance and conceit?" I asked.

"Walk up to the mirrors," He suggested.

"I would rather not," I said, "but it is better to handle it now than to allow it to grow."

"You are right, My child," He said.

"Will You go with me?" I asked.

"I am with you wherever you go," He answered, "but you will have to walk toward them yourself."

One foot in front of the other I figured was the best way. I lifted my right foot and then the left, slowly making my way toward the mirrors. I was expecting this to be ugly. Oddly, the closer I got, the prettier I thought I was becoming and the smarter I looked. It was nothing like I expected.

"No," He said from behind me, "it is not. But that is what pride sees, *I can do better*, or *I look better*.

WOW, how dare us, I thought.

"Keep going," He commented.

Another foot in front of the other until, "Whoa!" I yelled. The wind blew and a suction that seemed to come from the mirrors pulled me toward them like I was in a whirlwind tunnel. I was drawn swiftly to the glass. My face was pressed into one of the mirror and my body clung to it.

"That is what happens," the Lord said. "It is a shame it starts with what appears as inconvenience, then the next thing you know, it has you. Stuck like a bug on a windshield."

With my face splattered up against the mirrored wall, I awkwardly moved my mouth and said, "How about a little help here?"

He and the Pharaoh laughed. I had not seen any real emotion from him until then. It was interesting to see what his face looked like without a smirk. I still wasn't wild about him, but at least I knew he could be somewhat kind.

"What was all that about?" I asked as the suction released and I fell to the floor.

"One word," He said, "pride. Pharaoh knew it well, and truth be told, so do most of My children."

I knew it must have been known to me from the red marks left on my face, arms, and legs from the power of the suction. It made me think about God's fallen son, lucifer. What did the suction marks look like on him?

Quickly, the Lord turned to me and said, "We don't do that."

"What?" I asked.

"Judge or compare," He said. "He is an example, but do not think yourself sin-free for it can sneak up on you, especially if you start thinking you are above it."

"Yes, Lord, You are right," I recognized. Satan indeed was prideful, but I had just been sucked into a room surrounded in mirrors. I'd better keep an eye on the plank in my own eye. "Lord," I asked, "what about the heart?" I didn't want to talk about Pharaoh like he wasn't in the room; after all, the question did involve him.

"Might you be inquiring about my hardened heart?" Pharaoh offered.

"Yes, that worries me," I said.

"Do you remember the two horses that pulled in the chariot?" the Lord asked me.

"Yes, Lord," I answered. They were now drinking from the tub of water in the corner.

"Remember how you did not know that there were two because one was so much louder?" He said.

"Yes," I said. I had remembered being surprised to find out there were two.

"That is the way with your heart," He said, "the louder emotion gets noticed."

"Like pride, it stands out because it is more assertive," He explained. "To justify why you are hurt, there is another emotion. When you are hurt, your pride stands out. When you're bitter, then your anger stands out. But," He said, "if your heart is full of love, then kindness stands out."

I was having a little difficulty following what He was explaining. *Am I slow or something? Why am I not getting this? Obviously Pharaoh got it,* I thought to myself.

"There," He said, "you are comparing yourself with another again. I made each of you for particular purposes. You will have many interests, but one purpose. If My children find themselves unhappy with their purpose, they tend to jump ship into someone else's boat. Makes it very difficult to patrol the ocean with so many wanting another's ship," He stated.

"Now," I said, "that makes sense. Still not fully understanding the horse thing, though."

"Let Me put it this way. Pharaoh was prideful; therefore his arrogances showed more than the reverence He has for Me."

"OK, but why did You harden his heart?" I asked.

"Good question," He said. "Remember how you felt by just the thought of another's heart being hard? It made yours softer because of your concern for them? His hard heart brought compassion forth for others hearts."

"I believe my work here is done," Pharaoh announced. "I must go win wars and pillage lands." His chariot stirred up dust in his exit.

"Do his words bother You?" I asked the Lord.

"Yes, pride in any amount troubles Me," He answered.

"Lord, rid me of all pride that is not pleasing in Your eyes," I asked. I knew better than to comment any further on Pharaoh's words. It was best to keep looking at myself in the mirror.

-CHAPTER 26-

The Lion Suit

Therefore, if anyone is in Christ, he is a new creation; the old has gone, the new has come! (2 Corinthians 5:17)

"Do not grow weary of doing good, You say. I am tired. I want to do what is right and I want others to feel the same way. How can I get them to?" I asked.

"You can't," He answered.

"No!" I screamed. "It has to be easier. Not easier, but maybe not so draining."

"Rest," He said.

"How can one rest when there is so much to do and so many hearts to help?" I asked. "I want to cry. So many lives hang on the balance with no net to catch them."

"*I am* the net," He replied.

"But what if they won't let You catch them?" I asked.

"I have back-up plans," He added.

My heart is racing faster and faster. The 8x10 room is closing in around me until there is only a 3x3 space. I begin to run, growling at the ones I pass by. I'm a lion angered by the sight of those around me. Growling and snarling, I run over those who come into my path.

"Get out of the way," I snarled as I clawed my way through the small path that is now barely large enough to run through, faster and faster, madder and madder, taking down whomever I need to get through. "They have to move, I have to survive!" I screamed. I can't breathe for the lump in my throat. Hyperventilating, I run on all four with teeth showing and eyes flaming. "Move," I growl, "move!"

Focused on the people on the side, I let out a fierce roar to frighten and intimidate the ones I pass by. "Move," I roar loudly, not caring that I have stomped on them to get by. I have to get by and that's what matters. Running faster and faster, so focused on the ones to my left. Picking up speed until, THUD, I run smack into a large oak tree. I'm out cold.

While spread out on my back unconscious, a crowd gathers. Unable to wake, I hover over myself and see the crowd glaring down at me. "I'm taking this off," I say as I stood over myself. "This suit has to go," I tell myself. I begin to unzip the lion suit. As I take one arm out of the sleeve, I hear a gruff voice from behind me.

"You can't take that suit off. You have worn it too long; it is part of you," the gruff voice said.

I turned to see a lion. He had many scars and a smirk that made me believe he knew what he was talking about. "You have run in that fur for many years; you know no other way," he continued.

Determined to prove him wrong, I began to tug and pull on the suit.

"See," he said, "even with your determination you can't re-move it."

"Why?" I screamed. "Why?"

I looked over my shoulder to see the most precious Lamb sitting under a lusciously full-leaved palm tree. Every frond and palm leaf was the perfect hue of green. I began to cry from the mere sight of the creature. The smile was warm and the fur was white as snow. Not day-old snow, but freshly fallen from the sky snow—not yet touched by human hands or feet. There was a tint of pink to the Lamb's face. It was breathtaking. I stood there in awe of this Lamb.

Then He spoke, "You can overcome that hindrance, if you desire."

"I can? He said I couldn't," I said and pointed to the lion.

"Who are you going to believe?" the Lamb asked.

I was confused; I knew neither one of these creatures; or did I? I walked over to the Lamb, "Please speak again," I requested.

"Dena," the Lamb said, "you know Me, I am your Father."

Overwhelmed, I ran to the Lamb and fell into the soft, tall grass that surrounded Him. The meadow was gorgeous. *Oh, I gasped, we are back in the playground.* There was the butterfly and God was sitting on the swing set. Then I remembered, "Oh no, I know why we are here."

"Yes, your incident is taking place, but this is your whale... remember?" the Lamb asked.

"Yes, but why are we back here?" I asked.

"There is a battle for your heart," He stated.

"That is enough!" the lion growled.

His loud roar scared me and I turned, seeing the anger in his eyes. He lunged at the Lamb. Before my eyes the soft, loving Lamb turned into a strong and beautiful golden Lion. I stepped back in horror. They began to fight and claw at each other, rolling around in the grass. As the scared lion's fur hit the grass, it became dirt. Just as fast as the dirt flew, the golden Lion changed it back into green blades.

"What is happening?" I hollered.

I heard the Lord from the swing set repeat, "There is a battle for your heart."

Still standing in my own lion suit, I began to cry. I was scared. As they fought, I began to hyperventilate; my heart was pounding so hard that I thought it would burst out of my chest. I had never felt such an implosion in my chest. I didn't know what to do. I screamed, "Stop! I want out of this thing." I began to frantically rip at my arms and legs, trying to force the suit from my body.

"I told you it has been with you so long that it cannot be removed," the scared lion yelled as the golden Lion threw him on his back. Down came the huge paw of the golden Lion onto the neck of the scared lion.

"That is enough!" He said in a loud roar. It shook the swing set, and the blades of grass blew. I said, "That is enough." With one final blow, the scared lion flew through the air and landed twenty-five feet into the distant meadow. He laid there for a few minutes and then stood, trying to shake off the dazed feeling.

I turned to see the lush, golden Lion was now the peaceful Lamb again.

"I will be back," the scared lion said in a gruff voice. "I will be back."

This threat did not seem to faze the Lamb, for He continued to lie in the grass.

Looking at the Lamb, I became overwhelmed with guilt. Had all of this been my fault? I stood there not sure what to do next. My first inclination was to run. I have been doing that all my life. When things got uncomfortable, I ran—not sure what or who from, I just ran. But this time I was frozen. I couldn't lift my feet. All I could feel was my heart pounding and sweat from my nervous palms. One drip, then two, they fell into the meadow. *What do I do now?* I thought as I stood before the Lamb and the Lord.

"Transform," I heard the Lord say.

I knew that we as God's children were to be transformed into the likeness of Christ, and I knew the movie *Transformers,* but a lion suit? I was confused.

"You have been running from your perpetrator since the incident. Running from yourself and others. Fear keeps you running, believing that if you stay still, the event will reoccur. You are angry that it ever happened," He explained.

In a flash of light, we were in the Hall again. The faces were bleeding. Red liquid ran from the canvas and dripped onto the floor; there were puddles on the floor.

"No!" I screamed.

I felt the Lord wrap me in His arms. He took my face and peered deeply into my eyes. "Hear Me, Child," He began, "you know I must speak truth, but I will speak gently."

"I trust You," I said as tears fell from the corners of my eyes.

"You have been angry for a long time. That is the threat the enemy kept throwing in your face. With all deception that is half-truths," He spoke. "He was right, you have carried it a long time, but he is lying when he tells you that you can't take it off—you *can* take it off."

"Oh, thank You, Lord, I want to, I want to," I said, excited to hear the news.

He smiled. "Good, then first you must realize that you have been angry," He explained.

"Lord, I know, I see now." I thought of just moments ago running and growling at all who came my way. "I know," I repeated.

"Very well," He said as He turned His face away.

"What is it, Lord?" I asked, concerned.

"Now, comes the..." He stopped.

"Lord," I said, "I want to remember."

"OK, now you have to face those you ran over," He said.

My heart sank. My eyes moved to the wall lined with portraits. One by one I went down the hall, talking to my heavenly Father, asking forgiveness while He taught me about myself. I had not been proud of what I had done, but I knew grace that day. Somewhere others had their own hall, but I had to be responsible for mine. I was sorry. I no longer wanted to run or plow over others on the way. I hoped to take the hands of those in my path and help them instead of hinder. To not only seek forgiveness, but repent, turn from my old sinful ways and walk in the new way He continues to show me. Forgiveness is one of the steps. I wanted to take all of the steps.

"Then stay on My path," He said.

"Lord," I asked, "is there a happy Hall? One that features smiling faces and maybe laughter?"

"Yes," He said with great joy, "there is."

"I can't wait to see it," I said, hoping there would come a day.

"You will," He said with confidence, "you will."

He walked with me as I continued to wipe up the spills and blot off the canvas. I was sorry I had caused this pain. "I wish I had known," I said.

"Now, you do, you can do better," He said smiling.

I'm going to, I said to myself, *I'm going to.* I had been so involved in the insight and forgiveness, I didn't notice portions of the lion suit had begun to vanish. Where I had just been in such a panic that it was on me, I had barely noticed it was almost gone. Like a cool stream that softly washes over the rocks, that was the feeling I felt as the anger I had carried so long was being removed. Deep down I knew I had more suit to remove; but with the Lord and the Lamb, I was protected. I was cared for.

A Lemon Slushy

"Life hands you lemons and you make a slushy. The pressure to convert that small, yellow tart fruit into a drinkable, liquid treat that someone will enjoy can be enough to upset one's stomach," I said.

"What it is?" the Lord asked.

"I am over the top with pressure," I answered. "The day-to-day, minute-to-minute demands of life can bring me into a tailspin. How did Moses do it? He had a wonderful father-in-law and people who wanted to help, but how did he let go?" I asked. "And most of all, how did he manage them?"

"He had his moments," the Lord replied. "Dear, you will never have everything down pat nor have all the answers," He clarified.

"I think that is where I stress the most, Lord. I want others to be OK," I said.

"How about you?" He asked.

"What about me?" I questioned.

"Can I tell you about a wonderful woman who lost it one morning?" He asked.

"Yes, please," I answered. *I could use some company,* I thought.

"She was beautiful," He began. "She had a heart of gold and wanted nothing more than My Son Jesus to be loved. She washed His feet with the finest of oil at the cost of her being chastised."

"I remember her," I told the Lord. "I bet she was wonderful." She touched the feet of our Savior; no words could have expressed what that must have been like.

"She adored Him and wanted others to, too," He continued. "She was there when they…" He stopped and held His heart, "… hung My Son."

I could see the hurt in His eyes as a single tear rolled down His face. I began to cry. I could not imagine how horrible it must have been to see His only Son hang on a cross to redeem even those who spat on Him earlier. "Lord, He is so wonderful."

He gathered Himself and replied, "Yes, He is, dear." He put His arm around my shoulder.

I thought this so precious that He who suffered greatly over the visual of His Son was comforting me. *Should it not be me who held and comforted Him?* I wondered.

"Dear one, it is not your place to answer every question that others bring your way," He began. "Mary was with Jesus. She knew of Him and the things to come. Yet, when the stone was rolled away and the grave was empty, she wept. She didn't understand. All she knew was her Beloved was gone. Oh, how she cried. I held her just like I am you. I will hold every child who desires My touch."

"Lord," I cried into His shoulder, "they don't know, and I don't know what to tell them."

"Do you know what My son John wrote?" He asked.

"To be honest, he wrote a lot and I need You to be a little more specific," I honestly admitted.

"He penned that even I had not revealed everything in My Word; therefore, if I have left parts out, then how can you even begin to know everything?" He pointed out.

His words made perfect sense, but I wanted so desperately for the words I spoke to bring others to Him.

"They will," He assured me, "but if you knew every answer, would they not begin to come to you instead of Me?"

"You are so right," I said. "I'm so sorry."

"Please don't be sorry for a heart like Mary's, one that longs to be near My Son at whatever cost...and for not knowing all of the answers," He said. "Moses knew a lot, but even he needed My help when the ranks became more than he could bear. I do not want My children to live under an umbrella of pressure to be perfect. You are confused. Perfectly made does not mean perfect in every way."

I looked at Him as I let His statement sink in. He must have seen I was processing His words because He began to elaborate.

"Everything you are is made perfectly, but we are working out the things you do. Jesus' selfless action on the cross made you forgiven...but not perfect. We are working out the sins as we go. Look at it this way, if I revealed to you the pride I know harbors in your heart, it would crush you. So, little by little I reveal it. My prayer is that you will come willingly with Me to heal you of that imperfection. Our goal is a shameless bride on the return of My Son. Pure and unblemished," He concluded.

That sounds wonderful, I thought. *To be a radiant glow of my Father; to look like the family.*

"Yes, you do resemble Me," He said. "You have My eyes."

We both laughed. I longed for people to see a picture of me and say, "Oh, you look just like your Father." Yes, I thought that would be a good day. A family portrait, that was exciting. To stand by my Father, as his child looking into His eyes.

"Give yourself time, you are growing into the woman of God I already see," He said lovingly. "Give yourself a chance to learn… and yes, make mistakes. I can do some of My greatest work from what My children consider horrible mistakes. Children learn their mannerisms from the ones they spend time with. Spend time with Me, and you will learn to act like Me. Spend time with the world, and that is what you will look like."

I knew He was there for the long haul. I wanted to let myself off the hook and allow myself to grow. I wanted to look like my Father. "I don't want to be sad or overwhelmed about all of this," I continued, "but how can my perspective change from half full to half empty?"

"Lighten up," He replied. "Everything is not life or death. Will you do something with Me?" He asked.

"OK," I replied.

"Stand up," He motioned. "Now pretend you have a wheelbarrow and it is full of dirt."

"OK," I agreed, thinking this is a strange request. But I had learned He always has a good reason.

"Try to pick it up and move it," He directed.

"But I can't because it is very heavy," I said.

"Now try to dump out the dirt," He instructed.

"It is too difficult for me to lift *and* dump it out," I explained.

"That is where I come in," He said. "I will help you dump all of the dirt, rocks…even the cement you have accumulated over the years."

I looked down and saw the head of someone I knew in the wheelbarrow. It wasn't scary. He was talking although I could not hear him. He was jabbering away. "This person was very close to me," I said.

"Yes," the Lord said. "We get a lot of our perspectives from our parents or those who looked over us."

This made me think about married couples and owners with their pets often beginning to look alike.

"Similar, but not quite My meaning," He said jokingly. "If you are around a negative person as a child, you tend to view the world as such. If life is this horrible creation you are trying to suffer through, then your outlook will reflect such."

I thought about the person I was seeing in my wheelbarrow. Although I loved this person greatly, he did see life as a rough, serious road. "What do we do, Lord?" I asked.

He began with a smile and a loving cheer, "Spend time with Me," He said while clapping and dancing around.

His joy made me laugh. I really loved to laugh, even though my laughter occurred far too infrequently.

"See, it is already working," He said. "If spending time with people influences your outlook, then spend it with Me. Did you notice something else?" He asked.

"Yes, Lord, it is contagious," I said confidently.

"Yee ha!" He yelled. "I created life to be abundant, no negativity here."

His words made me want to sit with Him all day.

"Who can sit all day?" He replied. "We have to get out and do, enjoy the scenery, the people, life," He said with excitement.

I want to reflect my Father. To look and act like my heavenly family, the Trinities. Yes, that would be our family name. Early family members may choose to come and go, but my name is written in the baby book of my heavenly family. I am part of the Trinity family. "Yee ha!" I yelled.

"Yee ha," He repeated. "If you can't figure out what they want, you don't give them anything. You don't like people to know your business," He announced.

"Have we changed course?"

"No, one layer peels another by attachment," He said. "Wow, we are always peeling," I noted. "Fear they will distort what you say because that has happened before so you think if you don't say anything, it won't happen again. But you are wrong. People, unfortunately, are going to say things whether you talk or not."

"Then what do we do?" I asked.

"Be yourselves," He replied.

"We need to work on your fear of others," He said.

I knew He was right. "Why, Lord, do some people who appear to be nosey bother me?" I asked.

"You don't know what their angle is, where they are coming from. It makes you nervous because you cannot be prepared," He explained.

"What do I do?" I asked.

"That is a tough one," He replied. .

"Why, Lord?" I asked.

"Because there are so many layers. I believe you want a one-trick pony when you really need a whole carnival," He said.

"Can we start?" I asked. "I've been through layers before."

"Are you sure?" He asked.

"Yes, but it makes me a little nervous that You had to ask," I admitted.

"See, there is one," He pointed out. "This particular healing involves gloom—always thinking the worst will happen," He said. "My asking is manners. Parents do not just tell their children no or you can't, they tell them why. I want you to be part of the decision. I do not want to control, but involve."

"Ooh, ooh, I like that," I said. "I would love to dispel the reason I assume the worst."

"OK then, back to the wheelbarrow," He said with excitement.

"OK. Take a look at that large piece of cement in your wheelbarrow. See if you can pick it up," He asked.

I tried, but I couldn't.

"That is because it is stuck," He explained. "Fears had mixed with a personality trait and caused it to harden to the wheelbarrow."

"Cool in theory, not so much in healing," I said.

"Never fear," He said, "I have the right tools for the job. Bring your hard hat and steel-toed boots, we are going mining." He flipped a large light switch and a huge flood light came on.

"Cool," I said. We were in the wheelbarrow looking up at this big piece of cement.

"Don't worry," He said, "at this point it won't budge."

"I was wondering if it would break away and crush us," I said.

"Know one thing about fears combining to a hardened form, it is not going to move," He stated. "But once we start picking away at the elements within, there is a great chance it could crush you. That is why I chip away in layers or the whole thing could come crashing down, defeating the whole purpose," He added.

"Lord, "I said, "what is that purpose?"

"Freedom," He said. "My Son went through a lot to free My children from sin, debt, and to give them power and a joyful life. The door was opened. The veil was torn apart, but I knock and still some do not answer. Sin has been redeemed, but the effects still reside. I come with My mining gear to chip away at the residue, but I cannot trespass. They have to allow Me on their property."

"Well, have at it," I said. "Full access is all ours."

He walked over to the side of the wheelbarrow where I noticed He had propped up several tools. "This will do," He said as He picked up a pick. "Going to need these, too," He said as He picked up some gloves. "Want to keep my hands soft for when the children want to play patty-cake."

I smiled. *How sweet,* I thought.

"Do you know how embarrassing it is for one of those youngsters to call you out with rough hands?" He said, smiling.

"Yes, I can imagine," I said. "Kids say the darnedest things."

We both laughed.

"Yes, but I like truth," He added.

"Children can be brutally honest," I added.

"That is good...well the honest part," He said. "Parents can train the approach not to be unkind, but I wish they wouldn't steer them away from the truth part."

"We have done a lot of chipping away today," He said. "How about we rest for a while?" He asked as He propped Himself up against the wheelbarrow.

"Rest sounds good," I admitted as I joined him by the wheelbarrow.

POST-ITS

"Lord, somewhere I got confused," I said. "Remove the veil of deception and confusion and open my eyes to the real truth," I began to pray. It felt like lies were all over me, creating a dirty, ugly feeling. It was like having Post-it notes stuck all over me. I offered them up to the Lord, but I still felt some on my arms. I confessed the ones that were stuck on by my own hands and offered them up, thanking Jesus for His forgiveness and grace.

"What about these that won't come off?" I asked.

"What happens when you throw Post-it notes in water?" He asked.

"The ink disappears," I answered.

"That is what will happen to the lies as I throw the Post-its in the Stream of Living Water," He answered.

"Thank You, Lord. Is there more?" I asked.

"You are heavy from dirt," He said prophetically.

"How can I remove the dirt?" I asked.

"You can't, you have to be willing to let Me," He replied.

"Why do I still sense Post-its on my arms?" I asked curiously.

"That is the place they are before they become actions performed by your hands," He began. "Another common place to have them is around your lips. Not everything I tell you is your fault or something you are doing wrong. It can be just knowledge or to be able to relate better."

"I like that," I said. I noticed that there were some still stuck to my stomach. "Is it envy?" I asked. I wanted to get to the bottom of this mess.

"Girl, we just got started," He said, grinning. "What do you want, a miracle?"

"Well, yes," I said, laughing.

"Well, you're not getting one this time, at least not instantly," He said, still grinning.

"I can live with that," I replied.

"I'd rather you do. That's why you'll have your miracle," He answered.

"Thank You," I said.

"You are welcome, darling," He said.

CHAPTER 27

The Path

In all your ways acknowledge Him, and He will make your paths straight (Proverbs 3:6).

"Who am I?" I asked. Then it seemed to me that I was going about this from the back entrance. I mean couldn't I ask a question like, "Why do I get so upset when I think others are making decisions for me?" But I had learned that He knows best, even if I don't know it yet.

"Come with me," He began. "We are going on a trip. Grab your swim suit, a life vest, and a net."

Before me was the most beautiful, clear blue body of water I had ever seen. Looking over the horizon, the water went on and on, as if extending into forever.

"It does, you know," I heard Him say.

The sight, combined with the words out of His mouth, made me tear up. As we stood there drinking in the majestic scene, I noticed the warm almost therapeutic sand between my toes. It wasn't too hot from the sun that hung above like a perfectly round translucent orange. The sand didn't stick to my skin, something I had hated as a child. It was comforting, making me feel safe. The cool, gentle breeze that blew off the water was refreshing, not a nuisance like breezes can be when you don't want your hair to get messed up as you walk on the beach. No, this beach was pleasantly enjoyable.

"Nothing bothers you here," He said, jarring me from my thoughts.

"No," I said. "It is perfect."

"What is interesting…" He remarked, "…look to your right," He requested.

To my right stood about ten men gathered around a small wooden boat. It had rust around its hull and chipped red paint that apparently the sun had faded. I could hear them bickering over something—voices raised and hands reached to the sky, displaying their frustration.

"Is that all you see?" He asked.

"No, I was about to mention another man," I said. He was sitting alone in a dark blue boat just off shore. The boat was tied to the bank, but by what I was not sure. He was old in appearance: white beard; long, white, tangled hair; wearing a white gown. His face seemed weary.

"He is tired of waiting," the Lord explained.

"Waiting for what?" I asked.

"The bickering to stop," He answered. "There is a job at hand, but the men are so distracted over who should do what that they aren't doing anything."

"Why, Lord, is it peaceful to me over here?" I asked.

"You are alone," He stated. "Well, technically you are with Me, but alone from the Body. That is why My people retreat. They don't want to disrupt the peace. But nothing gets done that way.

"I am well aware that relationships are draining…heck, I get tired too." He laughed. "But what if I retreated?" He suggested.

I woke this day with an overwhelming sadness that I recognized as slipping into depression. I cried tears of a devastating loss. As the shower water ran, I lay in the bottom of the tub as a limp, numb shell of myself. With what little strength I had—or more the lack of desire I had—I turned off the water. With a total lack of care, I sat with a blank stare for too long. I believe that God had given me a very small taste of what it would feel like if He was no longer in my life. To lose all real Hope. Without Him, we are completely hopeless. He says He will never leave us. Let's not take that for granted.

I never want a day that I can't pray. I felt I had lost my best friend. I wanted Him back. "Show me, Lord, what You desire me to know and what I can say or do to wake up the Church! Then please come back to me. I don't like these empty feelings," I pleaded.

"What are you afraid of?" He asked.

"You not answering something and making me look stupid," I admitted.

"Why would I do that?" He asked. "What would I have to gain? You are willing to help Me," He continued, "why would I abuse that?"

"Common sense tells me You wouldn't, but my fear says You might," I stated.

"Perfect love," He replied. "You need perfect love."

"Yes," I cried. "Yes."

"Come here," He motioned.

I walked toward Him with my head down.

He lifted my head by my chin and began softly, "Child, I am here for the long haul. I will never leave you."

I wanted to believe Him, but I had felt left by Him before.

"We will take those things one by one and clear them up. Good parents aren't afraid to discuss confusion with their children, even if they may have appeared or actually been wrong," He explained.

"But Lord, You can't be wrong," I said.

"No," He said, "but you may have perceived Me to be. Now, sit, and tell Me what is on your mind."

"A time I had been hurt by a group of people," I stated. "I did what I thought You said, but it blew up in my face," I shared.

"OK," He began, "now honestly…"

"Yes, one time I jumped the gun in that environment, and I feel guilty for that," I said. "I'm sorry."

"Apology accepted, but don't be so hard on yourself," He replied. "I leave room for learning curves."

That brought a small grin, but I still felt I had ruined everything.

"No, no," He insisted. "Why is it My children only see what they did wrong instead of all they do right?" He said, shaking His head.

"Shouldn't I be the one asking *You* that?" I said. "In fact, I believe I asked that before. Why do we do that?" I asked.

"Let's look at it from another angle," He suggested.

"OK," I agreed. I was game.

"Why don't they live out the power of the cross?" He proposed.

"I'm not sure how the two mixed," I said.

"If you know the power obtained at the cross, you know mistakes are already forgiven…so it is unnecessary to dwell on them," He explained.

"Ah ha, forgetting the past," I yelled as I slapped my hands together.

"Forgetting is not dwelling," He stated.

"Yee ha!" I hollered.

"Hang on, there is more," He added. "If you know your mistakes are forgiven, they are no longer distractions taking your focus off the power."

"What is this power?" I asked.

"Oh, I love this question," He said with a giggle in His voice. "The power to do anything!"

"Wow, the thought of how endless and unlimited that was is powerful in itself. Please give me some examples," I said with excitement.

"There are so many, but the first that comes to mind is becoming a Daniel out of a Nebuchadnezzar situation," He said. "Those dreams that torment can be healed and become interpretations."

Wow, I thought. *The very dreams that had kept me up at night were now dreams that with the power of God had been interpreted.*

"Magical," He said.

"Yes," I gladly agreed.

"I want to commend you on recognizing that it is from *My* power you have *your* power," He added. "Things go bad when that is forgotten, and My children attempt to venture out on their own power," He explained.

Although that is true, I really wanted to stay focused on the good He had just shared.

"Just shared," He chuckled. "This news is over 2,000 years old. It just gets overlooked and forgotten."

"Why?" I asked.

"Because they focus on the bad, not the good," He said. "But like you did just now, My Word can be brought back to life. Recognizing that misuse of people's power for their own gain does exist, but choosing to focus on those that use it for the Kingdom, which is good."

"Some say that is ignoring the obvious or not being prepared," I stated.

"And where has that gotten them?" He asked. "More tangled up than when they started. Have you ever watched a steer try to get out of a rope that had been tossed around its neck?"

"No, I have to say, I haven't," I said.

"When that cowboy ropes that filly or a steer, its instinct is to fight it," He began. "It causes the animal to wear out and tie itself up worse. That is the philosophy of thinking you are ignoring something if you don't focus on the bad over the good. And there you have it," He said as if satisfied. "Why do My children focus on the bad instead of the good?" He repeated.

He was obviously pleased with the deduction. As for me, I would have to practice. I knew I had done this so long that to change my way of thinking would take time.

"And power," He added.

"Power?" I questioned.

"Yes, don't forget you have the power," He reminded.

Just as He said that, I saw what appeared to be a huge light bulb with legs. I rubbed my eyes to make sure I wasn't seeing things.

"Hey," the Light Bulb said.

"Umm, hello," I said oddly.

"Need any bright ideas?" He asked.

That was more than I could take. I burst out in a howl of laughter. They joined in.

"What in the world?" I asked with tears of laughter running down my face as I realized it was the Holy Spirit dressed as a light bulb.

"He is here to help you learn about your power," the Lord explained.

All of a sudden I heard a loud roar that made the earth shake. In the corner of my eye I saw the scared lion again. He stood there looking at me with his beady eyes and his yellowed teeth snarling at me. I turned toward the Lord to find the white, precious Lamb was back lying in the grassy meadow like before.

"What is this?" I asked the Holy Spirit.

"A standoff," He explained. "The enemy does not want you to know about the power you possess, but Jesus has come to protect you."

How could a soft, cuddly Lamb possibly protect me from this mean lion? I wondered. Then I remembered His previous transformation when the lion had attacked.

"Yes," the Holy Spirit said, "the Lamb is gentle, but when need be, He will defend His children."

"A good parent knows when each is necessary," the Lord added.

"Why is the Lamb just lying there?" I asked.

"He knows when to just observe," He explained. "Too often people jump in too soon. He knows when to react...and with Me, you can too."

"I would like that, too." As I spoke, I noticed out of the corner of my eye that the lion was still standing there. There was a paved street that ran beside him. Looking down the street I could see flames in the far distance. There were screams coming from this path. A smoky haze hung over the black, tarred road. He continued to stand as if waiting.

"What is he doing?" I asked the Lamb.

"He is waiting," the Lord said.

"For what?" I questioned.

"For you to make a decision," He answered.

I was not sure what I was supposed to be deciding, so I asked.

"Which path you will take," the Lamb responded.

I noticed the Light Bulb was looking intently as if waiting, too. *This decision must be important,* I thought. I looked at the road and noticed another option I had not noticed before. I stood at the point where two paths forked into two options. Looking farther into this second option, I noticed it was not paved but a path of soil. There were little rocks, but the sky above was a beautiful shade of pale blue. I heard singing and birds chirping. There was laughter and the sun shone at the end.

"I will take that path," I said as I pointed to the blue sky and the unpaved road.

"Then why do you run?" The Lord asked. He was standing in the distance behind the Lamb.

"I don't know," I said. "I know that in the past, in fact this very morning, I had avoided my time with Him because I was worried about what He might ask of me or tell me. So I had gotten in my car and ran errands. Errands as a whole are necessary, but I knew as I walked through Target, I was killing time. I felt horrible; He had been so good to me..."

He stopped me from continuing and began boldly, "When you run from Me, you are choosing a path. If the path does not lead to the son at the end, you have chosen the fire—there is no in between. My children fool themselves into thinking otherwise. Choose your own path or out of no choice, one will be chosen for you. Don't go down the wrong path out of default."

"What am I choosing?" I interjected.

"Go My way or allow the enemy to escort you to hell," He said without batting an eye.

"What?" I said, offended.

"You heard Me," He said. "The enemy can only take you where you allow him to take you."

"But what about sifting?" I said, questioning. "Letting things pass through your fingers."

"Look again at the roads," He said, pointing in that direction.

"Oh," I said. Now I could see dirt that branched off the paved road leading to the dirt road.

"I always give you a way out," He said. "The branches are ways I provided to veer off the dirt road. It is up to you to take them," He added.

"Thank You, Jesus," I said under my breath.

"You are welcome," the Lamb replied.

"What do I do now?" I asked.

"Remember when you have a situation…" He began.

"Like when someone says something against me," I jumped in the conversation.

"Yes, like when someone says something against you…you have two roads to choose from," He showed me.

"Light Bulb," I looked at Him and asked, "what do You do?"

"I give you insight and light to walk that path," He replied. "The road is dirt because We are honest in telling you it will be bumpy. Our adversary deceives with what appears to be a smoothly paved road, but when you walk it, you soon find out it is a lie. Look," He said pointing toward the road.

The paved road now had huge pot holes and in places, the road split open into a long drop downward.

Light Bulb continued, "He doesn't tell you this. Omission is not admission," He said.

It all seemed so clear. "Oh, I hope I remember," I said.

"I can help you with that, too," Light Bulb added.

"Why are you all doing this?" I asked. I appreciated His sentiment, but I had not had the same experience.

"You haven't?" He said. "Look down the road," He directed.

I could see people, family…my family.

He began to show me family members and how they loved me. In their own special way; my family loved me. The emotion was more than I could hold in.

"Let it out," the Lord cried.

"See," He said tenderly, "what you would have missed if you had kept running. Keep looking, child," He said.

The tears ran; I wiped them from my eyes to see my beautiful granddaughter running toward me, behind her was the vision of my grandmother. She was laughing and clapping for her.

"No," He said, "she is clapping for *you*. She is so proud of you. She wants you to enjoy your granddaughter as much as she enjoyed you." Looking back at this moment, I knew in my spirit, my future was going to be blessed with a grandson. And knowing my grandmother's love for children assured me she would want me to enjoy him too."

That was it, the flood gates opened as tears poured down my neck and dripped onto my shirt. It was the most beautiful thing I had ever seen.

"Child," He said softly, "there is good in everyone at some point, and everyone makes up a family."

"Why have You allowed me to see such things?" I asked.

"Because your heart was ready to receive them," He said.

"I love my heart," I said.

"You should, it has come a long way," He said.

I stood there looking at the three of them, my family. I was so appreciative of who and what they were willing to do for me. "The Trinity Family," I said out loud. That is one tree I don't mind branching off from.

"What about trees you don't want to branch from?" I heard the Lord ask in a deep tone.

"Yes, Lord, what about them?" I asked concerned.

"You are a family. Even though families often times have disagreements, they learn to work it out," He said.

I could see His point, but I had also known incidents where working it out had not been an option. *What then,* I wondered, *dare I ask?* He knew I was thinking it so I guess I'd say it out loud. "What about ones who won't budge?" I asked.

"Move around them," He answered.

Brilliant, I thought.

"Now," He continued, "that doesn't mean hitting them as you pass by or shouting a name at them."

I laughed; that was funny and yes, sometimes had been true. I knew now that would be a path choice.

"Yes," He added, "but how you walk that path matters too. Joseph's family was mean to him," He started. "He wanted them to come around, but at some point you can't wait any longer. You have to keep moving on your path."

I noticed where there was one dirt path now there were many.

"Everyone has their own path, but as you see, they all intertwine," He explained. "I will have others meet you on your path, and if all works as planned, your family will meet up with you as Joseph's did. Sadly," the Lord said, "it was the famine that made them come around."

"Yes, but they came not knowing Joseph was there," I pointed out as if He didn't know already.

"You are right, but why does that matter?" He asked. "Because," He said as I heard a drum roll, "I exalted Joseph even over his enemies."

"Yeah, yeah!" I cheered, and began to dance and sing.

"I am responsible for who comes along on your path and what you say to those you move around. So, since I know you like to flap that jaw..."

I would have been offended, but He was right and it sounded funny coming from Him.

"...Let me," He continued, "speak when necessary. I have all these people out there who think they are talking for Me, but if they would check themselves with the Light Bulb, they would know it wasn't My idea. Now about the movement part," He said.

"Yes, Lord, not that great with my actions," I admitted.

"It starts with your hands," He said.

I remembered the Post-its on my arms and hands.

What is the proper action?" I asked.

"Walk, run, skip, or crawl with Me...I will get you around them. I repeat, I will."

"Why the need to repeat?" I asked.

"Because just like the words, My children are out there moving around their feet in My name," He stated.

I looked up to see the Holy Spirit was now wearing a big tennis shoe.

"Look at the path," the Lord asked.

The sky was flooded with lights, some were bright and some dim. It was the Lamb walking alongside a man down the path.

"He will light the way," the Lord said. "He knows the dangerous areas and the tricky turns. But you must stay with Him because those paths I open to bring you from the paved road go both ways."

"Ooh," I said.

"Yes, fix your eyes on Him and set your feet to discern the Holy Spirit's direction," He advised.

"What are we doing in the woods?" I asked

"Quiet...they are sleeping," He whispered. "Hibernating."

I looked around and saw sleeping bags laid out. "Are we sleeping here?" I asked.

"You have been," He answered. "You are part of the awakening."

I saw someone sitting under a tree. "Who is that?" I asked.

"Elijah," He answered.

Oh man, I thought. Wait a minute, "Is my hair OK? Do I look all right?" I said as I fussed with my dress.

"Why does it matter?" the Lord asked.

"Lord," I replied with a surprised look on my face, "he transcended and never came back. He walked with You…" I was going on and on until He interrupted.

"Dear," He said, *"all* of My children are great."

"I know, Lord," I said, "but this is *Elijah.*"

"No buts," He insisted, "I feel that way about them all." Then He spoke as I had not heard Him before. He was direct, with little tolerance, but great purpose.

"To the Church. There is an uprising in the Body of Christ, not the *building* of Christ, but people who are demanding, hungering, and tired of hearing *about* Him and want to *know* Him, experience Him. Isn't that a big difference between the living Me and Mohammad and dead gods?

"Our God is alive," I said. "Should we not expect to be able to see, hear, and smell Him?" I added.

"There is going to be a coming-out-of-hibernation party," He continued. "They have not been sleeping, they have been preparing. Like a squirrel storing for the winter, I have been preparing My people."

"What have we been preparing for?" I asked, in awe of His words.

"To awake a sleeping Church," He continued without taking a breath. "I'm bored. Experience Me now; do not settle for waiting until after your death. There is no wait; ride with Me now. The

National Treasure movie doesn't touch the experience I have set for you. The roller coaster cart has pulled up to the turnstile gate. It is about to be released; there is a seat next to Me with your name on it."

I could see Him looking up from the seat in excitement and anticipation, waiting for me to jump in.

"Go...Go...Go! Don't let it leave without you," He shouted. "Don't miss the excitement."

I said, "The world has led us to believe that You sit holding a stick waiting to bang us on the head. No, You are a fun, loving, and joyous God. I want to ride. I'm in now, the harness has come down. Swish, we're off!"

"Hands up...it is funner that way," I heard Him say with a line from the *Madagascar* movie. "Let Him worry about steering or holding on, you just enjoy the ride," Jesus said.

I fell limp. The experience was emotional and out of my own realm. He had spoken not only to me, but through me. From Him, through me, to you; the Body. I cried out, "More, Lord, more of You." Never looking back or getting off the ride, I said, "I love You. Thank You for waiting and being excited when I came in."

My heart was elated for the anticipation of the ride, but broken for His children. I cried out to the churches, "What if I came to you today and said there is no more God? He is finished trying to show us His glory. Don't pray, don't journal—heck, turn the building into recreation rooms and malls and call it a day. We can't let this happen. We need You, God."

I was on the floor now, desperate. Many of us are too lost to realize it, admit it, or to take the time to seek Him. Face down, heart pounding, I had been in the glory. I could never go back; I didn't want to. I was on the ride.

As the words had been spoken with such conviction, meaning, and power, we returned to Elijah just as quickly.

I gathered this when He asked, "Can we get back to Elijah?"

Gathering my thoughts, I understood what He was saying, but I had long prayed to transcend into the open heavens. The thought of walking into them all with the Lord excited me to a giggle, because I had just experienced my own transition.

"Honey," He interrupted again, "can we just get back to Elijah?"

"Yes, I'm sorry," I said with a grin.

"Why is he sitting under the tree?" He asked.

"Yes," I remembered now.

"He is hiding," He explained.

"Hiding…like I ran earlier?" I questioned.

CONFIDENCE

"No, hiding because he has lost his confidence," He said.

"Oh, Lord, I had hoped once you got confidence you couldn't lose it," I said.

"Well," He started, "I hate to disappoint you, but just like we peel layers of the onion, we add layers of confidence. One trades itself for the other. Fear is replaced with confidence. Confidence because you know whose you are…and I am love."

"Cool," I said. "Fear made confident out of You, which is love."

"You get the idea," He stated. "Let Me elaborate. Being right breeds confidence, but even the thief can believe he is right. What kind of confidence is that?" He asked.

"That is why I hear people say, 'If I am wrong, I'll err on the side of Jesus,'" I said.

"Wouldn't you rather *know?*" He questioned. "How was Elijah confident in who he was?"

"Because he knew who I was," He answered.

"How do we get confidence?" I asked.

"By letting me remove those Post-its," He said. "This is the transformation I am talking about. Some will come off like a Band-Aid. While some have been there a while, the sticky is embedded. But there is no glue I can't unstick. Some may sting when they come off, but I have salve. Like when you skinned your knee as a child, you may need a kiss for that boo boo or a hug while you cry. I am a full-service parent. I know what you need before you ask, and I give it freely. Come to Me with your wounds as a child," He said.

"Where do we start?" I asked.

"Well, you are confident that you hear Me," He said. "And if I tell you what to say, then what is the problem?" He asked.

"People," I answered.

"My people need to deal with fear of people," He stated boldly.

"Rejection...that again," I said.

"Yes, it is deep," He said. "Over the years, things have settled to the bottom, because they were heavy. Weighed you down. To get to them, we have to go deep. That is why so many circle the same well. They skim off the top, never getting to the depth of the problem."

"Then deep it is," I said.

"Elijah," the Lord called, "untangle yourself from that vine and get over here."

Elijah came running. Brushing the particles from the tree off of his shoulders, he introduced himself. "Hello, my name is Elijah...and yours?"

"My name is Dena, nice to meet you," I replied. I wasn't as elated or nervous as I had thought I would be. He seemed average, not in a bad way, but normal like me. I thought he'd be taller.

"Like on a pedestal," the Lord chimed in.

"Yes," I had to admit. I had put him on a pedestal.

What do I do with that? I thought. "Lord," I asked, "what do I do?"

"Realize that all My children are great," He said.

I've heard that before.

"I said it again because the Body tends to *elevate* instead of *rejuvenate*. It is not about titles. That is for order. Not order over, but to keep order," He said. "The gifts I have given to you are equally important as the ones I have given to others. You know my body analogy."

"Yes," I answered. "The hand cannot function without the wrist." I threw my spin on it.

"Exactly," He said.

"Lord…" I began. I hesitated to continue because I knew it was a sensitive subject, and I didn't want to offend anyone.

"Yes?" He leaned into me.

"What about protecting the flock?" I asked.

"Hmmm, you are bold, little one," He said.

I took a deep breath and tried to calm my nerves. "Don't run," I heard in a loud voice. Startled, I jumped. It was coming from little Elijah. *Wow, such a strong voice from an average-size man,* I thought. I now saw, and heard, the confidence God had spoken about.

"Don't run," he repeated. "Don't run from man or woman," he said as he looked at God and shook his head. "If God says it, rest in that, and not a patch of grass hiding under a tree."

Point well made, I thought. "OK," I said, still a little shaken, "what about the flock?"

"If My leaders are on their faces before Me, the flock is protected," the Lord said bluntly.

My heart began to pound because I could see on His face there was more.

"Not everyone is called to work in the nursery," He added with pure tact.

"Oh, dear Lord," I said out loud. If I was going to hide, now would have been a good time. I was going to need many layers of confidence and a few onion layers peeled for this one.

"Dena," He said laying His hand on my shoulder. "My children are precious; the little ones need workers whose hearts I have prepared to care for them. It is an honor, not a training ground to see if the people are safe or qualified to move into another position."

I fell to the ground. His intensity had knocked me down. I was on holy ground. I began to take off my shoes. "Lord, may I speak?" I asked.

"Yes," He replied, "but do not look."

I did not understand, for I had seen Him before.

"You cannot take this intensity," He explained. "It will burn you."

"Burn me?" I questioned.

"Yes, the glow of My holiness will pierce your eyes and disintegrate your being," He answered.

That didn't sound good. "Will it always be that way?" I asked.

"That is why Elijah could not come back," He stated. "Once you have seen Me, you must stay. My home is holy."

I laid on the ground, hands over my eyes, face to the earth, waiting for what, I didn't know.

"I have spoken," I heard Him say and then He disappeared.

I looked up to find Him and Elijah gone. "Darn," I said, "they did it again." I realized that I didn't run. No tree for me today. My heart was still racing from the word I had heard. Panic was not an option. I took to heart Elijah's words and wanted to be firm in my footing.

"Where are You, Lord?" I asked.

"He has gone for now," I heard a voice from behind me speak. It was a rough, female voice.

-CHAPTER 28-

Jezebel

For our struggle is not against flesh and blood, but against the rulers, against the authorities, against the powers of this dark world and against the spiritual forces of evil in the heavenly realms (Ephesians 6:12).

Suspicious, I turned toward the direction of the voice. I knew from the black hair and evil look in her eyes, it was Jezebel.

"Do you know I could ruin you with one word?" she asked with confidence.

With my heart pounding I replied, "Do you know to whom I belong?"

"Oh," she said sarcastically, "you want to play *that* hand? I can call on my gods and have you done away with."

"If this is true," I replied, "then why haven't you done it?"

"Do not get cocky," I heard from a whisper within.

I cleared my throat.

"Aha," she said, "weakness."

"Are you kidding me?" I replied. I cleared my throat.

"Would you care to dance?" she asked as she pulled out a sword.

We were in fencing gear. Hers—black from head to toe.

Mine—I looked down—a sword, helmet, breastplate, gilded shoes, and a bronze belt.

"You come to me with the findings of man; I come to you with the presence of the Lord." He had not left like she had said. He had covered me like a sheet of 10-gauge sheet metal. No sword of her gods would penetrate the armor of God.

"Say what you will," I said with confidence, "for the voice of the Lord will out-speak you." Suddenly, I saw onion peelings hit the floor and the glow of the letter C on my chest.

"Confidence," she screamed, "not confidence."

"See," I heard the Lord say, "what she called confidence was false. Her words are spoken in intimidation. True confidence always resides from love because I spoke it."

I stood with my sword by my side. Eye to eye, we peered. "You have to go now," I said calmly. "I cannot allow you to get in the way of my path." I took a step to the side. Looking down, I saw the sneaker, the Holy Spirit, was leading the way. We moved around her.

Bewildered, all she could do was watch as we went by.

"If they won't budge," the Lord repeated, "we'll go around them. Nothing can block My faithful children, for they have heavenly strengths: confidence, endurance, and Us."

Amen was the only appropriate response that fit the moment. "Amen, Lord, amen," I said confidently.

Somebody Catch the Sheet

"Good morning, Lord," I said.

"Why yes it is," He replied, grinning. "I see you have found a secret to time. Match what needs to be done with the prompting of your spirit. Your spirit knows when and what needs to be done and yes in whatever area, season, or time of your day. She, your spirit, is not conventional, but radical."

"Why radical?" I asked.

"Anything that goes against the world's grain is viewed by unbelievers, and yes some believers, as radical," He explained.

This day I had awoken at 4:30 in the morning. Normally, I would have fought with myself to go back to sleep, reasoning that it is still dark outside and so I should be sleeping. I finally thought, *Why waste this time when I could be productive in my responsibilities?*

"Every day is not the same; therefore, every day will not demand the same rest. My people beat themselves up because they think they don't get enough sleep or try to catch up on their sleep," He said, laughing.

"What's so funny?" I asked.

"Can't you just see people running after a big bed sheet?" He said chuckling.

He made me grin. The thought of running after a bed sheet was funny.

"Your *who* is the Holy Spirit and human spirit. They work in sync," He stated. "If they are not content, there is an indicator. The *what* is your body. Mechanically there is a sequence to the way it should function and what it needs to function. If that is off kilter, you have signs. Signs and indicators," He repeated.

"Makes sense to me," I added.

Then there are ideas from people that say "*sleep during such and such hours.*" A little concerned I would be dead to the world by 8:00 A.M., I still opted to get up. "I was going to be tired whether I lay there and fight it or I just get up," I said.

"That is so true," He said. "You were at peace, not struggling with something that needed addressing. You were just full of sleep."

Hmmm, I thought, *full of sleep.*

"Yes, just like you can be full of food, you can be full of sleep," He said.

"I like that," I said. "It seems to take the pressure off of having to sleep during certain times."

"Know your body," He started. "I have given you many gauges and indicators."

"Like what?" I was curious.

"No, who," He chuckled.

"Oh," I said, "I know them well. I mean, that is what started all of this."

"Yes, peaceful dreams indicate full sleep. "If you wake in peace, you have full sleep," He said.

It seemed so simple, but I had known it to be true.

"Everybody lining up; up with me," He spoke. "That is peace."

I saw a beautiful, white with light blue tint cloud over the ceiling of my bedroom at my home while I lay snuggled in my bed.

"There it is," He said.

I looked closely; I had a smile on my face as I slept.

"There it is," He repeated, "peace."

It had been what had felt like a long journey; but I had peace. Sleep was no longer a place to fear, but a place to rest.

"Fill her up," He shouted. "Fill *her* up with sleep."

"Amen," I said. "I love You, Lord."

CAUGHT IN BAD WEATHER

"Before every rainbow, there must have been rain," He said poetically.

"Then why do I feel like I have been hit with a hail storm?" I asked. "I'm so distraught this morning. Why can't we see the day as a privilege not as bad? I'm so upset."

"Why, My child?" He asked.

"I don't understand why they didn't tell me she was going," I said. "It shouldn't have been their judgment call to make. They knew how much I loved her. I wanted to know. I'm torn between furious and tears. I don't like people making decisions for me," I said between gritted teeth.

"Do you know what gritted teeth are?" He asked.

"No," I said.

"Gnashing," He said. "Like flares used to indicating you are in trouble."

"Although I imagine flares going off in your mouth would be painful, I have to ask, what does that have to do with the pain I am bearing?" I questioned.

"It shows which way you are inclined to go," He said.

"Go where?" I asked.

"To retaliate or hide," He said. "When faced with adversity, My children tend to go one of two ways. They want to hide under the covers to avoid future confrontation, or they rally up their frustration and form an attack."

I knew that in my situation this was true. Recently someone accused me of something I felt I had not done and after, he talked to me, I retreated to the covers to hide my head. I didn't want to deal with the others involved because I didn't want additional pain. But if I was a gambling person—and I am not—I would bet that His use of gnashing meant I must have retaliated instead of hibernating.

"Why did I choose different options, going to retaliate in one circumstance and then hide in the other?" I asked.

"It has to do with your walk with Me," He said.

"Really?" I asked.

"When you were younger, you were not walking with Me, so you did as the world would do—you took matters into your own hands. Now you are strong in Me, so you go hide."

"That does not seem right," I said, "I mean that walking strong with You makes me hide parts of myself."

"Exactly!" He shouted with glee. "Walking with Me should have you in the middle, not defensive, yet not withdrawing. This happens when My children learn about their incorrect ways. They lean toward the other end of the spectrum. I don't want them to feel as if they have to hide their heads in the sand. I want them to lift their heads up and know I have their backs."

"Lord," I said, "that makes perfect sense, but how do we get there? The middle ground I mean?"

"I have the answer," He said with confidence.

"Please tell," I asked.

"Knowing who you are in me," He said with a big grin on His face. "If you know in your heart whose and what you are, then you can deflect any words and actions while standing in the middle ground. No need for hiding or retaliating."

"Hmmm," I said, "honestly I believe what He said, but I knew it had to be time consuming."

"Well," He asked, "is it worth it? That is the question that only My children can answer for themselves. I can tell you and I can send others to confirm that it is, but the final answer solely rides on the individual."

After serious thought, I knew it would be worth it. I had seen the transformation He had performed in my life so far, and I knew I could not go back to the old me. "That just isn't an option, so ahead it is," I replied.

"Going ahead," He said.

YOU CAN'T MOVE FORWARD LOOKING BACKWARD

"You can't go forward if you keep looking backward," He said.

I knew we had discussed that apostle Paul said to forget what was behind and to look forward, but I wasn't sure if that is what He meant.

"I am talking about continually looking back to the point you are not living in your future," He commented.

"But Lord, the future is not yet here," I said.

"Yes, it is," He said. "On that cross, your future was settled, but My children live as if they are in pre-cross times."

"Oh, that is good," I said. "Not that we live that way, but how you described it," I explained.

"Good or not, it is not the way the cross was meant to be exercised. My children have all they need at their fingertips, yet choose to settle for the scraps the world chooses to hand them," He said.

I was intrigued. "Lord," I asked, "can we sit?" I knew this was going to be very interesting and wanted my undivided attention on His words.

"Certainly," He answered. "Hmmm, where shall we go?" He asked as He scratched His head. "I know," He said after a few minutes, "the bowling alley."

"Are you sure?" I said with concern. "Won't it be hard to hear each other because of all the noise?"

"Exactly," He replied.

"Why would You take us to a place to talk that You know ahead of time is going to interfere with our conversation?" I asked.

"Yes, why would you?" He asked, turning the question to me.

"Excuse me?" I said confused.

"Why would My children come to me in the middle of a party of cheering for their favorite football team?" He said.

"Oh," I interrupted, "is this where we get to use the Colts as an example now?"

He laughed, but went on with His question. "As I was saying, where they are cheering for their favorite team and want to have a conversation. Please do not get Me wrong, I can speak during a game or during quiet time, but for a heart-to-heart, we need quiet time alone together."

I understood. It had been during our one-on-one time, just He and I, that I had experienced some of the most profound revelations that changed my heart.

"Isn't that what we are going for here…" He asked. "…a heart like mine?"

"Yes, Lord," I answered.

"So, how can you learn about My heart with the business of the world in your ear?" He asked.

He made a very valid point.

"What are we aiming for here, I mean with our hearts?" I asked.

"Put your heart in My hands," He began. "That's the Potter and clay."

"What do our hearts look like to You?" I asked.

"A green meadow where everything is flourishing," He replied. "The air is filled with happiness. Colors are vibrant and sounds are clear."

I saw a vision. A vision of trash. A river that is over-taken with pollutants until it stops flowing.

"Hardened hearts eventually die," He said. "This is the saddest of all because it could have been stopped. After the cross, no one should suffer this. I need workers who are not afraid of hard work, intense labor, or getting wet when plucking the trash from others' lives."

I saw a man in a jumpsuit on the side of the road with one of those poles that they use to pick up trash.

"They should not be concerned with other people seeing them," the Lord said. "Man sees the outside; I see inside. It is beautiful and harmonious."

"How do we get there?" I asked. "Lord, I want to go on a journey with You...with our hearts joined."

"I will take you. Don't rush it, enjoy it," He said.

"What am I missing about our hearts?" I asked.

"Me," He replied, "the key is communication, the missing piece is Me. I tell you things you do not know about Me and yourself. When we talk, your heart condition is revealed, and then you are prepared to see more clearly and hear more sensitively."

"Help me relay what You are saying. I will try," I said. "Will You help me? It's just...I'm finally with You. It's been such a long journey. I have never felt so much love in my life. Thank You."

"I am always with you," He assured me. "We will do this together."

-CHAPTER 29-

Parenting—
All in a Day's Work

Train a child in the way he should go, and when he is old he will not turn from it (Proverbs 22:6).

"Lord, it's daytime and I'm already worried about bedtime. I'm so afraid of getting in trouble. Even when I know I didn't do anything wrong," I admitted.

"Do you?" He asked.

"Do I what?" I replied.

"Know you didn't do anything wrong?" He questioned.

"I think so, but now I'm not sure," I admitted. The question alarmed me. I wasn't expecting it. I sure was hoping so. As I began to cry, I felt His arms wrap around my shoulder and embrace me lovingly. "I want to do right, Lord. I really do."

"Honey, I know you do," He said with a comforting tone. "This confusion comes from being told you were wrong, but not what you did wrong. Parents mean well, but if they are not clear themselves, they don't know how to pass it on. It is that generational thing again. Somewhere communication broke down between Me and the parent, and then the parent and the child. Raise children in the way that that they should go and they will return. There is so much confusion when the way they are trained is not *to* Me but *around* Me," He explained.

"I think I understand, but I'm not sure. I mean, about the *around* part," I said.

"Too many parents fear Me, but don't believe in Me. So, they teach their children to be afraid of Me—not to come to Me. It can become a mess to untangle," He said.

"How does that explain my not understanding what I did wrong, but just that I was wrong?" I asked.

"If parents teach children My way, they will know what is right; therefore, they will know if they do something wrong," He explained.

"That is brilliant. Knowing the difference sure would make it less confusing. OK, but what about grownups like me who are lost now?" I questioned with excitement.

"First, recognize that you are still that child to Me," He said, "and that I can still teach you the right way."

"Wonderful!" I shouted. "What a great opportunity to still be able to learn. What about the fear of making someone angry if you do wrong?" I asked.

"That is a deep subject," He said. "Are you ready?"

"I think so. You tell me," I said with a little hesitancy.

"Deep down inside there is a pile of rejection," He began.

"Why do You call it a pile?" I asked.

"Because it is not pretty. It has been heaped upon, rejection after rejection, sometimes accumulating more than you consciously remember. But your heart remembers it," He added.

"Lord, Lord," I asked, "how do I change my heart?"

"You don't change your heart, you repair it," He stated. "The fact that the rejection happened feels true to you, whether it was realistic rejection or not. We must mend that heart. That is My Son's specialty."

The sound of His voice and sweet memory of His presence came back. Oh, He is so worth waiting for. I drifted off. *He is so dreamy,* I thought.

"Dena, come back to Me," He said, waving His hands in front of my face.

"Sorry," I said as I came back to our conversation. "You were saying about Jesus," I said.

"He binds up what is broken and mends what was bruised," He said proudly.

"Why bind?" I asked. "But wait," I interrupted, "before that, what about the person who gets angry at you when you didn't do anything wrong? I really need to know."

"Sweetie, I am getting to that," He assured me. "But to make you feel better, first you have to know what really is right and wrong. That satisfies the *did I do something wrong question,* then you must deal with the fear of rejection," He explained.

"Fear? I thought we were talking about being rejected," I said, surprised.

"We are," He answered, "one naturally follows the other. When someone is rejected, it leaves a sting, a pained heart. My children, understandably, do not want to feel that way again, so they go into stealth mode."

"What? Wait a minute...did You say 'stealth mode'?" I asked.

"Yes," He said, beginning to laugh. "I know you think that is funny," He added.

He was right. It was from a television character my family found hilarious. It is so funny, but to hear Him reference its humor makes it even funnier.

"But Lord isn't this a serious matter to all of a sudden make a joke?" I questioned.

"No, it is the perfect time," He replied. "Taking what others say when it is not constructive or encouraging should be laughed off. Now, I said laughed *off,* not laughed *at.* Two wrongs do not make a right," He said.

At the same time we looked at each other and said, "But two lefts do." We laughed until we cried. That is another thing our family enjoys, the contemporary Christian music group Relient K. Their album titled *Two Lefts Don't Make a Right, but Three Do,* is one of our favorites.

"You really *do* know us," I said.

"I pay attention," He said, winking.

"Rejection hurts, there is no doubt about it, but putting the source into perspective and then..." He stopped suddenly and then said, "...let Me ask you instead. What would be next?"

"Come to you," I answered with some apprehension.

"Bingo!" He yelled. "That pile can be hauled away by Jesus binding it up. But as new situations arise that make you feel rejected, don't panic. Come to Me and let Me show you the truth. My awesome Partner, the Holy Spirit, is great at letting you know if you have stepped into an arena that may be wrong. Learn to listen and step out or better yet, don't step," He concluded.

"I have to be honest, I still feel a little nervous. I love my husband, and I don't want him or anyone I care for to be angry at me," I admitted.

"That is good," the Lord said, "because it shows you love them and you care. But let Me ask you a question," He said.

"OK," I agreed, as I laughed a little.

"What is so funny?" He asked.

"You asked if you could ask a question by asking a question," I answered.

"Yes," He said beginning to laugh, "that is funny. You got it," He added.

"Got what?" I questioned.

"What I illustrated earlier," He said. "You can laugh even though we are having a serious conversation. Sometimes it even makes it easier to handle," He said.

I laughed and agreed.

"So," He continued, "do you feel any guilt?"

"Wow, as a matter of fact, I do," I answered. "Why do I feel this guilt?" I asked.

"Often when children are told they have done something wrong, there is a shadow of guilt that is served with the punishment," He explained.

"Lord, why do you use the word *punishment*?" I questioned.

"Isn't that what you are secretly afraid of?" He asked. "Hypothetically, let us say, what if someone you care for does get angry at you; are you not most worried about what they will do, what the punishment will be?" He said.

A light bulb the size of a cantaloupe came on in my head. "You are so beyond right," I shouted. "Oh my goodness, this is unbelievable," I shouted.

"Children are told they are wrong and a punishment follows. The issue develops when they are not sure what they did wrong, or worse, how to do it right. They end up spending their adulthoods bobbing and weaving trying to be perfect, so they won't mess up again. But how can they not mess up...none are perfect? They are racing a race they cannot win; nor were they ever asked to even sign up," He stated.

I knew that saying, but I'm not sure to what You are referencing, I thought.

"They bob back and forth not sure who will get mad at what and then weave the punishment. It is very tiring to try to keep from being wrong so you don't get in trouble," He said.

"What hit the nail on the head for me was not knowing the right way," I realized.

"Very true," He agreed. "My adults need to teach our children the only way—My way. Anything less will only confuse and separate the family."

"Why separate, Lord?" I questioned.

"I will send my coins to show the little ones My ways, and hopefully they will learn. The family doesn't like this instruction. But it is necessary. I want my families back," He added. "And for that to happen, the chains that have kept them captive must be broken. That starts with learning and applying the Truth. It could all be avoided if they were taught the Truth from the beginning," He said boldly.

"Lord, I pray that will happen," I added.

"Me too, child," He agreed.

"We still have to deal with the fear of the punishment. Are you ready?" He asked.

Somehow I thought this was the part He originally asked me about before. "Yes," I said with confidence. I was not sure where that burst of confidence came from, but I was going to run with it while it was here.

"I want you to think of the one thing you fear the most of happening," He said.

"Man, Lord, You don't waste any time," I said.

"No, I don't," He agreed. "It has been long enough. The longer we wait, the more it has a chance to grow. So go," He said, pretending to press a stopwatch.

"OK," I said. "Off the top of my head, I fear being left," I said.

"OK, next question," He said. "Think of someone who, by leaving you, caused you to hurt," He asked.

"The first person who comes to mind is my grandmother. I don't understand that because You showed me her leading the choir," I stated.

"That gave you peace about her passing, but not for the pain of losing her," He said compassionately.

I was silent. His words were so true. The onion came to my mind. This must be the layer He and the others have been talking about.

"It is, child," He said. "I wish it was one layer and the core is exposed. Unfortunately, one painful event can sprout many painful emotions. This is why it is so important to stick with the process. Little by little the healing unfolds," He reassured.

"Well, I hope it unfolds quickly before I flop down," I chuckled.

He joined in my laughter.

"I love our laughter time," I said. I love to hear Him laugh.

MORE THAN LILIES IN THE VALLEY

"I could hardly wait until our time today," I began. "I have been pondering over in my head this fear of punishment that You were talking to me about yesterday. You were absolutely right. So, where do we go from here?" I asked.

"Let's start from the beginning," He suggested. "You know I like to do that so we cover all the bases. I believe if My children know all of the facts, then they are equipped to make the best decisions. It is evil that sets to conceal," He said. "Sin is twofold: one, it binds or ties up the person; two, it separates Me from that person."

"Lord," I interrupted, "but what *is* sin, what does it do?"

"Very nice," He stated. "It is..." and then He stopped, taking a moment to pause. "Let Me put it this way; throughout My Word I have given you examples of right and wrong ways to handle situations and people. In many instances, I have spelled it out plainly. I think it is very important to make things clear. Confusion comes when things are left to randomness. For example, the Ten

Commandments," stopping to take a deep breath then continuing, as if to be thinking of His choice of words, "they…"

"An image of Moses standing on a mountaintop with the stone tablets held high in the air with lightning striking does come to my mind," I admitted.

"There it is," He finally spoke. "That vision, although true in sight, is not all in interpretation. I had some very undisciplined children roaming around at the bottom of that mountain. I needed to get their attention. They were not listening to Me or respecting the words Moses was saying."

"Wow, that seems so much clearer now. Please go on," I said.

"The problem now is everyone is terrified of the Ten Commandments. I don't use fear and intimidation to win My children…I apply love and forgiveness. Those Commandments are to give My children consistency," He said.

"Consistency?" I asked.

"Yes, remember yesterday when we were talking about not knowing what is right or wrong and how confused you were?" He asked.

"Yes, I remember," I said.

"The Commandments take the guessing out of it," He said. "They are black and white, no room for misunderstanding; or at least I thought. The words are misunderstood, because the love behind them somehow has gotten replaced with intimidation. It is as some of My own Body uses My words to hit My children over the head. No wonder they don't come to Me. Would you want to spend time with someone who may slam condemnation over your head at any time?" He asked.

"Honestly, Lord," I said, "I wouldn't. There are enough here who already do that."

"I am a fair God. That is why I am the only One who should judge," He stated.

Hmmm, I thought, *that word—judge.*

"Here we go again," He said. "Judge is only bad if you have done something wrong. That is why there should be rejoicing over judgment. If you have been faithful, notice not perfect, then when judgment falls, you are sitting pretty. Judgment gives you the freedom to let what others do roll off your back because you know I am going to take care of it. It was supposed to be a blessing, not the curse that it has been twisted into. Again, I am a fair God." I heard His voice raise. "I do everything—even judgment—out of love. Let Me ask you a question," He said.

"OK," I said.

"If you had children who were doing something that you had told them not to do because it would hurt them, would you not correct them?" He asked.

"Yes, I'm sure I would," I replied.

"That is all I am trying to do. I tell you what is right or wrong and the consequences, nothing is left to the imagination," He stated. "This is what good parents do, too. They, without guilt, tell a child what they expect and what will happen if that expectation is not met. When parents waver in what they expect, or what the consequences will be, the child gets confused. Children cannot keep up with or understand what they are to do or not do, and they fear punishment because they do not know how severe it will be. Does that make sense?" He asked.

"Perfect sense," I said.

"Dear," He called me.

"Yes, Lord?" I replied.

"I know you have a question," He said. "Why don't you spit it out?"

"Lord, You tell us not to sin, then You are faithful to forgive us if we turn from that sin after asking for forgiveness," I started.

"So far I am with you," He stated.

OK, I thought, *stop stalling.* "The man at the well who you told to pick up his mat and walk…" I blurted out.

"Yes, I know him well…no pun intended," He laughed.

"You told him that he was healed and not to sin again or something worse may happen to him. What is that something worse?" I finally got out.

"First I want you to know this was not a threat, it was a fact I wanted him to be aware of. If My children continue to sin, it can be seven times worse. That merely means it is harder to come out of a sin once you go back to it," He explained.

"Why, Lord?" I asked.

"Because it grows," He stated. "The more you give in to that sin, then the more power it has over you. Do you understand?" He asked.

"Yes, that makes sense," I replied.

"Anything else?" He asked.

"I'm not sure. I don't feel like it is complete. Like something is missing," I said.

"There is," He said.

"What is it, Lord?" I asked.

"My Son, Jesus, you cannot talk about sin, forgiveness, and power without the remembrance of the cross," He said.

Yes, I thought, *I had heard the stories and felt the grace many times in my life. But what was He alluding to?* "What is it, Lord; what is it about the cross that is missing?" I asked.

"My people," He stated.

"I don't understand…Your people?" I questioned.

"The cross was an act of love, yet they don't come," He said.

I still don't understand.

He stopped and looked away as if frustrated, trying to put it in a way I would understand. "Do you know why you and so many others are having trouble understanding?" He asked.

"No, but I would like to," I said.

"Because it is old hat to you," He answered. "You have seen the play and read the children's books, but you haven't felt the heartbeat of the Word," He said.

Wow. I was silent. *I never thought about it that way.* "Please go on," I asked.

"My Son made a world where dead hearts could come alive again. They were bound and entangled by the mistakes they had made, but He made a way to be forgiven. The Commandments I gave would be impossible to follow if it had not been for Him, His sacrifice," He said.

"I don't fully understand," I said.

"There would be no second chances to do the things we had done wrong; right. It would have been one strike and you are out. Do you get that?" He insisted.

I could tell His blood was starting to boil because His face was turning a light shade of red.

"The very hateful way that people are viewing is exactly ten times how it would have been without the cross. The farther you move away from the cross, the harder your heart gets. That is the direction the world is headed. Get to the cross!" He cried out. "Rekindle your love for Jesus. Time is ticking, and I do not want to see anyone perish." His head fell into His hands. As He raised His head, He asked, "Dena, would you want to lose a child to a mistake he or she made?"

"No, Father, I wouldn't."

"Me either. That is the cross, the mistake forgiver. The place where wildflowers grow and birds sing. Fresh starts and new birth. I garden the souls of the pained. If they will just come," He said, hoping. "Everyone will produce fruit, good or bad. Respectful or sinful, it is your choice. I am the Gardener who will tend to and water you, but if you refuse to grow, well, that choice is yours."

I wasn't completely sure what I had learned this morning, but one thing I knew about God's word; it grew. As the days passed, I received revelation and great understanding. We are fields of fresh soil, which, if tilled and handled with care, can grow into gardens of fruit. Fruit unlike what the world grows, of character and righteousness. I wanted that fruit, rather...I wanted to display that fruit.

His light red face was not of anger, but urgency mixed with concern—a loving heart for His children. *He loves us,* I thought. *I hope we get that.*

CHAPTER 30

My First Bedtime Story

He makes me lie down in green pastures, He leads me beside quiet waters (Psalm 23:2).

While taking my evening bath, I suddenly remembered God's promise of a bedtime story that He had made earlier. Jezebel popped into my head. My first reaction was: "You promised, no scary stories."

He began, "No, I never promised such a thing. That happens a lot," He continued. "My children say I promised something that I never said, but we will address that later. As far as tonight, I want to tell you about a little girl who was from a broken home. Her parents worshiped idols and spent little time with her. She, like all My girls, wanted to be loved by their father. This posed a problem because her father was so wrapped up in his dead gods that she was neglected in her critical years. To make matters worse, she did not know of Me and that I would not leave her Fatherless."

This isn't a scary story, I thought. *This is sad.*

"Yes, it is; but it goes deeper than sad, it gets downright mean," He stated. "Her hurt and sadness grew into hate and revenge. She wanted others to pay for her suffering, and she was out to see it so."

"That's not good," I said.

"No, it is not," He said. "She wouldn't listen to Me or others I brought her way. She terrorized My children and abused her husband. I called her to be his helper, but all she did was help herself to his life. She wreaked havoc wherever she went with no apparent remorse. But I knew her heart." He stopped for a minute to reflect.

"Yes," He continued, "I knew her heart. It started as hurt, but grew into a monster full of anger. She was out of control and not looking back. Or shall I say, she was running from her pain, but it was with her everywhere she went."

"Lord," I interrupted, "You do know what people say about her today, don't you?" I asked.

"Yes, they call her controlling, manipulative, and jealous," He pointed out. "I am not denying those to be the case. However, I do hope that My children will focus more on how she got there instead of so much of what she did once she was there."

"Are you saying we should not be concerned about a Jezebel spirit?" I asked bluntly.

"No, what I am saying is to bring your hurts to Me before they take over your life. As far as the Jezebel spirit, be cautious, but not fearful. Elijah was fearful, no, downright afraid, but if he had come to Me, I could have saved him from hiding. All I want is others to recognize that she was once a little girl with big dreams and aspirations. She played in the sand and splashed in the water just like many of My children today. Her dysfunctional family started her off on the wrong foot, but I was there to change her path." His head dropped as He continued, "But she would not hear of it. I don't want to see any others fed to the dogs. That is not the abundant life set before them."

I meditated on His words for a minute. I had never given her a second thought except for the horrible things she had done. I felt sorry for her now. Her life didn't have to be like that. Why didn't she listen to God or the many He brought her way? "Why?" I asked.

"She was eaten up inside," He remarked. "Where a precious, thriving heart once beat, lived a shell. When people are given over to their sin, it is hard to get them back."

"Why, Lord?" I questioned.

"I will always be right there waiting to forgive, but they must turn. She never turned," He said.

I stopped for a moment and wondered why such a sad story right before bedtime. As I pondered this the answer came to my mind. "Pray," I said out loud.

"Yes," He replied. "I know that as you and your husband lay your head to your pillows, you pray. I have brought the names of some of My wayward adults to your mind. Pray. You do not know where they are in their hearts, only I do, but I ask you to pray. Don't give up on them. They have not met the dogs yet."

"Now, I lay me down to sleep, I pray the Lord my soul to keep, if I should die before I wake, I pray the Lord my soul to take. Why, Lord, did that prayer come so specifically?" I asked.

"Because those I am asking you to pray for were wronged in their childhood. They wanted to play, but circumstances begged to differ. Pray as a child for them. They are still children in My eyes," He explained.

There was complete silence as I thought about them as children. My heart was affected by this image.

"That is why I have asked you to look at them as such," He said. "As adults there is a tendency to be softer, more sympathetic to little ones versus adults. Remember, they were children once, and in many ways you all are still."

I don't know whether to be offended or thankful, I thought.

"Thankful," He replied. "Coming as a child is a blessing; living tormented as a child is painful. To become a child healed of hurt, the child must let Me help. I want to help," He stated.

I was getting frustrated, one because I didn't fully understand, and two because I felt sorry for them.

"Slow up, little one; now you understand how they feel." He said. "They are frustrated because they do not understand and because they don't believe anyone feels sorry for them. They are children trapped in adult bodies. When they allow childhood pains to be dealt with as adults, then they will be free to be children. Does that make sense?" He asked.

"Yes, Lord," I answered. "To have fun like a child, you have to be rid of bondages that hold you back."

"Yes, that is the sin; it binds them," He said. "So will you please pray for them?" He asked.

I knew that I would, but something was troubling me. "Lord, You know that the ones you have asked me to pray for are some who hurt me the most," I stated.

"Yes, and we will deal with that pain," He said. "For now, remember them as innocent children who through no fault of their own were abused."

I didn't like those words, but I wasn't going to ask for details.

"You can ask," He said. "I won't tell you their business, but I will tell you what abuse means to Me."

Wow, such directness. It kind of shocked me.

"When it comes to My children, abuse is anything that does not reflect My love," He said boldly.

That seemed pretty simple, but I thought how many would not like to hear such boldness.

"That is for Me to contend. I love My children, period. I make no excuse for My love," He said. "Dena, I know this is not the *once upon a time* bedtime story you were expecting, but I need My warriors out there praying for everyone, including the ones they fear. And while they are praying, maybe we could talk about why they fear them. Two healings at once. I can run a special," He began to laugh. "I like a two for one."

Boy was I glad to hear the playful tone again.

"Sweetheart," He added, "your once upon a time is in the making. We just have a little work to do in the process."

As He spoke, I thought of all the blessings He had placed upon my life. I am living my happy ever after. I trusted Him. If a sad bedtime story was what He felt necessary, then I would be happy that He wanted to share with me. At some point, I thought I really needed just to be grateful. And that sometime was now.

"There is your happily ever after ending," He said. "And she lived happily ever after. Good night, My child, sweet dreams."

I noticed that I didn't feel panicked or agitated that He had said "sweet dreams." I had a feeling I was going to have them.

"Good night," I said.

-CHAPTER 31-

All That Math Adds Up

Jesus looked at them and said, "With man this is impossible, but not with God; all things are possible with God" (Mark 10:27).

"You can lose sleep over things, not just people," I heard Him say.

"What?" I questioned. I had in fact missed many full nights of sleep over a math class I was currently taking. I hold no bones at telling anyone who will listen how much I do not...no, I have to say *hate* math. Give me an English class or composition of some type, and I'm all over it, but numbers, no thank you.

But how could this be? I wondered. Math was not worth not sleeping. I knew I wanted to do my best and pass the class, but not lose sleep. "How could something of no emotion or breath cause me to wake in a panic?" I asked.

"It has a tie," He answered.

"A tie?" I questioned.

"Yes, it in some way is tied to an emotion," He explained. "Do you remember the donkey that was beaten in the Bible story?" He asked.

"Yes, Balaam beat him three times," I replied.

"Why do you remember?" He asked.

"Because many people, including myself, think it is hilarious that God would use a donkey."

"Yes," He said smiling, "when it comes to iron sharpening iron, I can get very creative. The donkey had a purpose."

"OK," I said with a puzzled look.

"Your math has a purpose?" He continued. "Is it not just to get to the next step in your pursuit," He asked.

"Yes," I agreed. "But I worry I will not do well enough to pass."

"Aha!" He said with excitement. "There is the emotion. An inanimate object has taken on an emotion, your *fear* of not passing. It is alive," He said as if He were Frankenstein.

"Wow, You are so amazing," I said. I wanted to know what to do with this new insight, but I was so amazed with the knowledge I wanted to hang out in it for a moment. Once I closed my jaw that had hung open from this understanding, I asked, "Lord, what do I do?"

"You give it back," He answered. "Once Balaam recognized the donkey was just trying to do its job, he held no animosity toward him. Recognize the math has no ill-will. Has math not served you over the years?" He asked.

"Yes," I said, thinking about the basic need to balance my checkbook and add simple measurements when cooking. That I recognized, but I was still concerned about failing.

"OK then, it is not the math, but the fear that you will not pass," He pointed out. "I want to stop you right there for a moment," He said.

"Yes, Lord," I replied.

"I want to thank you for not avoiding or quitting because of the math," He said. "This happens far too many times in My children's walk. They reach a spot of resistance thinking it is an object that stops them. But if they investigate deeper, they find it is fear. Fear is *not* a heavenly strength," He said bluntly.

That's new, I thought. He had so far only pointed out the heavenly strengths, not ones that were not.

"Fear will strip My children faster than turpentine on a piece of antique wood, and it has the smell to boot," He stated. "I want My children to stand and deliver."

"Deliver?" I questioned. "Lord, that seems like a lot of pressure. I mean, what if I try and fail?"

"Whoa right there," He said. "Have you not learned that you can do the math?"

"Some of it, but to be honest, I haven't mastered it all," I explained.

"OK then, smarty pants," He said, laughing, "what about the relationships with those who have helped you along the way?"

I smiled because I knew what He was getting at. During my math class I had developed bonds not only with my husband, but also with my daughter and son-in-law that far outweigh a grade on a test.

"Yes, My dear, it is about the relationships," He said proudly like a papa bear. "If I wanted you to add, you would add. It is not about the numbers, but the overcoming of fears and loving those you meet. For that, dear one, you have passed."

I blew a sigh of relief. *Would I sleep tonight?* I wondered. Maybe, but one thing was for sure, I knew now that if an object caused me sleepless nights in the future, I was going to the Lord to find out where and why I had given it an emotion.

PEELING AWAY MATH

"That is why you dread math. It is not because you can't do it or don't like math...it is because it brings back painful memories,"

He explained. "Just as I used the donkey, I can use math to peel layers," He stated.

"I don't like journaling on this computer, and I don't like math," I complained.

"Right now you aren't in favor of much of anything," He stated.

"You're right. I'm on the verge of a temper tantrum," I replied.

"Math is not worth all of this fuss. We can and will work through this if you will just calm down and breathe. I've got you," He assured me.

"Then why am I on the verge of tears?" I asked.

"Because it is uncomfortable," He said.

"I saw a little girl. Someone is with her. They are mad at her because they think she made up not feeling well to keep from getting into trouble," I explained.

"You avoid things to keep from making others angry," He said.

"What?" I said.

"You get nervous when you don't understand something be…"

"STOP!" I screamed, interrupting His sentence. "It is not the math; it is all of this stuff it is stirring up."

"Yes, we know that, but you cannot logically walk your way through this," He said. "You are going to have to feel it."

"NOOOOOOO!" I screamed.

"What is it?" He asked, concerned.

"Nobody would listen, and no one would take the time to help me," I cried out.

"Although that may be true, it is deeper than that," He said.

"How deep?" I asked.

"Pretty deep," He responded.

"Please lead," I asked. "I can't do this alone."

"Nor should you," He said. "Go back to the vision of someone accusing the little girl," He directed.

"OK, I'm there."

"What do you see?" He asked me.

"The person is mad. I can tell by the look on their face." I said.

"Was there someone you remember having the a similar expression?" He asked.

"Yes," I said loudly, "a relative who used to help me with my math homework. They would get frustrated and angry at me because I didn't understand what he was trying to show me."

"Look at yourself when you ask your husband to help you," He said redirecting the conversation.

"Yes, I give him that same look," I said sadly.

"Why do you do that?" He asked.

"Because I'm impatient and frustrated because he isn't getting it," I answered.

"That is why they did the same thing to you," He stated.

"So what do we do?" I asked.

"Let Me show you how to stop this pattern," He said. "All patterns are not *big* or shall I say, noticeable. Some are hiding in the crevices. It isn't until a dam breaks that the cracks are noticed. I will see you pass this course, but I want you to learn a new behavior during this final run of Algebra," He said.

"Yeah," I said, "final run!"

Once an incorrect behavior has been revealed, you can begin to learn My way," He began. "I will teach you a new approach; one that does not get angered or frustrated. I want to stop the passing down of unhealthy generational behaviors."

"OK," I said. "This is exciting. What are those approaches?" I asked.

"A good parent doesn't just tell you why to stop, but how as well," He stated. "When you do something like someone else, ask why that person does it that and see if it lines up with My Word."

"That makes perfect sense," I said. "I did hate math, but I thought it was because it was hard for me."

"It is hard for you because it makes you uncomfortable," He explained.

"Are you saying that once the memories are dealt with I will be a wiz at math?" I asked.

"Not necessarily, but at least you will not dread it," He said. "You will be open to learn it because you have no personal ties to it. It will just be math, not hurt."

"Tell me about my math issues," I asked.

"That is what we are doing," He said. "You know of the frustration; now we will chisel away at the causes of that feeling. Do you want to begin?" He asked.

"Yes, I think," I responded.

"What about the anxiety you are feeling now?" He asked.

"Failure. That is what comes to the surface," I said.

"Why are you so afraid of failing?" He asked.

My head fell into my hands as I said, "I will disappoint people."

"Who are you worried about disappointing?" He asked.

I noticed that the first two people who came to my mind were men in my life, and then I noticed that there weren't any women. Yes, there were two in particular.

"What is similar about the two who have come to your mind?" He asked.

"I love them with all of my heart," I said.

"Yes, you do," the Lord agreed.

I began to cry. The thought of letting either one of them down killed me.

"What do you think will happen if you let them down?" He asked.

"Bottom line, they will leave," I answered.

"Child, you cannot live a life trying to keep them in it. Just like they have free will to choose Me or not, they have the same choice with you," He explained.

I knew this; but others had left even though I hadn't done anything to cause it—they chose to leave anyway. I have to watch myself and... "Dang!" I yelled. "I'm tired of this. I just can't do it anymore."

"Do what, dear?" He asked.

"Jump through hoops," I screamed.

"Do you remember the child who was trying to figure out what her parents wanted, yet in her home environment, things were so sporadic she couldn't?" He asked.

"Yes." I nodded.

"That is what you are accustomed to as an adult," He stated. "You are trying to figure out what others want when they probably do not know themselves," He explained.

That makes so much sense. "Money," I blurted out.

"What about it?" He asked.

"My husband handles the money; and if I fail, I have wasted his money," I explained.

"First of all, it's *My* money, not his," He clarified. "We need to work on your view." He asked.

"I am trying to be or do what is necessary to get to a day when I can make it worth his patience," I stated.

"Hmmm," He said. "Make what worth his patience?" He asked.

"Me," I said in a low voice.

"Why do you feel you are not worth it?" He asked with kindness in His voice.

"If I made enough money, wore the right clothes, had a successful book career," I said solemnly. The what if's were too many to count. "What would it take for others to stay?" I wondered.

"Oh," He said with His hand on His chin. "You are worth it to Me. We spin around that same topic a lot," He pointed out.

Yes, He was right, but it wasn't like I wanted to. "Holy Spirit," I began, "what insight can You give me about my need to be worth others putting their time in keeping me?" I noticed He didn't swoop in with a telling costume or a big grin on His face. Instead He just stood there looking into my eyes.

"I see your heart," the Lord said.

There it was; I saw the Holy Spirit as a heart, red and vibrant, but with a sad face.

"He is representing you," the Lord explained. "You are vibrant, but your face is sad. My goal is to get what *I* see to match what *you* see."

"Let's go with Your view," I said with a half giggle.

"Yes, that would be best," He agreed.

I felt defeated. There was so much to conquer to get me straight. Worth, failure, disappointment, and the list seemed to go on and on.

"Don't get discouraged," He said. "We can tackle these one at a time."

"It seems like it will take forever," I admitted.

"I have the time," He said, laughing.

It wasn't funny. I was tired of math and all that came up from it.

"Madam," He said, "this is going to be uncomfortable. I wish different, but if you have a sad face while we work on the vibrant heart, it only makes it take longer and honestly be no fun."

"How could all of this pain be fun?" I questioned.

"Just watch," He said with a grin on His face.

I saw the Holy Spirit doing what looked like a jig. Jumping around and laughing. "How and for goodness' sake why?" I asked.

"Why what?" the Lord asked.

"Why would He do that?" I replied.

"Because it is fun," He answered.

"Oh, fun," I repeated.

"Yes, you should try fun," He said. "I think you would like it. An adult child doesn't know enough fun to overcome the serious."

"You have something there," I said. "Can You teach two things at once?"

"Oh girl, I am so good at multitasking," He said excitedly.

"Great, then let's have fun healing me," I said. I was actually excited. "How can we make my fears of disappointing exciting?" I asked.

"Because I am going to tell you," He said. "You are going to have truth and tah da..."

I heard a drum roll.

"...FREEDOM," He announced with great excitement.

As great as I knew that to be, it was hard to see it through the hurt. Could a child of God get to the point where he or she could sing like the apostle Paul did in prison? I had believed it was available for all His previous children and His current children too, so the answer had to be yes.

"Lord," I said with my chest stuck out and my head held high, "I want to sing in the midst of my prison."

He smiled, "You got it, Baby!"

Season to Love

"Lord," I said, changing the subject, "what about that dream I have that someone I love dearly is dying? Are they going to?" I asked. "I love them. No, Lord, not yet," I screamed. I began to hyperventilate. "NOOOO!" I cried as my hands shook.

"What do I do with this?" I asked. "I want to make sure this is what I think it is. Is she going to die?" I cried out again.

"What do you think it is?" He asked.

"You are preparing us, our family, for her passing?" I asked.

"No, no, My child," He said.

"Are you sure?" I asked trying to calm down.

"Yes, I wanted you to see the difference between someone passing without forewarning and when you do know," He explained.

"Is she OK?" I asked.

"She is fine," He assured me.

"I'm not sure I'm hearing You right," I said.

"No…you are not sure if you trust Me," He said.

"I'm sorry," I said, "this is just so big. I mean, if she is leaving us, I need to tell people so they do not miss the opportunity to talk to or see her," I explained.

"Shouldn't they be doing that anyway?" He asked.

"Yes," I agreed.

"Tell them to love their loved ones, for one day they will come home to Me," He said.

"Lord, what about those who live in fear because they let ones go without loving them?" I asked.

"Guilt," He replied. "It seems we started with that, didn't we?"

"Yes, Father, we did," I agreed.

"There is guilt taken, and then there is guilt given," He replied.

"Please explain," I asked.

"If someone does something to you that is not your fault, but you take their act upon you, then it is a guilt taken. But if you do something that is your responsibility, it is guilt given to yourself. The enemy likes you to get confused about which you are doing because you will be so wrapped up in which one it is that you won't give it to Me. See, I can take the taken or the given. My Son saw to that," He said proudly.

"Thank You, Jesus," I said.

"My children recognize that the cross was for forgiveness, but they don't always remember to bring the repercussions of that sin to the cross," He explained. "It covered it all. When My sweet Son uttered, 'It is finished,' that is exactly what it meant; it is finished. You fill in whatever *it* is to you. If you were on bad terms when someone passed away, that guilt is finished. It is the enemy's pleasure for you not to fully benefit from all of the treasure in those wooden stakes. The body of My Son replaced the sinful body of My Church. Yet they still walk around as if they do not have the answers. All of the questions have been put to rest. What you ask is answered at the cross. I ask you and all of My children, 'What is your *it*'?"

My heart sank as I blankly stared into the distance. I began to mutter, "I didn't tell her goodbye. The night she passed away, I hadn't said goodbye. For years I had blamed others for not telling me she was going to die; but the truth be known, I didn't go in there. Others did. I have carried this guilt for so long." I began to cry hysterically. "I loved her, yet I let her go without saying goodbye. I let her…"

"Child," He said as He put His arm around my shoulder, *"you didn't let her go. I did.* The others thought she might go. Do not take their part on in this play. However, you can give Me your part."

The next thing I knew we were in the room my grandmother last stayed in before she passed away. She was beautiful even though the cancer had wreaked havoc on her body. She was glowing. I saw two beautiful angels perched above her bed. I thought of another special woman who was precious to me. I could see two angels over her bed the day she passed away.

"They do not go alone," He said. "I have special angels that wait and comfort them as I prepare the great feast for their arrival."

I could hear a trumpet blowing in the background. He smiled. "A child has come home. It is a wonderful reunion when they come home."

"What about us left behind?" I asked.

"Oh, dear, you are not left behind; you have angels, too," He explained.

I thought about Sara whom God had allowed me to see. She watches over me at night. She brings great comfort. As I got my thoughts together, still standing outside the room my grandmother was resting in, I noticed green slime in the palm of my hands. I looked at my Father and asked, "What is this?"

"It is the guilt. It has become such a weight that it is oozing from your hands," He explained.

The green mess began to flow between my fingers and drip onto the floor. "We'd better go before I make a mess," I said.

"No, not yet," He said. "Go over to your grandmother," He said.

Softly and slowly, I walked toward the bed. She had a peaceful grin on her face. She was resting. "Grandma," I began, "I am so sorry I did not tell you goodbye. I miss you so much." I looked over my shoulder to see my Father still standing there. When I looked back, I saw other people in the room. They were the individuals I had blamed for not telling me.

I heard the Lord say, "You know what to do."

I began to walk around the room and one by one I asked forgiveness from God for blaming them. I gave Him my guilt. I began to cry because the weight of it all was wearing on me. I put my head in my hands, not caring the slime was still there.

When I lifted my head, we were back in the temple. I knew I was to go to the suitcases. There it was: a green bag the color of the slime with GUILT written in black, bold letters. I heard a loud POP. It startled me, and I jumped back. It was the guilt suitcase. It had flung open.

"You had it sealed shut for so long, it took great strength for you to open it. I am proud of you," He said.

"I noticed the elephant's foot had lifted some from my head," I said.

"Yes, you have owned your part and did not justify it by what others did or did not do," He said. "In a perfect time someone should have told you, but you had a choice to go. No one in this case is to blame. All were trying to survive a very painful time. The cross gives grace, but My children have to be willing to go forward. Let yourself go and those you brought along," He advised.

I turned back to the suitcase. I hated that bag. I went over to kick it, but the Lord stopped me.

"Please do not do that," He asked. "You are hurt; that is under the guilt and blame, but you must realize that it is coming out in the form of anger. Would you like Me to show you what to do?"

"Yes, I would," I answered.

"Then come with Me," He motioned.

I followed Him to a suitcase labeled JOY. It was the most beautiful mint green and pale yellow that I had ever seen. "Why these colors, Lord?" I asked.

"The mint represents My healing water diluting the ugly green from the slime," He explained.

"And the yellow?" I asked.

"It is the diluted bright yellow of coward now transformed into pale, calming courage," He said. "You had been afraid to face the truth, but when you go deep, the bright yellow and the dark green are softened by My well."

The sight of that suitcase was absolute joy. It made me smile.

"Put your hands in the suitcase," He motioned. "Wash that sin and despair away."

I leaned down and bent over the bag, as I dipped my hands in the water, I noticed two perfectly manicured and soft sets of hands in the water beside mine. I looked up to see two angels helping me wash off the slime.

I looked over my shoulder.

Our eyes met and He said, "I have angels to help those, as you said, left behind. If My precious children only knew the help they have at their disposal every day, they would fear no one but Me."

I stood up, and one of the angels handed me a white, soft hand towel. As I dried my hands, I asked Him, "Fearing You, isn't that what You wanted them to understand about You?"

"No, no, Dear," He replied, "I didn't want to be the villain that the Body has begun to see Me as, but they do need to fear Me."

"What is the difference?" I asked. As I asked the question, I noticed I felt lighter. I looked at my hands to see that there was no more ugly, green slime on my hands or the towel. I smiled.

"There are some suitcases you want access to…but not to carry," He said. "Joy is one of them."

I loved that joy suitcase. I would have to remember to visit it again.

"Villains seek to fear people for control," He began. "I have given the control to you because I want you to fear Me out of love. Because you love Me so much, you would fear to lose Me. Think about good parents. They build a relationship with their child by teaching. That teaching comes by example. Over time that child loves the parents and comes to desire not to hurt them because of that strong bond."

"This sounds a lot like the 'much is given; much is expected' principle," I said.

"Very similar except the reference part," He answered.

"That word always confuses me," I stated.

"Yes, it can be cumbersome, and you know I like simple," He said, grinning.

We both laughed.

"*Reference* means you are aware of what I can do, but out of your love for Me, you do not want to see Me have to do that," He explained.

"Wow, I like that," I shouted. "I know You can stop the earth today, but I don't want to cause You pain because I love you so much. Love the Lord so much I fear Him. I can live with that."

We both laughed again.

-CHAPTER 32-

Trust

Trust in the LORD with all your heart; and lean not on your own understanding (Proverbs 3:5).

"I want to trust people," I cried. I really do. No such luck on the sleep last night. I hadn't seen this one coming.

"Oh, I did. I opened a can of worms," He said.

"What do you mean?" I asked.

"It is that math again," He said.

"Yes, I want to trust them to do what they have agreed to do," I said. I had realized that during the night. How can I live until the end of the semester waiting to see if they fail me? I can catch myself if I wait until the last minute. "What do I do?" I pleaded. "Please help me, Lord. They mean well and want to help, but I can't seem to let myself let them."

"Ones before are dictating those current," He said.

He was right. I had suffered at the hands of those who said they loved me, but ended up bailing out at the last minute. No, let me be blunt, they lied. They said one thing and then did another. All at the expense of my last-minute scrounging around to catch up the time I had lost. The responsibilities of each event still had to be done; it just now would fall on me to play catch up, race, and angrily panic. "I am furious!" I screamed.

"You know what we need to do first," He said.

"Yes," I replied. "I know that anger is only a protection." I was well aware that it served no current purpose, although it might have been legitimate at the initial time. "I don't want to be angry anymore," I said. "I want to be like Moses and allow others to help."

"I find that interesting that you brought up Moses, because he would be a great example of letting go," He said. "But on the other hand, let's talk about Pharaoh first."

"Why him?" I asked.

"Because he wouldn't let My people go," He answered.

"Hmmm, You have my attention," I replied.

"He wanted what he wanted and at whatever the expense," He began. "That was his first downfall. Others are not there to use for your gain or benefit. He did not see that. He wanted to rule to secure his own needs. Where Moses wanted to rule to serve *My* needs."

Wow, that hits hard but truthful, I thought.

"Why do *you* want to serve?" He asked.

I didn't completely understand.

"This math, why do you want this math class?" He asked, clarifying His position.

"We talked about this before. I want to further my education to help others," I stated.

"Bingo!" He yelled.

"Isn't allowing others to be part of the math helping?" He asked. "Let Me explain. Moses knew by the insight gleaned from his father-in-law that others had callings too. For him to hoard all of those responsibilities to himself, he not only wore himself out, but denied others their opportunity to walk their path. Not to mention Moses would be distracted from his path. It took them all to make it happen. Moses let My people go. Pharaoh, on the other hand, feared things not getting done his way."

Oh, I thought, *He hit on something there.* I had watched those willing to help do it their way, and it made me a nervous wreck.

"There are more ways than yours to accomplish the task," He said.

He was right, but what did I do? "I need the help and really want to let them," I said.

"Then let them," He said bluntly. "Pharaoh ran people off by his need to keep them. Moses trained them and then responded only if they needed him. One ruled with an iron fist while the other loved with a cushioned glove. Which would you rather have stroke you?" He asked.

"The soft glove sounds much nicer," I admitted.

"May I tell you something?" the Lord asked gently.

"Yes, of course," I replied.

"You know how you hated the saying about the onion, but are you growing to love it?" He asked.

I nodded yes.

"You will grow to appreciate math, too. If you hang in there, you will look back on this class in gratitude because you will see your transformation from Pharaoh to Moses. That is, if you let yourself go," He said.

I had commented that I would not let myself let others. "How could I possibly with the chance I might have to pick up the pieces later?" I asked.

"That is a very good question, and many wrestle with it," He replied. "Let's talk about your alternatives. You are tired, sleepless, and if we are honest, you are stressing the ones around you. I don't want to see relationships ruined over a book of equations," He stated.

Nor do I, I thought. "Then what is the magic remedy?" I asked.

"There is no magic potion, nor would I allow such a trick," He commended.

"I open your eyes, you see, and we peel," He stated. "This is the way of healing. I sent many eye-opening events and people to Pharaoh. He was hardheaded. Some he saw, while others he chose to ignore. I continued until he broke. Not because I wanted him to suffer, but because the very opposite—I wanted him to heal. In his stubbornness, he held himself back from letting go and brought a lot of unnecessary plagues upon himself and others."

And others, I thought.

"Yes, the ones around him felt the wind and the locust just as he did," He stated. "My people who are free do not want to be around those who will not let them go. Isn't that the very essence of our time lately…to stop controlling?" He asked.

Dang, He hit the nail on the head again. I had seen His vision of how a controlling spirit is rampant in the Body and prayed diligently to see it dissolved. How then could I stop holding those back from their walks and keep from hindering my own? "What do I do?" I asked humbly.

"This is not as much a realization about others as it is a truth about us," He said. "If I may be blunt," He began, "the hard fact is not the trusting of others as it is the not trusting of Me. I have called you to love your brothers and sisters and trust Me with all your heart. What part is missing?" He asked.

He had the ability to point out something so harsh, but my heart would receive it in love. I wanted that. I wanted to speak such facts in a way that would be delivered with a cushioned hand.

"I don't like to get off-track," He said, "but I feel I need to here. You, too, can deliver such truth in a gentle way when you do not have the need to solve the person's problems with that delivery," He explained.

He doesn't miss a thing, I thought. I have had many conversations with ones I love where I walked away frustrated because they left with their problem.

"It is not yours to solve. That is My job," He said. "If you are the solution, then where does that leave Me?" He asked.

His question radiated in my mind. Wow, it wasn't for me to mend the problems of the world. "What did Moses do?" I asked.

"He gave them the facts and let them choose their actions," He answered.

"I love that," I cheered.

"While, you are cheering," He began, "let's go back to My last question. Trust Me with all your heart; what part is missing?" He repeated.

"I don't know," I replied.

"Very good," He rejoiced. "You don't, but when your eyes are open, we can examine what part or parts are missing. Hidden in the onion layers are areas that have yet to be revealed…that are missing trust in Me. When we peel the layers, there are opportunity to replace that missing part with trust."

I had not looked at the peeling as an opportunity. It made it seem a little more enjoyable.

"Where there was a layer of misplaced trust in others, we can replace it with the only true trust, that which was meant to be— with Me."

"So," I began, "it is a process."

"Yes, My child, it is," He agreed. "My children are too hard on themselves. They believe that trust should be instantaneous, and when it is not, they understandably feel defeated. The cross conquered the old heart, but time with Me reveals it. Give yourself grace just as I am asking you to give those willing to help you some, too."

"Lord, I really want to," I insisted, but I could feel the fear rising up in my stomach of the original question, "What if they fail me and I end up failing the class? How do I live each day waiting and hoping it works out?"

"Take a trip with Me," He said.

Willingly, I took His hand and we began to walk.

"Do you recognize this place?" He asked.

I did. I had just received a call from a local college. I had been accepted. I was excited.

"Do you remember what happened next?" He asked.

"I was told I could not go

"It is all good," He answered. "Did we not discuss that the disappointments of the past now hindered your present?"

Yes, we had, I thought. "What do we do now?" I asked.

"If you are willing, we explain the past so the future can move on," He said.

"Very well," I said, still angry.

"Pick up the phone," He said.

I stood there holding the phone.

"What did the lady say from the college?" He asked me.

"I needed to take the entrance exam," I answered.

"Can I be honest with you?" He asked.

"Yes, please," I said.

"You would not have passed," He said.

I stood in silence.

"Do you know why?" He asked.

I nodded no.

"Because of math," He answered.

"Promises should have been kept," the little girl in me screamed, her loud voice covering her broken heart. Over and over she had worked hard, only to be let down. "When will it stop?" she cried and stomped. "When will it stop?" The adult rationalized the fact she would not have passed the entrance exam, but the little girl was far from satisfied. She was angry, hurt, and in need of a temper tantrum.

"I can help you with that," He said.

Part of me wanted to comfort the little girl, while the other wanted her to stop crying about it. I don't know why, but that made me laugh.

"I am glad you are taking it so well," He laughed. "The issues you are currently having with math would have still been there, and you did not have the tools, nor did you have Us to help you overcome them. I say all that to say this; yes you were let down, but there are always other factors involved. That is why our time together is so important. I am the only One who knows all of the factors and circumstances."

I had to admit I had a peace about it.

"I do not only peel layers, but I do it in a specific order," He said. "I will not give My children more than they can handle."

"Wait...I was no longer angry, but flooded with a desire to cry.

"Come now, Dear," the Lord said as He embraced me in a tender hug. "Now we can peel away the hurt."

"What do You mean *now?*" I asked.

"Before, you were angry, and that kept you from feeling the hurt. It walled you in while also walling Me out," He explained.

THE WALL

I felt vulnerable on the inside, but safe on the outside...only because of His hug.

That vulnerability opened the door into the fortress of a brick and mortared wall I built for protection. "May I come in?" He asked.

Crying, I responded, "Please."

"Goodness," He said as He walked in. "You have done quite the remodelling job in here."

I assumed He was referring to the shape of my heart. I knew it was rough, I had lived pretending it was tough. He must have seen that.

"Yes, Dear One, it is quite soft in here to Me, but what I notice most are the poorly healed scars," He replied. "You must have done many of these yourself, for they are not the mark of My Son."

His assumption was right. In those times like the disappointment of college, I had nailed and boarded the open wounds the best I knew how.

"And no one is blaming you," He added. "You did the best you knew then, but now you know Him. He can heal current wounds, future wounds, and even old wounds. It is often past wounds that infect the present wounds."

"Come with Me," He said, again taking my hand.

We stepped onto a blushed, soft surface that slightly swallowed my feet when stepping into the room. On the light, rose-colored walls were raised, red marks. Some were apparently infected due to the pus that slowly dripped from them. "This is it," I remarked, "the inside of my heart."

"Yes, nothing like the movies," He said.

"No, not at all," I agreed.

"This is what I am working with," He began. "But let Me make it very clear," He stated, "each and every one is worth it. I love them all that much."

"Thank You, Lord," I said, not feeling like I truly knew how much I would thank Him later. I watched Him stand in the center of my heart slowly turning for a 360-degree view. He was aware of the work ahead. The question would be, "Was I?"

CHAPTER 33

Anyone for Basketball?

For our struggle is not against flesh and blood, but against the rulers, against the authorities, against the powers of this dark world and against the spiritual forces of evil in the heavenly realms (Ephesians 6:12).

"Not sure where to go with us today," I said.

"That is the great thing," He said. "We don't have to have a laid-out plan. We can be whimsical."

"We can?" I questioned. "I thought everything was strategically laid out."

"Oh, there is a plan, but we can be carefree as we go," He explained.

"I would like that. How?" I asked.

"Light on our feet," He said with a great big grin on His face.

"Go on," I said with anticipation.

"I know you have a question," He stated.

"Yes, I do. I want to know more about moving around those that won't budge? And what does that have to do with being light on your feet?" I asked.

"Everything," He said.

Oh my, I thought. I looked around to see we were on a basketball court. It must have been regulation because the basket was high and the floor was wooden, perfectly polished.

"What are we doing here?" I asked as I looked around and saw several men playing what seemed to be a fun game due to their laughter and smiles. There was one man with a golden ball, while the others had red balls. He was in a low position dribbling the golden ball, eyes scoping his opponent trying to determine if he would go left or right to dribble around him. I watched in amazement as he was patient and strategic, yet having a great time. "How can he do that?" I asked the Lord.

"Keep watching," He answered.

Fake left, bounce, bounce, I heard the ball. Then like a butterfly, it appeared his feet never touched the floor. Around him he went. The man never knew what happened. Down the court with a jump, slam—the ball went effortlessly in the basket. "Score!" I heard someone from the press box above our heads holler. I stood there in amazement. As I looked at the Lord, He was clapping for the man.

"Good job, son," He yelled, "good job."

The man waved, grinned, and headed back down the court.

"What just happened?" I asked, still astonished by the weightlessness and ease he had shown moving around his opponent.

"Wait...there is more," He said, motioning for me to keep watching.

Looking across the court, I noticed another man dribbling his basketball. He was unhappy, I could tell by the frown on his face. The ball left his hands to make a thud on the floor. Slowly, he dribbled as if the ball weighed a ton.

I could still see the man who was light on his feet dribbling on the other side of the court. One, two, opponent after opponent, he dribbled by them with the same ease. But this other man was having trouble. He had no air under his feet. Every time an opponent would oppose him, he froze. Still bouncing the ball, his next move could be detected by the way his body shifted. There was no weightlessness, only heaviness in his presence

"That is it," the Lord broke in. "He is moving in his own weight, not the weight of the Holy Spirit. Every step, every bounce he is taking is full of dread and doom because he is in his own flesh. He sees a Goliath," He said.

"What?" I asked.

"Oh yes," the Lord said, and I heard a crowd roar. Looking around, I saw the bleachers full of cheering fans.

"Don't be deceived," the Lord said, "some of them are not fans. Or let Me be clearer, not *your* fans. The one who opposes has fans, too," He stated.

That sent a shock down my spine. Now I have those to worry about, too.

They are not in the game, merely on the sidelines." They are on the court."

"Then what do we do?" I asked.

"Do you remember the first man, how patient he was as he sized up his opponent?" He asked.

"Yes, I noticed that," I said.

"He was waiting on the Air Jordan of the Holy Spirit," the Lord said chuckling.

I began to chuckle too.

"Oh, yes," the Lord said. As He finished His sentence, I saw the Holy Spirit beside the man who was light on his feet. When the Holy Spirit leaned to his left, then the man would, too. There was a slight delay.

"Yes, that delay is the time it takes for the Holy Spirit to whisper the game plan to the man, then he moves in the direction that was shared," He explained. "It is team work."

"Cool," I said out loud.

"Yes, but now look at the contrast of the other man," He said.

"He was standing *in front of* the Holy Spirit," I said.

"Yes, he has gone ahead of Him," He pointed out. "The Holy Spirit might as well have been in the stands." As He made the statement, the Holy Spirit now sat in the midst of the fans. "He can cheer the man—and you—on from there, but just like the fans, He is not on the court with you," the Lord said.

"I want Him on the court with me," I said with great conviction.

"Yes, that was what I had planned, not behind…but beside," He stated.

I looked past the man with the golden ball; I could see Jesus at the end of the court. "Why is that?" I asked.

"Jesus goes before His Church," He said. "He knows when you need to fake right or break. The Holy Spirit guides you through the opponents in the direction that leads to Jesus."

"Man, I love that," I said with excitement. "OK, we have to have patience and the Holy Spirit on the court beside us—then what?" I asked. I was excited to hear more.

"Then it is eyes and ears," He said.

"Tell me, tell me," I said as if a child engrossed in a bedtime story.

"Ears to hear the direction of the Holy Spirit and eyes on Jesus," He explained.

"Yee ha!" I said with excitement.

"What is next, Lord?" I said, jumping up and down.

"Now are the feet and mouth," He said.

"Hmmm, why the two together?" I questioned.

"Your feet follow the path that leads to the Jesus, but your mouth praises Me," He said.

"I had never thought to praise You when an opponent is before me," I said. "I always thought I had to *set them straight* or defend my walk."

"No," He said flatly, "those are both flesh needs. Your flesh wants to retaliate and boast on your walk."

"Boast seemed such a strong word," I said.

"If you defend Me, it is about you," He said. "I need no defense."

"But Lord," I started, "I want others to know I stand for You."

"Then praise Me in the prison," He said. "Did you see Paul stand up sword in hand and yell obscenities about how he had traveled to and fro proclaiming Me?" He asked. "No, he sang," He answered. "It was his calmness that turned the prison guard to Me, not a bunch of standoffs and miscommunications."

"Miscommunications?" I asked.

"Yes, if My children start declaring who they are, the opponents will begin to attack, declaring who they are," He explained. "I am nowhere in there. I get misunderstood by the good intentions My Church seeks to display. You can show more of Me by silence than a rant to prove who you serve. Others do not want to follow someone who stirs them to rant; they already have that. Show them someone who can sing while shackled—then you have their attention."

I stood there with my mouth wide open. I had it wrong all these years. I had been a Pharisee yelling my Father's name when I needed to be a Paul singing His praises.

TAMING THE GOLIATH

"The Pharisee walked in the flesh, spoke in the flesh, and served in the flesh. They sought to belittle and intimidate the Samaritans, when it was them who knew Me. Humbleness...I cannot say it enough. When one lives with the rule of the flesh it becomes its own giant, taking down what it desires, when it desires, and how it desires; there is no room for Me. And honestly, they do not want Me there. In their arrogance they claim they are doing it in My name, but boy are they wrong. How did David kill Goliath?" He asked.

"With a stone and a sling," I answered.

"Very good church answer, but it was in My name," He replied. "The stone and sling were the tools I supplied him with to take down the giant. When you have an obstacle in your path and you are walking that path in My name, I will always offer you a stone and sling. I guarantee it. The key is in the waiting. Like the basketball player who waited on the direction of the Holy Spirit, my Body should wait too. They do not know the obstacles to come except for what they see in the present. Too many times they created additional obstacles that didn't need to be there."

I had to take a step back on that one. *Man,* I thought, *how many times have I done that?*

"It really comes down to wait...or add more to your path," He added.

"Why is it so hard for us to wait?" I asked.

"Your emotions run rampant, and they cause your flesh to cry out. You want results now, and often the best result comes from doing nothing," He answered.

"Nothing?" I questioned. "I'm not wild about that," I admitted.

"OK then, but why do you need to do something?" He asked.

"To set them straight," I responded. I couldn't even finish my reply; I had just proved Him right. "My flesh wants to show that I'm right. What do I do with that?" I asked.

With a flash of light and a thunder clap, the Holy Spirit was there in a flash. He was dressed as a super hero in red tights with a large S on the front of his shirt. "What, pray-tell, does that S stand for?" I asked.

"Silence," He said with His hands on His puffed-out chest.

I laughed so hard I almost cried. *No, He did not just say that,* I thought. *Did He?*

"Yes," the Lord said, as if He held a microphone to His mouth. "He can save you from your jibber jabber and swoop in with silence." His voice echoed from the microphone like at a sporting event. It was priceless.

"Silence is all I am asking until you are sure," He said. "When in doubt, don't shout." He laughed in response to His creativity.

With the Holy Spirit still standing with hands on hips, the Lord continued, "I have to give My Body a lot of credit; most want to do right, but are not sure what that is. The Church has confused themselves. Do this, don't do this. It goes on and on. I am here today to tell you when you are not sure—see Me. I would rather help you get help in the moment than see additional obstacles pop up."

"Lord, I'm so glad You are willing to help us," I said.

"Oh, it isn't just Me," He added quickly, "you have My Son, the Holy Spirit, and your spirit. Look at all the help you have. You have quite the team backing you."

I had never seen them all together, all standing there wearing basketball jerseys that said *Team Hoover.* The sight choked me up. "Why Hoover?" I asked.

"Because you represent a family," He said. "It is not about one, but the whole group. What you do affects others. Just as We represent you, you represent Us. We are a team."

I loved being part of their team. *Never alone,* I thought, *never alone.* For some reason I thought about the team being benched, which prompted a question. "Lord," I asked, "do You ever bench Your players?"

He smiled and said, "Sometimes I have to. I want the best for them, and sometimes that means sitting them down to think about what they have done. But I always sit with them. Sometimes they are so angry they won't even look at Me, but I will wait. I love them too much not to."

"You wait, too," I replied.

"Oh, you bet," He replied. "I wait on My children all of the time; even those who run ahead. I wait for them to come back."

"You are amazing," I said.

"Thank you, you rank right up there, too," He said.

"Lord," I started.

"Full of questions today," He added.

"Yes," I said almost blushing.

"Go ahead," He said, "you know I love a good question."

"Why are we taming our Goliath if David killed his?" I asked.

"Good one!" He added. "Have a seat," He said as He motioned me to the bleachers. "The flesh is a chameleon, it adapts to its surroundings. In this case it appeared as Goliath, and in that obstacle he killed it, but in another it appears in a different shape that may only need to be tamed. When David lusted over Bathsheba, it was the window. Just like I have tools to help you, the enemy has tools to hinder you. He wants to trip you up. If he can get you to slip up and name call as you pass by, the attention comes off Me and onto you. I am not saying don't look out of a window…I am saying to know what you are looking at."

She's Gonna Blow

I could feel the anxiousness and irritability rumbling in my chest. One more word from another, and I could blow. Not because that person was out of line, but because I was on edge. I knew this feeling. It comes when there is an issue I need to take to the Secret Place.

"So, here I am, Lord," I said. "I lay it at Your feet, or maybe a better way to put it, I'm going to spew it out of my mouth. I am so grateful that I can bring it to You, as raw as it may be, in an attempt to keep from taking it out on some innocent bystander.

"It is math again; I hate it, and I don't want to do it. After pondering the *whys*, it boils down to: why do this? I have no guarantees it will turn out good. I notice myself avoiding, putting off, and dragging out other chores to postpone the beginning of a responsibility I don't want to tackle. Why? Why avoid and ignore only to find it pilling up? Fear of it then piling up to the point beyond recovery. So, why not just not do it? I mean, I probably won't do well anyway. Why put myself through the letdown? All the work with the possibility of a letdown..."

"OK, stop right there," I heard Him say. "You are doing a great job of talking yourself right out of trying."

"You're right, but why try with the possibility of doing all of the work only to fail?" I remarked.

"Who said you would fail?" He asked.

"No one," I said. Truth be known, He had already told me I would make a B.

"Then it must be a trust issue," He added.

Yes, it normally was. I felt badly that He had told me about the final grade, yet I still wanted to throw in the towel. I had a good idea from where the problem stemmed. There have been many times when I was told I would receive this or that, yet when I had done my part, the other individuals had fallen short. Oh heck, let me call a spade a spade; they flat out lied and bailed on me. I began to scream and stomp my feet, as I yelled, "Can just one person do what they say they are going to do?" I had had it.

"So you take it out on math," He asked.

Not thinking that was funny, I felt my blood start to boil. "It is not the math," I yelled—not at the Lord, but out loud.

"Thank you," He replied. "Now we can get started."

A little confused as to what He was talking about, I restrained myself.

"You are not angry at the math, you are angry at the feelings the situation that happens to be around math brings," He explained.

Well, yee ha, I said to myself in a sarcastic manner. *Either way,* I thought, *I hate math.*

"Well, young lady, that attitude will get you nowhere," He said. "We can address your anger, or we can wallow in your temper tantrum. The choice is yours."

When He gives me this type of ultimatum, I know I want to address the issue. I also know I need to check my attitude at the door and let Him do what He is so graciously willing to do—help. "Lord," I said in a calm voice, "I need Your help."

He smiled as He hugged me. "Very well, let's get down to business."

Just His tone and willingness to love me, even as I had my fit, quieted the rumbling in my chest. Oh don't get me wrong, it was still there, but it was not louder than His voice now. I could hear and wanted to hear Him.

We walked into a room with gray walls and dark, almost muddy red carpet. The entire room was surrounded with couches. These couches were built into the walls and circled the perimeter of the room. The couches were gray and black tweed material topped with red pillows. "Why red?" I asked.

"This red represents anger," He said.

There were men lying on the couches as if they had nothing to do, their faces emotionless.

"What is this about?" I asked.

"They have given up," the Lord replied. "But they do not see it that way because they have convinced themselves not to try to the point that they do nothing but lie around. They appear to be content, but inside they are angry. They want to do something, but have avoided, manipulated, and frustrated others to the point that no one asks anymore. Pretty pitiful, wouldn't you say?" He said.

"Yes, I would; but it seems others shouldn't be angry at them," I commented.

"Why not?" He asked.

"Because they chose not to do something shouldn't bother someone else," I stated. "They are the ones left in this room."

"Are you sure about that?" He asked.

I looked around the room and noticed there were blue windows eye-level around the room made into the walls. Outside the room, people were peeking in.

"Look closer," He said to me.

I scanned the room to see a little window about three feet off the ground. A little girl was peering in with tears streaming down her face.

"Go to her," He said.

I walked to the wall and knelt down. As my eyes caught the attention of the little girl, I realized it was me. I began to cry. Our tears where in sync, one tear after another in harmony. My heart ached for her, for me. Still kneeling, I looked over my shoulder at the Lord. He was already there. He stood behind me, and I noticed He was behind her too. The pain seeped through our eyes. Someone had decided to avoid something, and we were left hanging.

"Yes," the Lord said, "when others put off until they have run out of time to catch up, it affects the ones who are depending on them. That is why others are frustrated with them. They were hurt."

"Why would they do that?" I stood and asked.

"Many reasons: fear of failing, fear of the result, over-booked, and over-promised," He blurted out. "But instead of admitting they fell short, they fall out. This leaves others confused, frustrated, and often scrounging around to make up for the piece not taken care of by that person. If you get anything out of this," He continued, "please know that it is not the math. The math is a small piece to the bigger piece. If My people will look further than themselves, then they will know that where they are presently standing gets them to the larger story...and then it is bearable. No, math, a part-time job, or a desire to eat better may not be fun in the moment, but the result is the payoff."

"Yes, but what if we do all *we* are supposed to and someone does just like those in the room?" I said.

He handed me a mirror.

I looked into the reflective glass to see myself in a room just like the one in which I was standing.

"Grace," He said. "Everyone has opted out of something that another was depending on...all have fallen short."

In a strange way, I was both humbled and grateful to see myself in this mirror. I felt no shame or guilt, but sympathy for us in the room. What did we miss by bailing out? "Lord," I said, "I don't want to miss a thing You have for me, and that includes math."

"Let's go," He said.

"What about the little girl?" I asked out of concern for her.

"Look again," He said.

I glanced her way to see a smile on her face. I smiled back and waved. She waved and then turned around and walked off with the Lord.

"Child," He said to me, "I am with My children when they are disappointed or playing. I knew what others did, but I also knew there would be times that little girl would enter that room because she was disappointed too. Grace," He repeated again. "Grace."

Not clueless to the strain it was going to be to open that math book, I wondered about motivation.

"Motivation comes from keeping your eye on the prize," He jumped in. "Come on, we are going running, get your sneakers."

"Sneakers? Running? Have You lost Your mind?" I said, joking. I looked down at my feet to see gold sneakers and white socks. "Oh my, this is not stylish," I said.

He laughed, "We are going to have fun."

"Are you sure?" I asked, "Because this is running, You know."

"Yes, I will teach you to pace yourself," He said.

"I could use that," I replied. I knew that if I didn't resort to avoidance then I drove myself crazy trying to get whatever I didn't want to do finished as soon as possible so I could move on.

"But what about having fun while you did what you didn't really want to do?" He asked.

How could that be? Could it be? I looked down again to see a black pavement and yellow lines. *They clash with my gold shoes,* I thought.

"Then turn them to white," He suggested.

"The shoes or the lines on the pavement?" I asked.

"The lines, of course," He said, laughing.

"How? Why?" I asked.

He handed me a piece of white chalk. "Write it down," He said.

"What?" I asked.

"What it is you want to accomplish," He said. "To pass math, to be a teacher, whatever you desire to be or do," He suggested.

I bent down to write as He continued to speak.

"My son, Habakkuk, is known for doing this. I told him to write down something I had told him."

"For what benefit?" I asked.

"Accountability," He said. "Others knowing does many things: It proclaims your desire. It shows courage that you seek to accomplish your goals, and others knowing keeps you from being too quick to stop. But most of all, it keeps you from forgetting why you are doing so many math problems when you would rather be doing anything else."

I stood there on the race track replaying His words. I wanted to accomplish my degree, and to do that, math had to be passed. *Oh no*, I thought as I panicked, *What if I write it for all to see then I don't succeed?*

"Do You have an eraser?" I asked the Lord.

"Oh no, you are not erasing that," He insisted.

I knew He wouldn't make me if I didn't want to. Then I thought, *Why don't I ask Him to help me overcome that fear and then I could leave the chalk on the track?*

"I am a step ahead of you," He interjected. "So what if you don't complete the degree?" He asked. "What do you think will happen?"

"People will think badly of me," I answered honestly.

"Yes, I am sure there will be some who might," He replied.

"Hey, I just remembered we were supposed to be having fun," I said.

"Let's start running," He said.

"What? That doesn't seem like fun to me," I said.

"The running isn't the fun part, Silly...it is what we are going to pass along the way," He said. "Perspective," He said with a grin.

I didn't believe how running and seeing the scenery could make me want to open a math book.

He looked at me and said one word, "Others."

I began to cry.

"I have you in math for *others,*" He said. "I have My children in places that they may not want to be for *others.* "I do not know any other way to say it except…" He stopped running and bent down.

I stopped and turned back toward Him. I walked over to see Him writing on the pavement. Listed were my dreams: to write a book; to teach multitudes of women how fun and amazing our God is; to be a godly mother and a supportive grandmother. The list went on and on. I stooped down and cried. I had wanted those dreams so badly. But I was afraid to do them. If I avoided math, I would take a chance of not seeing them come true. I would have an excuse. My heart sank as I whispered, "I get it."

With the chalk, He wrote *others* and drew a line pointing to the dreams.

"Your dreams are not just for you," He said. "A heavenly strength does things not just for themselves but others. When you can't bear to open the book or study one more problem…remember, others." He stood up and asked me, "Can we continue our run now?"

"Yes," I replied.

Slowly we lifted one leg then the other until we were running along the track. We passed people on the sidelines, some waving, some crying, and some with no expression at all.

"Lord," I asked, "who are they?"

Softly, He answered, "Others."

I had lost my perspective, the reason I was doing what I was doing. Yes, math was not my favorite thing to do, but it was a step to the porch I wanted to sit on. I need both the things I like in life and the not-so-great things to get to the prize; the end of the race.

"You have a heart created in My image," He said. "Through its development, it seeks to help others. Your walk heals you that you may turn and heal others. It isn't about the math," He said as He hugged me.

MATH

I was so angry that my jaw hurt like I had been grinding my teeth all night. "He was supposed to have helped me with that quiz," I screamed. I felt if I were to open my mouth I would literally growl. Thank goodness we as humans cannot make the echoing, ear-ringing, furious sound that a leader of a pride can. "Or can we?" I asked.

"Yes, you can," the Lord broke in and said. "The words you speak in those moments can rip the flesh of the heart like the big, razor-sharp nails of that furious lion, and they can leave the scars to prove it."

I knew He was right. If I didn't check this anger at His door before opening my mouth, there would be scars to deal with later.

"Very good, child," He said. "Check it, not stuff it. You are fair in your hurt, which has surfaced as an angry lion, but to let it out before you have calmed down by My peace would be harmful for your relationship. And I do believe you care for that relationship," He said.

"Yes, Lord," I agreed, on any other given day I loved this person beyond words. It was just today that those words were not nice.

"Then let's walk through feeling like a lion to speaking like a lamb," He suggested.

His words so far had been wise, fair, and honestly, soothing. I felt myself actually take a breath. I had not realized I had even been holding it. I had a choice, to react from my anger or take it to Him. I was thankful that I had done the latter.

"Often, My children do not have time, due to responsibilities, to work through the hurt; but if they will learn to check in at first sign, then we can move toward our time together. But here is the catch," He said. "Watch your thoughts. If you allow your thoughts to go back to the anger, the lion will roar again. If you will stay focused on My Word, your heart will wait."

"Why do you say heart?" I asked.

"Because that is where we are trying to keep both the scars on you and the person you were hurt by and not creating new ones. Our goal, sweet one, is to be free of placing scars."

"He called me sweet one," I said out loud, surprised. I had just said I wanted to growl and He still called me His sweet one.

"Oh, child, you *are* My sweet one, no matter if you growled or not. My love for you is unconditional. Where My discipline is universal," He stated.

My head fell into my hands. "Lord, I don't want to feel this way," I said.

"I know, sweet one, but you do...and that is understandable," He said. "Now, let's work through it."

That sounds like a reasonable idea, I thought. "What do we do?" I asked.

"Start at the beginning by telling Me why you are upset," He said.

"I needed his help on a quiz, and he didn't do well...and I feel let down," I said.

"Disappointment," He asked.

"Yes, Lord, exactly," I said.

"Then what?" He asked.

"I don't know if I can trust them at all," I answered.

"So you are saying that because he disappointed you one time you are ready to throw your hands up to it all?" He said.

"What do you mean?" I asked.

"Well," He began, "if you stay angry and they can never do right again, that is going to cause a huge rift to say the least, and may end up costing the whole relationship."

"Oh, no, I don't want that," I pleaded.

I saw myself lying in my bed. My face was turned toward the dresser. Between my face and the dresser was the accuser, our enemy. He stared at me as I did him. I laid there getting angrier and angrier. I heard the Lord say, "Do not go to bed angry," several times. *I don't care,* I thought as I threw back the covers and made my way to the couch. *I never get this mad,* I thought.

As I lay on the couch I looked into my bedroom to see the enemy as a lion standing beside my bed. He stared as to wait. I became angrier until I rolled over facing the back of the couch. I turned to look over my shoulder to see the lion was now in my bed, on my side beside my husband. *I won't have it,* I said to myself as I jumped off the couch. I lay back down beside my husband, shook him, and began to discuss what had upset me. After we had resolved the issue, I looked at the door of our room to see the tail of the enemy swishing right to left as he walked out of the room.

"I don't think most of My children want that when it starts. But too often when anger starts, it grows, and then they have a garden so full of weeds no one can get through," He said.

"But You...right, Lord?" I asked.

"Yes, no one but Me," He answered. "But too often they have grown so hard with pride that neither, or only one, will come to Me. That is why it is so important to come first thing. Even if we do not have all the time needed, we can at least get started."

"Thank You, Lord, that You are willing to help us from hurting ourselves even when we don't see it," I said gratefully.

RUSH

"Lord, would You help me with my need to rush?" I asked. "With this need to get something over with?"

"It makes you feel uneasy," He said. "You want it over quickly because you are not secure in what you are facing."

Again, I thought about math. Give me English; I was confident I could figure it out; but math was like standing on shaking ground. And I wanted off.

"Fear you can't catch yourself if you fall," He asked.

"Yes, the depending on others," I agreed.

"Your flesh wants it over with quickly," He began, "but if you wait on the communication between Me, the Holy Spirit, and your spirit, you will be prepared. Communication is key to building a relationship with Me or any relationship. You must listen, not just talk. We have a lot of people talking, but very few people listening. When the only voice we need to hear is Us."

"Why is communication key?" I asked.

"That is how we get to know each other," He replied. "That is how you build a relationship," He repeated.

"Then let's start building," I said.

"That is what we have been doing," He said laughing.

-CHAPTER 34-

Throw Me a Rope

To the LORD I cry aloud, and he answers me from his holy hill (Psalm 3:4).

Well then, all I can think the closer I get to the class finally being finished is, *What the heck am I doing?* as I become more panicked. The words *quit* and *why am I doing this to myself* keep screaming in my head. I am beginning to wonder myself. Could it be possible that what a friend or enemy can do to us is far less than what we do to ourselves? Then this question popped up in my mind. *What am I doing to myself?*

"Holding back," He answered.

"Don't you see I'm doing the best I can?" I remarked. "I have gone to every class except *one* because I was sick. Then I asked everyone I knew to help me; and lost hours of my life over what...a stupid math class? This had become ridiculous. Will I ever get out of this furnace? I have been pressed, knocked down, and shaken until I was about to lose it," I ranted.

"Yes, but you are not over," He interjected.

"But I'm done," I said, beginning to cry. "I can't give anymore." I saw myself falling into a deep hole—my arms extended as far as they would go on both sides, trying to catch myself. It was apparent my efforts were no longer working due to the fingernail marks I was leaving on the sides of the hole as I slipped down, farther and farther. I could see people standing around the opening of the hole. "Why aren't they helping me?" I cried out.

"They can't read your mind," He said.

"But can't they see I'm at the end of my rope?" I questioned.

"No, honey, they just see someone spinning in circles," He answered. "They are afraid to step in."

"Why?" I asked. "I need them to...I need help." Below was dark, and I had no idea what would happen when or if I got there. *I won't get there,* I thought. That is when the memory of an evening when I was in my early 20s came to mind. It was like any other day, at least to all of those standing at the top of the hole could tell. I had taken care of all my normal morning responsibilities and headed to a job that I should have been able to do, but fears had me believing I couldn't. Midway into the morning, I had made a decision; it was time to stop. I couldn't do what they needed. I couldn't be all that everyone wanted, and I was tired of letting everyone down. There, it was settled. I couldn't cry wolf anymore.

"Do you know you never cried wolf?" the Lord interjected.

"It seemed that way to me," I said. All the signs were there— defeat, crying, isolation, and to almost all their faces. I kept over and over disappointing them. I could not take it anymore. The people at the job never saw it coming. I created a story to leave early from work, and out the door I went. It was settled. I purchased my bag of things from the drug store and headed home.

As I walked out the store's door, I passed a dear friend I had known since grade school. We made light conversation. He didn't see it coming either. No one saw it, or at least that's what was said afterward. I never understood that. It was so apparent to me. I was drowning right in front of them, yet no one offered me a life vest.

So in my mind, there was no other choice. I had caused them too much pain already. With nothing on my mind except cleaning the house, I began straightening up each room. I didn't want them to come home and find a mess. I called who I needed to call, un-plugged the phone, and took the things I had purchased from the drug store into my bedroom.

As I lay in my bed, I began to talk to God. I had only recently met Him. Not raised in a church-attending home, I had as an adult been introduced to Him. I began to tell Him that I was sorry and that I hoped He would be OK with my decision. I must have faded out sometime after that because I woke to a family member standing over me shaking me.

Hmmm, I'm still here, I thought when I came to.

I would spend many years after trying to find answers to the very question that motivates me today, *Why do we do what we do?* My relationship with God, as you hopefully can see, is amazing, with a side of only getting better. I know that my fear of failure and the thought of disappointing others, mixed in with an incident that took my innocence as a child, led me to that day in my bed.

"No one knew," I said as I sat in silence. As I type these words, it reminds me of how I described that period in my life; it was like I was screaming in a crowded room, but no one heard me. That is how I feel as I see myself falling down farther and farther into this hole. I am clawing, but no one is helping. There is silence again.

"Do you hear that?" the Lord asked.

"Yes, it is silence," I said. I looked at my mouth and it was not moving. "Had I not asked for help?" I asked the Lord.

"No, I am sorry to say so bluntly," He replied. "Your first words of help were when you spoke to Me on that bed."

"But," I began, "I thought they knew."

"Oh, there were signs that maybe one might pick up on—that is if they knew to look for them," He explained.

"Then it is my fault," I said almost sick to my stomach.

"Oh, oh, no," He said, comforting. "The things that happened to you were true; it is what we do with those events that gets us help or not."

"What should I have done differently?" I questioned.

"Ask for help," He answered.

I looked around at the faces at the top of the hole. None did I feel I could tell. "Wait," I said. "None that knew what to do; I didn't trust them."

"Why?" He asked.

"I don't know," I replied, as I began to cry.

"Can I give you a little insight here?" He asked.

"Yes, please," I answered, feeling beaten down.

"You were not helped when you were molested. There was no one you felt you could trust; therefore, you took that same deduction into every situation you got yourself into from that point on," He explained. "Since then, you have trusted few to none, and instead of fighting through it with help from others, you would find a reason to stop."

His words rang true. Looking back, I remembered times that I would not go out for a team sport unless I knew I would make it. The thought of failing or not being good enough was more overpowering than trying. I realized in that moment how many fun opportunities I must have missed.

"Yes, that is why I pray you will stick with the math," He said. "You are learning why you do what you do, so that I can teach you the right way—My loving way."

"What do I do about me falling down this dark hole?" I asked. I could see the people's faces still standing over the hole peering down, just watching me fall.

"If you will let Me," He began, "we can address each of those faces and replace them with ones, because you have peeled away layers, with smiling faces you can trust. Each layer peeled has the potential to reveal another layer. Lies cover lies until the Truth is reached."

There was hope. I could see three smiling faces already standing over the hole.

"Hey," my husband said, hollering down into the hole, "would you like some help with that?"

"Oh my gosh," I hollered through my tears. There were no sweeter words he could have said at that moment.

"What can I do, Mama?" I heard my daughter say.

"Me too," my son-in-law added.

There were friends calling, hanging over the side, wanting to help me. It was unbelievable to see so many who cared.

"I need help," I cried out.

"OK then," they said.

"Let's get to it," my husband said.

The next thing I knew they were holding a rope, shimmying it down the hole to within my reach.

"If you are at the end of your rope, grab mine," my husband said.

I took that rope and held on while they slowly hoisted me up.

"Why are they pulling slowly?" I asked the Lord.

"They don't want to lose you. Slow is good," He added.

"My children are one rope after another that starts with Me," He said. "That is the way it is supposed to be. Like your husband offered his rope, I started his rope. I want My Body to be one continuous rope. They are stronger that way. I need them to see when others are reaching their end plus those who are approaching that end, to ask for help, not assuming it is understood. I know not all will listen, although that breaks My heart, but if you ask, I will ensure that you see a smiling face at the top of your hole," He said smiling.

All that I felt was appropriate was, *Thank You*. What else could I say to a God who loved me so much to guide me through such a painful healing? He was and always will be amazing to me. His wisdom left me humbled. I like it there.

THE YARD

"Make them get off of my property," I yelled. "They have no right...nor are they welcome. Who said they could come in my yard?" I asked.

"They just want to get their ball that rolled onto your grass," the neighbor replied, trying to be kind.

"Didn't your mother teach you better?" I questioned. "If not, can't you teach them?"

I hated my tone; I hated the feeling I had deep in my gut. *Why was I so mean?* I thought as I slammed the front door.

Giggle, giggle, "Come play, Johnny," said Sarah, a little girl outside.

"Why are those kids so loud?" I screamed. "Don't they know I can hear them in my house? I have not asked for their noise. If I wanted the sound of kids in my home, I would have invited them in. Maybe that is what I need to do, invite them in and teach them some manners and respect."

"They are only playing," the Lord said.

"Why is everyone defending them?" I screamed. "Where is the love for my side?" I cried, falling to the kitchen floor. "Where is the compassion and concern that I am being violated?"

I felt His arm wrap around me as He sat down beside me on the floor.

With rage, I rejected His embrace and stood up with force.

"I needed You then," I cried out. "I was little once and no one cared that he violated my space," I screamed. "Where were You?" I hollered. The impact of the past came crashing down. I cried into my hands, cupping my face. In the darkness my hands provided, I could see Him standing behind the very one who had come into my yard when I was young.

For the first time, I could see Him there. It was more than my body could withstand. If there was a deeper way to fall into the floor, I was doing it. "I wanted to play," I began to say. "I wanted to giggle and have people defend *me*. Ones who would stand up for me when he came into a place he wasn't welcome. Or was he?" I asked as the tears dried up instantly. "Did I invite him?" I had never asked that before.

"No," the Lord said, walking toward me. He had not let my resistance hinder His compassion for my hurt. "No," He said again. "In no way did you ask for his gestures," He said firmly.

"Gestures?" I yelled. "What happened weren't *gestures*," I said.

"No, I do not mean to make light of the situation; not at all," He said. "What I want is to get you out of it now. You are still there," He said.

"What?" I asked. "Don't you see me right here?" I questioned.

"Yes, dear, of course, but every time a child giggles or a ball rolls into your yard, you go back," He explained. "Sometimes you return quickly, and other times, like today, you crash. I want to help you stay here."

With a blank stare, I said, "I don't see how."

"Are you willing to give Me a chance?" He asked.

"Yes," I said, picking myself up and making my way to the couch. "Do your best, because it is going to take it," I said honestly.

In the back of my mind, I wanted to rejoice with the sound of children laughing and throw the ball with them as they had fun. But I had not had fun. Not then and not many years since. Be quiet, be seen but by all means do not be heard. I was tired of not being heard. I had a voice, and I was going to use it. And *they would hear me or they would be sorry*, I thought as the anger began to rage.

"You are right, this will take My best, but that is all I ever give," the Lord said as He sat down beside me. "Did you know that a parents' anger can be passed down to their children?" He asked.

"No," I replied.

"If they see that something is irritating to their parents, they believe it must be up to them to feel the same way. Have you heard the story about the puppy?" He asked

"Yes," I replied. I had heard a well-known speaker tell the story.

"Well, let's review it again. There was a puppy who had to have her back leg removed. She hobbled along, but managed to get around very well. When she had puppies, they learned to walk the same way their mommy walked. They saw how she walked and believed it must be the right way. In your relation to children playing and people coming into your yard, others think this must be the right way."

My heart sank. *How many things had I passed down that were my issues, not others, which had been taken on by my child?* I thought. *I hate to even imagine.*

"I can help you...and them," He said. "There is no guilt when I reveal. It is to heal."

"Heal me, Lord," I said as I knelt to pray.

Lord, Thank You for the revelation of the reasons why I do the things I do. Please forgive me for where I have wrong and help those I have been influenced by my lack of knowledge. Help us all to see our shortcomings and give them to You. Thank You for Your love and willingness to heal us all. Amen.

Bam, bam—I felt something hit my shoulders like a bucket of rocks.

"Stand back," I heard a man say, "there are more where those came from."

Bam, bam! The weight was heavier. I could hardly stand.

"Shame," the enemy, said. "Don't you feel badly now?" he asked. "You have ruined your daughter's life," he said, taunting me.

"No, no, I did my best," I replied, agitated that he would propose such a thing. "I love her. I wanted what was best."

"Yes, but it appears you did," he said. "Even the Lord said so."

"No, He didn't," I screamed back. "He just pointed out what I had done wrong."

"Yes, but isn't that the same as saying you did wrong by her?" he added.

"Stop! Stop! Stop that talk," I demanded.

"Why, is the truth hard to handle?" he questioned with a smirk on his ratty-haired face.

"No, no that isn't the truth," I said. "Lord," I called out, "that isn't the truth, is it?"

"I was waiting for you to call on Me," He said. "No, it isn't the truth, but My fallen son would love for you to think so," He said as He roared so loudly that His breath blew the matted hair of the enemy.

Still standing there, he glanced at me with a smart-alecky look.

"Flee!" I said. And he was gone.

"He uses every opportunity when shame rises to twist and confuse My adults," the Lord explained. "He knows how dear to them their children are, and if he can get them to believe they have failed as parents, he is quite the happy camper."

"Oh, he makes me *so* mad!" I said, stomping my foot.

"Take that anger and turn it into energy," He suggested.

"How?" I asked.

"Talk to your children. You know how important communication is," He reminded me. "Tell them when you believe you have fallen short. They can learn a lot from their parents' mistakes.

One, that it is OK to make a mistake; two, that even mommies and daddies are not perfect; and probably most important, telling them builds trust that creates a bridge they can feel comfortable to cross when they have made an error. Any other way is pretending, because all fall short. To act differently would be a lie. The list goes on," He said. "Explain to them your revelations, and if you want, invite Me. I love to sit in on family time."

How sweet that sounded. I remembered times when my daughter was young; we would sit at the dinner table reading a story called *Sticky Fingerprints*. She loved that story. "I know You were there with us during those times," I said as I saw Him sitting in a high-back, burgundy chair that sat by our fireplace.

"It was difficult to get comfortable," He said, joking. "You kept moving the furniture."

That made me think of a friend of my daughter's who had mentioned something very similar about our clock. I couldn't find just the right one, so I kept changing it. She had noticed and commented on how it was different every time she came over. I know now that I was trying to create the perfect setting in our home to make me feel safe, but at the time, all I could think about was that it wasn't the right clock.

"See, My dear, you did not know why you did what you were doing. It is the same way with things my adults incorrectly show their children. But you sought Me, and we worked it out. You know better and you're doing better," He said. "And not only is that a heavenly strength, but it makes Me very proud."

The Lord being proud, that was so much better than the enemy's shame. Yes, give me His blessing over the enemy's lies any day. This realization was hard to swallow, but necessary. I wanted my whole family free, no matter what. The phrase, "Do as I say, not as I do" came to mind.

"Yes, let's talk about that," the Lord said.

"OK," I agreed.

"Why would you want to be two different things?" He asked. "Because you do know one day your two worlds will collide, right?" He asked.

"I had never thought of it like that before," I admitted.

"If you say, 'do not smoke,' yet you smoke, then what is the real message?" He asked. "If you say that movie or video game is not played in our home, yet when they go to bed, it is popped in the player, what is really happening?" He asked.

"I don't know," I said curiously.

"You are lying," He said bluntly. "Doing as I say and not as I am doing it is a lie. I hate to have to be so brutally honest," He said, "but My Church is suffering. That is why the world wants no part of church. They see some in the pews...then at the bars. What are they to think?" He asked. "I need followers whose walk matches their talk."

"I want to be one," I said.

"Very well, then here is what you do," He began.

Oooh, I can't wait. This is going to be good, I thought.

"Put what My Word says into action. Be a doer, not just a hearer," He said.

"That's it?" I said under my breath. "I thought there would be a song and dance or flashing lights."

"Why?" He asked. "Why if it is so simple does it appear to be so hard?" He asked. "And why does it need a parade to get My children to hear and do? I do not understand," He said, "for I have given them all that they need. They possess the keys to My Kingdom, yet day after day they jeopardize all that is theirs. For what," He asked, "a cheap thrill here and a passing feeling there? With Me it can be a blast even in the trenches."

"I don't think they believe that," I admitted.

"Do you know why?" He asked. "Because the very ones who are supposed to be reflecting don't believe it either," He explained.

"What can we do?" I asked.

"Stick it out," He said. "Don't be so quick to give up. It took time for you to get into the mess you are in, be it by your own doing or another. Give Me time to get you out of it."

Again I saw a large, deep hole. I was at the bottom this time. Many people were above getting gear together to hoist me up. It took some time so that they would not harm me more than I already was from the fall.

"That is it," He said. "We want to take our time and do it right so that once you are healed, it is done. I don't want to add insult to injury while pulling you out of your hole. Impatience gets in the way," He said. "My ways are not your ways...you come to Me expecting by your ways. I know best. They have to trust Me. Sheep don't ask their leader where they are to go...they just follow. One day is a thousand to Me. They doubt when they don't see results soon enough for their liking.

"Some things will not be seen until the Feast," He replied. "Then if they don't see, they don't believe, and it spirals out of control. Talk it over with Me; let's detox your influences."

That makes so much sense, I thought. "You are so wise and caring," I said.

"OK, grab your pillow and have a seat," He said, smiling.

"Yeah!" I said as I plopped down at His feet.

"There was a man named Saul. I had told him of the great things he would do and he did. I even sent him a young man to help him. You remember meeting them, right?" He asked.

"Yes, I have fond memories of them both," I answered. I could hear stories about David and Saul all night.

"Well," He continued, "I sent Saul a helper named David. They were so compatible, both intelligent, hard workers, and desiring the things of the Kingdom, but their relationship went sour," He said. "One was to help the other be all that he was called to be. To lift each other up, not tear each other down. But one song from a group of women created fear in the heart of Saul, and from then on, he was suspicious. Jealousy can and does rip good combinations apart," He added.

"Combinations?" I asked. "Why do You use the word *combinations*?"

"Because I know what and who fit together best," He answered. "A perfect match, you might say. Think about a child's toy block set. The top of the container has a circle, square, and other shapes. The shapes are made to fit in those holes. But a circle won't fit in a square unless forced," He said. "With Me, there is no forcing."

"That made me think of a time when my husband and I were looking to buy a condo. We would go out with the realtor, only to be discouraged with what we saw. Not because there weren't any condos available, but because none of them ever felt right. I had even mentioned to my husband that it felt like we were trying to swim upstream. Fighting the current," I said.

"That is it exactly," He said. "If you have to force it, please check with Me. I flow...the flesh pushes. David and Saul were like a circle cut out in the top of the container with shapes to match. But when jealousy comes in, the shapes get confused and start to force their way into areas that they were not meant to go.

"It is that way with marriages," He continued. "The old saying that there is someone out there for everyone is true. But why My children feel the need to force relationships instead of waiting on the right one is beyond Me," He concluded.

"Lord," I began, "I want to flow in with the shapes You have planned for my path...to work with those who are my combinations. All in the name of the Kingdom," I cheered.

CHAPTER 35

Approaching

Whatever you do, work at it with all your heart, as
working for the Lord, not for men (Colossians 3:23).

"The exam is approaching. The results are almost done. Is there anything left to discuss?" I asked.

"What troubles your heart?" He asked.

"They won't love me if I fail," I admitted.

"Oh, dear, sweet little one, that is far from the truth," He replied.

"But they didn't," I said. "I would try my best and I could never seem to come up with enough," I cried. "I wanted them to so badly. Do you know how heartbreaking it is to look into someone's eyes and see over and over how you disappoint them? That is why I quit things that I would fail at. I couldn't take it."

"Let's talk about conditional love," He said. "You do know that is what you were dealing with, right?" He asked.

"No I didn't," I said. "I just knew I couldn't seem to get it right. I couldn't do well enough."

"It was not you," He said, "because their views changed with the wind, and it left you flapping and waving in the breeze. Honey, My breeze is constant, for I do not change. What you do for My love is the same today as it was yesterday. It will not change."

"What do I do?" I asked.

"Be you," He said.

"But what about those who I want to love me?" I asked. "What if I fail and they are disappointed? I don't want to hurt them."

"Honey, if your math score hurts them, then they need time with Me, not you."

"Fix me," I cried out. "Please make me better."

"Oh…oh, My dear child, come sit on My lap," He said.

I saw myself as a little girl. I was so cute, but no one said so. It was about my weight and how smart I was. If I was smart, maybe I could offset the weight. I was so confused. I couldn't see for the hurt. "Hold me, Father," my heart cried out.

"A daughter needs her father's hugs," He said. "She needs to know that his love is without conditions. That there is a place on his lap for the times she may fall short and the times she gets it all right. Daughters need that," He stated.

"What do we do if we didn't get that?" I asked.

"*My* knee is always open," He said tenderly. "I love you no matter what. There is praise and forgiveness on My knee."

"I just wanted them to love me," I admitted. "I would have jumped through fire if it would have meant that."

"Hmmm, fire," He said. "Come with Me."

I took His hand, and we walked toward a furnace. "I know this," I said. "Shadrach, Meshach, and Abednego."

"Yes, but this is different," He announced.

"How?" I asked.

"Because it is yours," He explained, "each child has their own."

"But why was there three of them?" I questioned.

"Very good question," He said. "There are two with you right now. The parent or caregiver, yourself, and of course; Me. See it is your furnace, but the ones around you go, too. As a child grows and walks through their furnace, the parents go too, even if they do not realize it."

"Go on," I said, intrigued with how this was going to turn out.

"The question is, who will get burned and who will walk through smelling of roses not smoke? In your case everyone smelled of smoke," He said.

That was so sad, but I knew it was true; neither myself nor those around me were happy.

"Happy is not the case," He added. "You can walk through it and not be happy. It is love that we are after. It is my desire that through the fire you will have a heart that loves like Mine. Unconditional love. When parents and children walk with Me through the trials of their lives, there are no conditions, only understanding. They may not see why they are in the fire, but they hold on to each other and Me through it. But too many times family members throw each other under the bus."

I saw a yellow school bus with happy, screaming children in the seats. There was a mob of angry adults circled around the bus, but the bus was moving. "What is this?" I asked.

"The children know how to be happy, but the parents are angry," He answered. "The parents are angry at each other, and the children are getting the brunt of it."

I saw the parents pointing fingers and cursing toward the bus. "Look," I said. It was the Holy Spirit at the steering wheel.

"He will take them through that fire," the Lord said. "The children have no clue."

Wait—there was one little girl at the back of the bus. She was sad. "What is wrong with her?" I asked.

"She knows…she sees the parents yelling," He said. "She has seen it at home. She knows those looks. She has seen the angry eyes."

"Wait," I said as I saw her walking down the aisle of the bus, hitting the children in the back of the head as she passed by. "What? No," I began to cry.

"She is angry now, too," He said. "She sees the adults and imitates their actions. What they do reflects how she and other children handle the fires."

I sat in silence, not knowing what to do from here. I wanted love, but now all I saw was the angry little girl hitting others on the bus.

"Stop," the Lord said, "you are missing the revelation. You wanted to be loved, but it was impossible to receive from an angry heart. Their hearts are not like Mine."

"Then what is a parent to do?" I asked. "Can one ever reach a heart like Yours?"

"Yes, they can; but do not panic," He said. "I am not in any way saying parents need to have reached completion; I am saying they need to reach *Me*. Knowing their hearts are not there yet is half the battle. The other half is won in the fire. I will gladly walk through the trials, showing them how to hold their child while I hold them. That is what families do. There is no pushing, shoving, hoop jumping, or yelling; only holding."

It felt good to be held as I sat on His lap. I knew now that we can't get love that is rooted in flesh, but love that is like His is filling. I felt full. If someone loved me less over a math problem, then they needed Him. I knew that because I had been with Him. We all need to go to Him because a furnace could be right around the corner.

I would rather come out with clean-smelling clothes than to have tracks over my back from bus tires. I saw a clothesline with white sheets dancing in the breeze. It was held by wooden clothespins. The crispness of the sheets enhanced the green pasture and indigo sky. There was peace there. It felt good. *I could do math there,* I thought.

"Good observation," He said. "Where there is peace, one can think clearly. Where there is peace, one can breathe."

I took in a deep gulp of air. It was cool and clean, going down the back of my throat.

"Breathe Me in," He said. "Once you have inhaled My freedom, you will recognize when it is gone. You will learn you can't and you don't want to live without it."

I knew what He meant. Coming from a life of drama, I had learned there was better. I needed His peace, His calmness, not everything being a production. Love like His was pure. I wanted a heart like that and ones who loved me that way.

A new standard set forth that day. I was the princess of the King. I am worth it. Anything less is not of His heart. I sat for a while on His lap soaking in the look of love—eyes that glistened, not shooting flames. No heated arrows here, just cool breezes. I wanted to remember the feelings and sounds of the sheet waving in the breeze so that when the screeching of a bus came, I knew to get back to the meadow. "Thank You, Lord," I said.

"Anytime," He said. "I am always here waiting."

CLEAN-UP

"Anyone need a clean-up?" I heard a familiar voice say. It was the Holy Spirit. We were on a basketball court again. He had come in to clean the floor from where I had dripped sweat from panic. He was there, and I was so glad to see Him. Running up to Him, I hugged and thanked Him for coming. "I need You," I said as I hugged tighter.

"Ahhh, Dear," He said as He hugged me back. "What has you so troubled?"

"I don't know how to play basketball," I answered.

"Oh, sweet one, you do not need to know how to play. That is why I am here."

"Yes," the Lord said, "we will teach you. First we need to address the things that hinder your game."

"Lord," I said as I pulled tenderly away from the hug of the Holy Spirit, "today is the math exam. The day we have suffered for months. But as I woke I realized a panic for which I was not prepared. Logically I knew I had studied every day for weeks. How much more prepared could I be? Then it hit me, a memory I had not thought about before. I had known that the incident had occurred during the night. I had awoken to this person beside me," I said.

"Yes, child, that explains some of your panic when you first wake," He pointed out.

"Yes, we had discussed how I wake up, then once I get my bearings, I am confident to continue with the day," I said.

"But when you do not feel prepared, you instantly scrounge to get prepared. But who can really be prepared for what is unknown?"

"What am I to do?" I asked.

"Walk with Me," He said as He walked toward the basket. "Try to throw this basketball," He said.

I took the ball and with all my might, I heaved it toward the basket. It was no surprise to me that it missed, even the backboard.

"Do you know why?" He asked.

"Because I can't play," I said again.

"No," He replied. "The game, just like math, has nothing to do with it. Remember, it has not been about the math."

"Yes," I said. "Lord," I began, "I feel this weight on my left shoulder."

"That is him," He said. "He is why you cannot play."

"Who is he?" I asked.

"The man who harmed you," He said. "You have taken him everywhere you go. His weight keeps you from hitting the basket and making those problems add up."

"Are you saying that if he wasn't there I could be a basketball star or a math wiz?" I asked. I almost felt sarcastic asking such a question. I knew that wasn't the case.

"No," He said, "it isn't. I am saying that when he no longer goes with you, you then have the opportunity to try things like math and basketball freely."

"I want to be free," I said out loud. That is when it hit me, the meaning of this math. I would take math a million times if it meant being free. I wanted to be free. Adding one and one could be done; but walking around, waking up, and living free of this weight needed to be done. "I want freedom," I said.

"I want that too," the Lord said. "Shall we do this?" He asked.

"Yes," I answered, sitting on the basketball court floor. No couch this time; it was time to get down to the nitty gritty. "What do I do?" I asked.

"We go for the truth," the Lord said.

I saw the Holy Spirit wiping, cleaning certain areas of the floor. "What is He doing?" I asked.

"Preparing the way," the Lord said. "Over the years many messes have been left behind, with Truth they can be cleaned up."

"Truth it is," I said.

We began to recount the morning I woke to someone lying beside me. We talked, I cried. He healed me, I cried. One by one the cleaning ended. The Holy Spirit sat beside us holding the damp cloth with which He had sopped up the tears and sweat. I knew that my dreams—the torment of my rest—were the indicators to why I do what I do, a question I had devoted many hours to researching.

Why do we do what we do? I questioned many times. I wanted to play basketball, do math, or whatever my path presented, free of the past. If that meant going there or whatever, I would do that. I knew the people who loved and cared for me. They had confidence that it could do these stupid math problems; why didn't I?

"Because you couldn't stop this man from sneaking in," the Lord said.

"Then help me," I said, frustrated and sick of this whole thing. "Let's get down to the core," I screamed.

"You are angry he was let in," the Lord said.

"Yes, I am."

"And if you keep him with you, he can't sneak in again," He pointed out.

"I don't want to take him with me anymore," I said, falling back onto the court.

"Then look him in the face," the Lord directed.

I turned my head to see this person. He was passed out like the first time I had seen him. "I hate you," I screamed as I began to wail on him. I didn't want to be this angry, but the more I hit, the more I wanted to hit him. "I want to stop," I screamed. I hit him until I thought my arms would fall off from exhaustion. There was still this anger even after hitting him.

"That is because it won't help heal your heart," the Lord pointed out gently.

"Then how do we do that?" I asked. "I blame him for my innocence being taken; I blame him for me not being able to do math, I blame him for…" I went on and on. Blame! Then out of nowhere, I turned to the Lord and said, "I blame You for not stopping Him."

Oh, I didn't want to, but it was truth. "If You won't stop him, how can I believe You will help me remember these stupid math problems?" I asked. I fell into the fetal position sobbing. "How?" I asked whimpering. "How?"

"I guess you can't," I heard Him say.

"No!" I said, angered and shooting up from the floor. "You're not going to give up on me that quickly...with no fight," I screamed. I was mad! "What do You think You are doing...You are God," I asked. "You save and You know how to do those problems. You can't leave me here," I said crying. "Answer me, darn it!" I said, sobbing into my hands.

There was silence. Had I made Him angry? Was He really gone? But His Word says He won't ever go. I cleared my throat, and asked, "Where are You? Where were You?" The question made my stomach drop. Where had He been? There lies the moment. I didn't believe He would do what He said He would do in this math exam, and I had to prepare myself to cover it.

No one had stopped this man. I had to be prepared. I was tired of being prepared. I just wanted to do the problems like I had just wanted to sleep that night he came in. I still heard nothing. I could see the Holy Spirit still sitting across from me. His eyes filled with tears as He watched me suffering. I thought of Mary, the mother of Jesus. How she must have felt crouched down at the foot of the cross watching her Son suffer and knowing there was nothing she could do.

"Many question why I didn't start over that day that Adam ate the apple. While others ask why I created a population knowing they would sin. All valid questions," the Lord said. "But what about forgiveness? Where would that have fallen?" He asked. "What about the love that I have for each one of you, where would that be?" He asked.

I sat there crying, wondering to myself, *Where was the love when others sin at our expense?* I knew I had been one of those skeptics. *Where do we go from here?* I wondered. Could we be at an impasse? Oh, I hoped not. There was silence again. I didn't like the silence. *Which was worse— going into a situation, like an exam, hoping He did what He said He would, or going in knowing I'm on my own, in silence?* I questioned. The latter, I had to admit, left no room for disappointment. But how could that be the best choice? I mean, I love Him. And to be fair, He had kept His word many times.

"Blame," He said. "Just as you blamed your perpetrator for the reason you cannot do math, My children blame Me for things I did not do."

I didn't think He would play the victim, but it almost sounded that way. It stirred an aggravation in my soul.

"I am not playing the victim," He said. "I speak the truth. With that being the only way I can be. Honestly," He said bluntly, "you are."

"No," I said. "I have prided myself on not being the victim; I have made sure of that."

"In your attempt, or you may say, determination, not to be the victim, you have accomplished the opposite," He said. "You have been the victim. Would you like to turn that card in?"

I was fuming now. I had *not* been the victim.

"Yes, you were," He said. "You were, that is very true," He explained. "But you are not any longer. You are a grown woman who can do math or throw a basketball. Please notice, I did not say ace either one. That is pressure you put on yourself that we can address another day."

I knew to be honest; I hated those who played the victim. I had sucked it up and they should too.

"Should they?" He asked. "Do you not believe you and others deserve their moment of acknowledgment that they were victims?" He asked.

"Yes, but then move on," I said.

"Hmmm," He said, tapping His finger on His chin. "How has that played out for you?"

I hated those questions that He knew the answer to, but wanted me to say out loud. OK, I would bite. "It hasn't, evidently," I answered.

"You have gone many days plowing through," He said. "Not enjoying, but getting it done."

"Like today," I admitted. "I just want it done. What is my alternative?" I asked. There was silence. I sat there. I knew that when He didn't speak it was often so I could hear myself. So I listened. Surprisingly, I heard myself in a joking voice say, *Self, what do you think?* How could I joke at a time like this?

"That is the alternative," the Lord said smiling. "You have an exam...fact. You will pass. I said so...fact. Why spend the day dreading?" He asked.

I had no answer. "Why did I?" I asked.

"Because it is what you do," He replied. "It has become a habit."

"Ta dah!" I heard the sweet voice of the Holy Spirit say as He jumped up from the floor. "I can help you break a habit," He sang as He broke out into a tap dance routine.

"You are quite good," I said, laughing.

"Thank you," He sang as He continued to dance.

"Do you *trust* Me?" the Lord asked. "Notice I didn't say believe."

"Yes, I do," I said. "Why do I trust You but have trouble believing? What is the difference?" As the words rolled off my tongue, I began to panic. The clock had been ticking while we had been talking.

"I can't go...I'm afraid. I can't go to bed," I hollered. "He may come in again." I began to hyperventilate. I had spent my life medicating myself with cold medicines to help me sleep. I couldn't do it any other way. "I can't, I can't. Help me, help me! Somebody help me." I started to run around in circles on the court.

I went to a memory of when I was young, and I would wake up screaming, in panic. The door to my bedroom was closed. Someone help me! I began to take deep breaths. "I can't go," I said, afraid to leave for school. My breathing was heavy now. It was all I could to keep from passing out. I want to crawl into bed, but it wasn't a safe place. I need a safe place. I thought their house was safe, but I had been wrong.

"Where is a safe place?" I said, panicky, running in a circle. I couldn't breathe. I fell to the floor unconscious. Limp, I laid there.

"Get up," I heard a mean voice say. "You have chores and school work to do." The voice was loud.

"Oh," I said, startled. I'd better get to them when all I really want to do is stay there on the floor a minute. Just a minute. I want to be the victim for a minute. "Can I just do that?" I asked softly.

"No," the voice screamed, "you have responsibilities, there is no time."

I was torn between wanting to yell stop and dragging myself up to continue. That is what I had always done, picked myself up to continue. Until that one day when I could not drag any more. I tried to end it that day. *What a baby,* I thought. *You are an embarrassment. They would suffer through life. Why couldn't you?*

"Because I did not want to suffer anymore," I answered.

"I can't do it alone," I screamed.

"It was never supposed to be that way," the Lord said. "If you will let Me, I will go with you," He offered.

What do I have to lose? I thought. "Please go with me," I asked. Maybe I will get lucky and pass the exam and You will come through. I hated that feeling of needing luck. Or hoping He would come through. I didn't want to hope, I wanted to *know.* "How?" I wondered. There was that silence again.

"No," He said, "no silence this time, just facts. How do you trust someone?" He asked. "You give them a chance," He answered. "That is all I am asking."

I thought I had given Him a chance. Maybe I hadn't. I had learned all about what I brought to our relationship: anger, blame, fear, and a lot of panic. He had been with me through all of that. But the burning question still flamed, "Where was He?" How could I trust He would be there today? I guess I didn't trust Him like I had thought. I felt bad for this harsh realization, but I knew He would understand. How could I know that, but not that He would help me in math? Was it left to wait and see?

"Do you build a relationship with others often waiting to see?" He asked. "If you agree to meet for coffee, do you not go to the coffee shop and wait to see if they show? Why am I not given the same opportunity?" He asked.

His words rang true, but my friend had not stood by and let a man harm me. Oh, that burned to say it. I didn't want to admit it. Will He leave me over this ugly thought?

"No," He said. "I will work through it with you."

I saw the Holy Spirit holding the cloth again, ready to sop up the mess. Not the mess of what I had said, but the mess that created the thought. This time I was silent. I wanted to wait to hear. I was going to the exam, like I would go to the coffee shop to wait. Then it hit me. That was God. I can't bear to be disappointed by Him. Others, I had grown to expect; but Him, it couldn't happen.

"Wow, that is a lot of pressure," He said. "What if there is a mistake by you or someone else involved?" He asked.

"There is no room for that," I said.

"Ding, ding, ding, there is that pressure," the Lord said as the Holy Spirit rang a triangle bell. "I won't be held accountable to your standards," the Lord said. This time He sounded a little miffed. "I am blamed and accused," this I understand, "but I will not be put in a box limited to the thoughts and ways of My children. You have issues that cause you to think you have to be perfect—I *am* perfect; therefore, I am free. Would you like to be free to make a mistake?" He asked.

I could tell by His tone, it was completely up to me. I also knew the thought of failing the exam scared me to death. I had maneuvered many events in my life to what I knew I would not fail at. This time I had pushed through all my fears and didn't quit. I wanted to push through this fear of failing too. "Please," I asked, "I want to be able to make a mistake. I want this pressure gone."

I felt as if I was in a wind tunnel. The fan at the end of the tunnel blew constant, forced air that when I tried to walk toward resisted my movements. I kept pressing forward, only to barely budge.

"I can turn that fan off," He said. "Or I can turn it down; it is up to you," He said.

I saw the Holy Spirit holding a switch.

"Just as events happen in My children's lives that turn on by a switch, I can turn them off with the switch of Truth," He explained.

The switch the Holy Spirit held was a big flashing sign that blinked *Truth* in purple bulbs.

I want the fan off, but my words said down. *Why would I do that?* I wondered.

"You are afraid of what off is," He explained. "You want to play it safe and test the waters by turning it down first."

I saw the Holy Spirit move His foot as to simulate dipping His toe into a body of water. "Jump in," He said excitedly.

I stood there wanting to jump. "OK," I screamed. "Turn it off."

"You don't believe," He said.

I knew I was trying to trick myself into believing I wanted or could turn it off. I realized that the time was still ticking. The time for the exam was coming, and we were still talking. "Do you not see?" I asked.

"Yes, but I know what is of most importance," He said. "Do you?"

"I can't fail," I cried out.

"Why not?" He asked, standing to His feet.

"They won't love me," I blurted out again. I had known that I received the most praise when I did well on my school work. I didn't want to disappoint. The panic crept into my chest. "Make it stop," I cried out.

"Code blue," I heard the Holy Spirit yell. Bam, bam! "We are going to have to use the cart." They wheeled in the machine. Bam, bam! I heard as my chest rose then deflated quickly. I watched myself lie on the table out cold and helpless. *Let her rest,* I thought. *She gave a good fight.*

"Are you ready to give up?" the Lord asked as He turned from the table to look at me.

Should I let her go? I wondered. I knew she was tired. *Was there any fight left?* I wondered.

"Hello," the Holy Spirit said. He was wearing a clergy outfit. "You have a choice to be deceased or move on. That is the decision all the Lord's children face when they opt to take the easy way or fight through the fears. There were many times when you did not try something because you were afraid of failing. Today you can choose to get off the table and fight for your freedom. Which will it be?" He asked.

"I want to fight," I said calmly. "Why am I calm?" I asked.

"You are right in knowing you are tired," He continued.

"It isn't supposed to be that way," the Lord interjected.

"Then how is it supposed to be?" I asked.

"We are glad you asked," They said.

"Take my hand," the Lord said.

When I reached out, I saw transposed over His, the hand of the Holy Spirit, Jesus, David, Saul, Paul, Mary, and Esther. "When you take My hand, you get the family," He explained. "We are a package deal," He said. "Together we can see each other through. You have been trying to do it on your own. That would make anyone tired."

I looked around the hospital room. There were many faces of people who cared for me.

"They want you to make it," He said, "but it is ultimately up to you."

"I don't want to let them down," I said. "If I fail this test, I am letting them down."

"Give them a chance," He said.

Panic ran through my body. Will I have to fail to prove a point? *Oh no, Lord, can't You just poof—and I believe? Not really failing,* I thought.

"Oh, child, why do you fear Me doing that?" He asked. "Do you not know I will do what is best?"

"Lord, please don't make me fail," I said, beginning to cry.

"Paddles," I heard the Lord yell. Bam, bam! My chest deflated again.

I watched myself suffering on that table. I wanted to help her. "Help me. I don't want to fear failure anymore," I cried out as I sat down in the middle of the hospital room floor. "Are you going to punish me by failing me? I tried to do right." The day I missed due to having the flu came to my mind. "I'm sorry, I should have done more. I should have gone in sick. Please don't punish me."

I saw the belt. I had tried to be a good little girl. "I will try to be better next time," I said angrily. "I disappointed you." I cried in the midst of the silence. "I will try to do better," I said again.

"I will not punish you for trying," He said. "I am not like earthly fathers. Again, the ways and thoughts, the limits and demands My children put on each other are not My ways."

"I want out of this box," I said. I could feel the walls of the box closing in. It was a pretty package from the outside; silver with red metallic ribbons and a big bow on top. But inside I was suffocating. "I can't breathe," I said. "Help me. I want out."

"Bust out," the Lord said. "You can do it."

I took my arms and flew them outward, busting the sides of the box wide open. I stood there with my arms and legs sticking out of the box. I had to laugh at the sight of this box covering my torso. It must have been amusing, because they laughed too. "How do I get the rest off?" I asked.

"Untie the bow," the Lord said.

Reaching to the top, I pulled the red metallic ribbon, and the box fell to each side of my feet. "What now?" I asked.

"Step out," He said.

With one foot then the next, I moved away from the pile of cardboard and ribbon. It looked so simple now, just lying there. The fan was off.

"Shall we go now?" the Lord asked.

"Yes, but why am I still afraid?" I asked.

"You are vulnerable," He began. "As suffocated as you were, you knew it. Now you are exposed."

"Oh, no," I said as I saw monkeys swarm around me. "Get off," I said as I swatted at them. "Get away."

"Do not fear, child," the Lord said. "The enemy knows you are free and has sent his helpers to scare you in hopes you will try to tape that box back together."

"They aren't scaring me, but they are annoying," I said.

"Then shall we go?" He asked again.

"Lord, I want to go, but what do I do about me on the table?" I stated.

"She will be fine," He said. "She will come along."

"But I don't want her to," I admitted. "She makes me tired."

"Ha ha," He laughed. "Dead weight," He said. "Very good. You have chosen, like Paul, to leave that behind. You will be lighter now."

We were in the temple again. I saw another suitcase melt away.

"You won't be needing that one anymore," He said, smiling.

"But what about that one over in the corner?" I asked. It was huge! So big it blocked out the encouragers behind it. I didn't need to, but I walked over to the big piece of luggage to see it said MATH in big white letters. "I am sick of this," I said, hitting the bag. *What if others do not think I did enough?* "Where did that come from?" I asked.

"Look at the ID tag on the luggage," He said.

It said *accused*. "What is that about?" I asked.

"Have you not been falsely accused of not trying hard enough," He asked. "And to be honest, was it true sometimes?"

"Yes, but the lines have gotten so blurry, I don't know which ones are true and which are lies anymore," I said.

"This is the problem with guilt," He began. "Both true and imposed guilt feel the same. But I can tell you how to tell the difference."

"Oh, please do," I said.

"True guilt comes with conviction and leaves with admission," He said.

"Oh, I love that," I said, clapping. "What about imposed guilt?" I asked.

"Imposed guilt weighs a ton, and when truth is revealed, it's undone," He said.

"Oh, another good one. So what do we do?" I asked.

"Ta dah!" the Holy Spirit said. "Step into my office."

We walked into a plush red room. The couch, walls, and ceiling were red velvet, but the floor was wooden. "Why red?" I asked. "And why so many reds," I asked.

"Because this room is full of love, My love," He said. "But just like my Word has many words for love, like agape and phileo, the color also has many shades and meanings."

"But what about the wooden floors?" I questioned.

"My children enter with hard hearts," He explained. "But…"

"Let Me, let Me," the Holy Spirit said with excitement.

"OK, go ahead," the Lord agreed smiling.

"They leave by way of Heaven," He stated.

As He spoke, a golden spiral staircase slowly dropped from the ceiling. "What is all this?" I asked, mesmerized by the beauty of the staircase.

"Oh, if you think *that* is amazing, wait until your heart is healed," the Lord said.

"I want it, I want it," I said, excited.

"Then have a seat," He said.

We sat on the couch for what seemed like hours, but felt like minutes. "I can do in seconds what can take people many years," He admitted.

He took my hand as we began to make our way up the steps until we wound toward the top. Slowly, through the clouds we made our way. I could see above the clouds now. The fear in my stomach became more intense. "No, no, I want to believe, I want to go," I said.

"Child, no one is stopping you," He stated.

"Then why am I panicking?" I asked. "What is happening?" I felt like if someone poured water on me, I would melt.

"What is this?" I asked. "Stop. Lord, what if they say I didn't try hard enough?" I thought about the time I was writing when I should have been studying. "What if…"

"Did I not call you to write?" He asked.

"Yes, but…"

He placed His finger over my lips, stopping my words. "Fear of people," He said calmly. "It stops many from making it to the top of the steps."

"I don't want to be one of them," I cried out. "Please." I could see me on the hospital table again.

"Knife," He said, "I am going to have to go in."

The Lord began to cut my chest from top to bottom. I was not in pain as I lay there. One by one He began to pull out what appeared to be organs.

"No, no," He hollered to me from the table. "This is what lies look like. They have been here so long, they appear to belong."

"Get them out, Lord," I said. "Get them." I was excited. That was different.

"Yes," the Lord said while still removing the lies, "you are beginning to see the benefit from our time, so it outweighs the fear. You are counting it joy."

"Can I help?" I asked. "I want to help me be free."

"Come on over." He motioned. Slowly He guided my hand from one lie to another, removing each. I felt guilt and shame leave my body. If I failed, it would not be because I didn't try. Then it hit me, *What would they think?*

"Hold on," He said. "Sutures," He called. After closing my chest and cleaning up, He walked over to me.

"Thinking, that is a good question," He began. "We can remove the lies from your heart, but if you still *think* the same way, they will seep back into your system."

"Then let's go into my brain," I said, ready for more surgery.

"Hold your horses," the Lord said.

I heard the sound of horse hooves galloping. Then "Whoa." It was Pharaoh, and he had Saul with him this time. "They know each other?" I asked.

"Remember, we are family," He said.

"What do they have to teach me?" I asked, trying to hurry this along. I only had a few hours until the exam, and I really needed to study.

"You know it...the material, that is," Pharaoh said.

"How do you know?" I asked, remembering our last encounter.

"The Lord told me," he answered.

"Well He told me too, but..." Oh as the words came to my tongue, I gulped. "But I don't believe Him." I turned sadly to the Lord.

"Why does he believe You, but I don't?" I asked.

Saul got off the chariot and placed his arm around my shoulder. I began to cry.

"He knows because he has been to the top of the stairs," Saul said. "When we live in the natural, as you call it, that is all we see. Your mind puts these things together from what it sees. We need to see from the *spiritual*."

"I want that," I said.

"Take all of your baggage and let's go to the exam. The rest will be revealed there," the Lord said.

"Lord, I'm more confused," I admitted. "Why are they coming?"

"So you will not feel alone," He answered.

"But why them?" I asked, meaning no disrespect.

"They have been where you are. Fear of people, failure, and not trusting Me," He explained.

"I don't want to go afraid," I said. "Can't we take care of it now?" I asked.

"But are you not worried about studying?" He asked.

"No," I admitted. "I am more worried this will all be for nothing. All of this writing whether the math is a defiant. I can see it on my transcripts. I had known someone before whom I told the Lord would provide and her response was, 'Great but I have to feed my kids while I wait on Him.'" Was I doing that; waiting to see? "Lord," I asked as I thought about what Saul had said, "can I see this in the spiritual?"

I took a moment to shower. I have a really good friend who heard the Lord best in the shower. He reminded me about another exam I had today. I had disregarded it because I knew how to do the work required for it. Why had I not worried about failing or panicked about disappointing over that one?

"Because you are having to depend on someone other than yourself—Me—to do the math where in your other class, you feel you can do it alone," He explained.

But I would realize I was wrong. Yes, I was better in the first exam, but there was a day that I panicked to accomplish what this class required. Wow. "Lord, I want to know I can depend on You in the second exam as much as I do did the first."

"That is seeing it in the spiritual. Knowing you can depend on Me no matter what the test is," He said.

"I want that," I said.

"Then let's go see it happen," He said.

Yes, there was twinge of concern of disappointment and what ifs, but I was going to give Him a chance. I would wait at the coffee shop. Maybe this would be the key to changing my mind.

WALKING THE TIGHT ROPE

"I can't fail. I have no one to catch me if I do. I can't take the negative voices anymore," I said.

"You can't?" He asked.

"Wait," I said, "one of them is me. How do I stop me?" I asked.

I saw a trapeze net under me as I tried diligently to put one foot in front of the other on the tight wire I was standing on. "Don't look down, don't look down," I said to myself.

"Why?" He asked.

"It's too scary," I answered.

"But what if it isn't?" He asked.

"I know it is," I replied.

"How do you know if you haven't looked down?" He questioned.

"Because they said so," I remarked.

"Hmmm, who are *they?*" He asked.

"People...you know, relatives, friends, co-workers," I answered.

"OK, and if they said jump off a building you would believe them?" He asked.

His humor was not appreciated, seeing that the bar I was holding was not helping me balance.

"Let Me ask you something," He said.

"OK, but not too loudly, this rope is sensitive," I answered.

"Why are you taking their word for it?" He asked. "Aren't you curious?"

"Yes, but what if I'm wrong?" I replied.

"But what if you are right? Take a chance and see," He said.

Hesitantly I looked down not moving my head. "WOW," I said. Instead of a net, His hands were there to help balance me.

"You can jump or stay; your next move is up to you," He said. "I can help you balance, or you can keep going on the words of others. They may fear looking down, but you do not have to."

From above, I could see food, shelter, and balloons in His hands. "I understand the food and shelter, but the balloons?" I asked.

"Don't you want to have fun, too?" He asked.

I had not thought about that. I had been trying so hard and concentrating not to fall that fun wasn't a thought. *Fun it is,* I thought as I leaped off the rope, throwing the pole to the side. Splash. I hit His hand. I was floating in a root beer float topped with marshmallows.

"Anyone for the back stroke?" I asked, giggling.

-CHAPTER 36-

The Big Top

Trust in the LORD with all your heart and lean not on your own understanding (Proverbs 3:5).

I had always tried to teach my daughter to be independent of me, but dependent on God. "Lord, do you see me depending on others?" I asked. It worries me. People don't come through. "God, I want them to. How can You help me?"

"Ta dah...the ONION," I heard the Holy Spirit announce.

"Oh my goodness," I said, noticing that He had a ring leader's attire and megaphone in His hand while standing in the center of the middle ring. We were in a circus tent.

"Come one, come all, welcome to the big top," He said into the megaphone.

"Please take a seat," the Lord suggested as He waved toward the wooden bleachers.

"How can I trust them?" I said as we sat.

"Time, give them time," He said. "Now quiet down, we are going to miss the show," He said politely.

In ring number one was a man with poodles. They were cute, white, and fluffy. "Jump, Sheba," the man said. The poodle ran from one end of the ring, jumped through the hoop, and then waited on the other side for direction.

In the far ring was a clown. He had a bright red nose and a horn that, to be honest, was annoying. Honk, honk was not fun about the fifteenth time.

Then there was a fairy princess in the middle ring. She wore a pink, satin dress that flowed to the ground with a long train in the back. Her beauty was breathtaking.

"Oh, Lord, who is she?" I asked.

"She is the one you can trust," He replied. "She is elegant, beautiful, and takes your breath away because you appreciate her, because you know how rare and important she is."

"Then what about the poodles?" I asked.

"They are the ones who come a dime a dozen because they jump through whatever hoops You place before them," He said. "They are trainable, but no fun."

"And the clown?" I asked, almost knowing the answer.

"He gets nothing done for having what they call fun," He began. "And yes, it can get annoying."

"What are we to do?" I asked. I heard the Holy Spirit spell out onion again.

"OK, I get it," I said, laughing.

"Give them time to do it," He said. "Some things have to be played out to know. And as they play out, come to Me for peeling," He said with a grin.

"I want to know," I said.

"Surround yourself with ones you can trust to do their parts," He said.

"How do I know that?" I asked.

"Let them do it," He said. "Give them space and encouragement."

"This trusting people is hard for me," I said.

"Do you know why?" He asked. "Because ultimately you are trusting Me in the event they fall short. I am your safety net. No one else should be. Come to Me and I will give you wisdom to discern who you can trust."

"What can I do to make it less painful?" I questioned. "It feels like my insides are being stretched."

"Focus on what is yours," He advised.

"But I am responsible for so much," I replied.

"Yes," He agreed. "Moses put responsible people in place and then let them fulfill their roles. Let them, Dena," He stated.

"Help me," I asked.

"I am. You are growing, that is stretching.

"Yes, your plate is too full," He said. "If I give it to you, then you can handle it. When My people take from others' plates, they get frazzled. You need Me as the protein to sustain the variety on your plate."

"Please help me learn to focus on my plate, letting others eat off theirs," I asked.

"Gladly," He answered. "When you stay on your own plate, you sleep better at night. Too many items fill your plate and your dreams."

FIXES THAT DON'T FIX

"Where do I start this morning that doesn't involve tears?" I said. "I have this overwhelming desire to go shopping. Not because I need or wouldn't enjoy a new shirt or bag, but because I am panicked...frazzled.

"Then go if you would like," He said.

"No, Lord, I know I will just end up crying anyway," I replied. "Can't we just hit this head-on?"

"I would love that, My daughter," He replied. "I know you are troubled, and buying more clothes won't fix it. So let's do just what you have suggested. Fix it. What if I told you that many of My children use things to distract them from something?"

I thought about shopping. I love to shop, but often I noticed that I'd be restless over a situation and then would run to a store out of the anxiety I was feeling, like I was doing right now.

"Avoidance in the name of an errand," He said.

Oh, that stung. My head fell into my hands as I began to sob. "Have you ever wanted something so badly, but the fear of losing it made you insane? Not crazy, but desperate? Like your skin was squirming and your mind raced to find a way to make the thought of how bad it would hurt go away?" I asked.

"Yes," Jesus said, "as I prepared for the cross. I asked My Father if this could be taken. I even had a legion of angels I could call upon…but deep down I knew what had to be done. You may not know what has to be done, but you know who can do it. It is not new clothes or that bag of M&M's you ate as you craved sugar in hopes to feel better the other day. Nothing but hitting these issues head-on will make it better," He finished.

All of His words were right, but how a shopping trip sounded nice. I had done that before, and then I'm a few dollars less and still in a panic. "Lord," I said as I sat on His couch, "help me be free."

"Gladly," the Lord replied as He sat down beside me. "Tell Me what troubles you this morning, My dear."

"I love someone so much," I began. "She had chosen to leave before. Although our relationship is the best it has ever been, I fear she will go again."

"Go on," He said.

"There is a fear that if she doesn't believe me, she will go," I admitted. "I don't know what to do. I am at my wit's end. I know not to control her in hopes she will stay, but my heart fear is she will go, and I don't know if I can live through that pain again."

"Your heart is resilient," the Lord said. "It is tougher yet softer than it has ever been. We just need to get your mind to know what your heart already knows."

"What does it know?" I asked, not ever thinking about what it may know.

"It knows you hurt, but it knows you have Me," He explained.

"Then why am I panicked?" I asked. "Why am I afraid she will go?"

"Because you do not believe," He answered.

I sat there fighting the urge to run to the shoe store. I had seen the cutest boots. They would look great with my new jeans. *No, I told myself, you have to stick this out, you, know, like Jesus did.* He had angels to call down and didn't. Surely, I could sit here and work this through not calling on boots. As silly as that sounded, it was what I was about to do. Call on a pair of boots to comfort me when what I needed was Truth. What is the truth about my fear of losing her and my lack of belief? I thought laying it out there would be the best approach. I was squirming inside, and I needed relief; real relief, not a temporary pair of shoes.

He never ceases to amaze me, I thought as the Holy Spirit entered the room dressed as an onion. "Are You kidding me?" I asked, laughing as He twirled and danced around.

"No, as a matter of fact I am not," the Lord said. "You could take a pointer from the Holy Spirit. Being an onion can be fun. It is all in how you wear it."

"What?" I asked. "Wear it?"

"Yes," the Holy Spirit said. "If you fight it or avoid, it can be yet another hassle in your life. But if you embrace and wear it with a smile, knowing it helps you, then it becomes so much lighter," He explained.

"I want that," I blurted out. "I want to wear it with a smile."

"Hmmm," the Lord said as He began to laugh, "it appears you got something new to wear anyway."

He was right, I realized, as I laughed too.

"The onion is a great indicator as to what needs to be peeled and a great tool to grow us closer," the Lord stated.

That brought a smile to my face. I could see why the Holy Spirit was smiling.

"Would you care to dance?" He asked while offering me His hand.

"I would love that," I said, taking His hand.

He twirled me as He said, "Another one bites the dust."

I found that funny and very appropriate seeing that another fear was biting the dust. I had grown to see the onion peeling as an opportunity to dance rather than something to dread.

"I know," the Lord said as the Holy Spirit and I continued to dance. "Whatever you fear; if you view it as a good thing instead of bad, healing comes easier."

WILL SHE STAY OR GO?

"I could tell you that she is going to stay, but you would not believe Me," the Lord said.

It pained me, but He was right. "Why is it that sometimes I just know what You said is true and I believe, but other times with Your same voice telling me, I still do not believe? What is this?" I asked, confused.

"When it comes to past experiences when you have been burned, you tend not to believe My words," He said. "You know what it feels like to lose her, and when the subject comes up, you go to that past pain."

"Where does Your Truth come in, and why don't I just believe?" I asked.

"Because I do not raise robots," He said. "You have a mind of your own. I am glad, because when you come to Me it is because you want to, not because I pushed a button. Now back to the hurt," He said.

We didn't have to go too far back, I thought, *it was right on my sleeve.* "She left," I cried. "I can't do it again."

"What if I said you wouldn't have to?" He asked.

I began to cry as I answered, "I wouldn't believe You. I want to, Lord," I yelled, "but I don't."

"Do not worry, Child, belief has layers too," He said. "We will get there if you stick with Me."

"Thank You," I said, wishing I would just believe. "What do we do with this mess?" I asked.

"We can talk," He replied. "Communication is the key, remember?"

"Yes," I answered. "Where shall we start?" I asked.

"We need to go back to the source," He said. "To the time she left."

I gasped as the thought of the pain that might flood from the dam I had so strategically placed around my heart. I had walled that hurt in well. I knew because every so often I would have to plaster a potential crack.

"You have to be willing to go to the wall and allow Us to brick by brick, mortar by mortar, begin to disassemble it. Are you?" He asked.

Shopping still hung in the back of my mind and a bag of chocolate cookies didn't seem like a bad idea, but I wanted to end this once and for all, not temporarily. I grabbed my hard hat and pick. "Lord," I said as I looked Him in the eyes, "let's do some demolition."

With a smile from ear to ear, He picked up His bucket and a baseball cap.

"Why a bucket and cap?" I questioned. "Aren't you afraid of getting hurt?"

"No, My child," He replied. "I do not want to lose any piece of the wall. That is why I have the bucket. The wall tells about many parts of you. Like a baby book. We can learn and spend hours talking over them."

"And the baseball cap?" I asked.

"Yes," He said with a grin, "you will need that when you realize this can be fun and want to put your hard hat down. That hard hat is just another way of protection," He explained.

After standing there for a few minutes, I handed Him the hard hat. "I want the whole experience," I said. "Better yet, I want to experience this Your way."

"Very well then," He said as He handed me a baseball cap.

"No way," I squealed with glee. It was a Colts hat. This was more fun already.

"My children," He said as we walked toward the wall, "think addressing their past is all painful. This keeps them from coming to Me way too often. I am not saying it will never cause a tear to be shed, but the heartache is far outweighed by the joy."

"I can agree with that from personal experience," I said.

"Yes, but isn't it joyous when you have walked through the tears?" He asked.

"Yes," I agreed. Then I saw the most beautiful waterfall. It cascaded over a rock. As I walked through the sheet of water, a gorgeous meadow was revealed on the other side.

"That is what healing is," He said, "walking through the rain to see the rainbow."

I could see the rainbow through the water, but not until I took my first step.

"Yes," the Lord said, "you cannot see the colors until the film is removed from your eyes."

"Please tell me more," I said.

"Let's start chipping away while we talk," He said.

Chip, chip, we both began hitting the wall with our picks. Small pieces began to fall.

"Yes, they start small, but the more we chip away, the bigger the chucks start to drop," He explained.

"You were saying about the film?" I stated.

"Yes, hurt darkened your view of the world, yourself, and sadly, of Me. But a few cleansings from the waterfall and your vision becomes brighter. The problem for Me is getting My children to take that first step," He explained.

PRESSURE FOR ANSWERS

I could not sleep. Realizations of my need to rush to get to the answer, or my impatience with someone else not getting to their point, was rattling.

"Some need to rattle," He said.

"Why is it I can't allow them that?" I asked. "Why do I rush those who want to help me? Most of all, why am I not sleeping again?" I asked, being very annoyed.

"So many questions," He replied. "Looks like you need some time."

"Yes, Lord," I agreed. "Why can't I grant that to others as well?" I asked. I thought of a song by Shaun Groves that goes, "How can I have all the answers, when I've got questions of my own?" I too had many questions. He was right about that. I wanted Him to take the time with me. So why couldn't I do that for others and for myself? Did I think I would miss something? I didn't know, but I knew through this restless season, He would reveal what was necessary to heal my shattered heart. He is, of course, the mender of broken hearts.

"New issues have risen to the top," He said.

"What?" I asked.

"You asked why you are not sleeping," He stated.

Not only have I been awake, but moments of panic have slipped in again, I thought.

"They have not slipped in, they have risen," He said. "You have many fears and frustrations, and when you are willing, they rise to the top. We have spent many times together, so you know you can bring them to Me. Now, we start sorting them out."

"More issues," I said discouragingly.

"Oh, don't be discouraged, little one, it is a good thing," He said. "You are having less and less. From glory to glory you are walking your salvation out."

CALL IT FINISHED

"I don't even know how to begin," I said, stepping out of bed. "I slept OK, but have awoken to a dread. I just want the math to be over. It has drained enough of the life out of me and those around me. What is left to do?" I asked.

"Be patient," He replied. "You are on the verge of your breaking through this bondage."

"Can I be honest?" I asked the Lord.

"Of course," He replied.

"I am drained and even questioning that will ever end," I began. "I have so many other things to do, and this is keeping me from them plus keeping me down."

"Well, just like all of My children, you have the choice to terminate the class," He pointed out.

"I would like to terminate it with a light saber like those in *Star Wars*," I said, half joking.

"Very funny," He laughed, "but seriously, you decided you were going to ride this out," He reminded me."

"Of course I am," I replied verbally, but inside I had wavered.

"That is it," He jumped in, "the wavering. Once My children make up their minds, they need to stand," He said. "The wavering takes energy and distracts them from moving on because they are always questioning if they should quit. So are you onboard?" He asked.

"Yes, Lord," I said. "Then what about the dread?" I asked.

"You fear something about it," He answered.

"I know what that is," I said. I felt there was no need to beat around the bush; I might as well jump head first. I mean, I knew what I feared.

"What is it, My child?" He said lovingly.

"That I will fail," I answered.

"And," He said.

"That You will fail me," I blurted out in tears. "You have encouraged and spoke Truth, but now we are at the end and what happens if I fail?" I questioned.

"First, dear one, the difference between Me and those who have let you down is they did not encourage you prior to the let down. If you recall, they only said what they would do if you did your part."

I thought for a minute. He was right. They had not been there to support, just to place conditions on what I was to do. I began to cry, "I always fell short."

"NO," He said boldly. "Those who control do not *want* you to succeed. They will change at the drop of a dime. They leave their prey confused and feeling guilty. What they do is a menace to My Body," He said, frustrated.

I had felt guilt over this class. I missed one class due to the flu, and it had haunted me ever since. I questioned myself, *Would this be the one thing that would cause me to fail? The what ifs were tormenting.*

"That is so true," He agreed. "What ifs are relentless. That is the hold of dread. You are not sure what will happen, but you fear something will. Your mind gets to spinning and there you have torment."

"What do we do?" I asked through the tears.

"I can't make you believe Me," the Lord said softly. "But I can show you that you can. There again, it is your choice. With time together, we can build the relationship that resembles the Garden. I say resembles because until judgment day, there will be sin on this earth. But we can have the closest thing to the Garden. Like you made a decision to stay in the math class, will you make a decision to stay with Me?" He asked.

There is no doubt I want to, I thought. "But what do we do with all this stuff that keeps surfacing?" I asked.

"We purge through it," He replied. "I know the Truth; you do not, but I will share it with you. I want you free," He added.

"So what do I do in the meantime?" I asked. "I hate feeling so unhappy while so much happiness is going on in my life. I do not like that this class has taken so much energy to survive. What do I do? I really need an answer. How can I live in *joy* if I am dreading each day?"

I would wait. I needed to know. How could it be that yesterday I was on top of the world and today I am walking in dread?

"Yesterday you did the entire homework assignment alone; and well, today you fear how you will do the next one," He added. "You are just as worried about disappointing others as you are that I disappoint you."

"What if I do?" I asked. It had not gone well in the past. I would be blamed for not trying hard enough. "My enough never seemed to be enough," I hollered. "I can only do my best," I screamed.

Again I saw myself hanging on to the top of a hole. I am clawing the dirt to keep from dropping. Looking down, all I see is a dark hole with no end visible. I could see indentions where I must have slipped, but caught myself to grab the side in time. I am tired of catching myself in the nick of time.

"I want help," I screamed. I was angry now. How did I get in this hole, and why had so many people walked by to leave me there? "Aren't we the Body?" I screamed. I could see holes as far as the eye could see.

"Yes," He said, "but do not be tempted to bucket everyone in the same group. The ones you are addressing were not of the Body. They were out to control their own selves in their own holes. They are just as angry, fearful, and tired of the whole thing. No one trusts the other, so they stay in their holes trying to keep from falling," He explained.

"Look," I said, pointing to a snake slithering toward the top of another's hole.

"He will give you a lift if you are willing or desperate enough," the Lord said. "He knows you are hanging by a thread, and in that desperation, you will probably take him up on his offer."

"What offer?" I asked.

"To help you out," the Lord explained.

"That doesn't sound so bad," I said.

"No?" He questioned. "You should look closer."

I noticed coming from the tail end of the snake were white strings; more than I could count.

"Yes, strings," the Lord said. "Strings like debt, guilt, fear, and conditions. If you let him help you, you owe him a debt that will accumulate over time. You can never pay it off. That is why you need My Son. When you sign up for the snake's help, you sin. Basically you place your name on his contract as a partner. He knows when his payday is, and he hopes you will go with him."

"I don't want to go with him," I shouted.

"My children make choices every day, either Me or him," the Lord announced. "There is no in-between."

I had seen a pattern forming here. Whenever the Lord would offer His freedom, the snake had a counter offer.

"The Church is hanging by a thread," He began. "They have decided if they are going to err, it will be on the side of Me; determined not to give up. They will hang on to the side of that dirt hole, praying not to fall. Do you see what I do?" He asked.

"What?" I asked.

"They are hanging on by their own strength," He answered. "They do not have the endurance on their own to hang there forever. They will fall, it is inevitable," He said. "There is more," He said. "Those of the church who are hanging on by hope—hope that it is all true."

"What is the difference between the ones hanging by a thread and hanging by hope?" I asked.

"The ones who hang by a thread are past hope. They are working from motivation and determination; their own actions," He explained. "The ones hanging by hope are weaker in action because their hearts hope it will all turn out to be OK. It is only a matter of time before both groups become like the third; those who have given up totally; hope and determination have given way. Honestly, child, neither one is better than the other. Neither really believes."

"I believe we want to, or at least I know I did," I added. "But how could we believe yet fear at the same time?" I questioned with a lump in my throat. The pressure that I didn't believe Him enough was starting to cause guilt in itself. What had I not done enough of? What had I missed? "Why wasn't I enough?" I cried.

It isn't that I don't want to. "I just want to be good enough," I whispered.

"You are holding on in your own power," He said tenderly. "The years of jumping through others' hoops has taken its toll on you and My Church. Even those who are in My Church hold the plastic rings in the faces of My Body. As a Father, it is very upsetting. They do not have the authority to hold those rings. I don't hold rings," He added.

"You were more than enough when My Son came. Did He hold up a ring? No!" He answered Himself. "Do your best...that is all anyone can ask. I accepted you when you were not doing your best. Would a good parent not want to teach you how to do better?" He stated.

"Yes, Lord," I agreed, "but what if fear and guilt were used in place of the teaching?"

"I understand and am very hurt that this does happen, but I am patient," He said. "I know My children worry about what is at the bottom of that hole."

"Yes, I don't know what will happen if I drop," I commented.

"Look again," He said.

Looking down into the dark hole that I hung above, I now noticed a faint light and a hand.

"I will catch you," He said. "You just have to be willing to let go," He said. "I am patient...I will wait. My children, like you, want to do the things that are comfortable, like you writing the book. But you do not realize that without math and others' situations, there is no book. That is what I mean when I say make it work for you not work for it.

"Like the donkey was working for Balaam. Know who is in control," He said. "Confidence is math serving you, not vice versa. Don't give your keys to another or a thing," He said. "You are in control of where you allow yourself to drop or if you take the snake up on his offer. What will it be?"

I had this overwhelming sense of excitement. The math was just a vessel used to free me of past hurts and best of all bring me closer to God. "Cannon ball!" I yelled as I jumped backward into the thin air, releasing my grip from the ledge. I heard Him giggle, but not move His hand an inch. He was going to be there; I just knew it. Hitting His hand felt like falling onto a trampoline. I bounced up into the air to fall securely back onto His hand.

"That is freedom, My dear one," He said. "The freedom to know I am there to catch you while having the room to live."

"I love that," I said, smiling and giggling as I continued to enjoy the fun of bouncing.

"Fun...there you have it, My child," He said, smiling. "We have done it. You are seeing Me as fun," I heard Him say, almost crying. "I want My children to know how fun I am."

I began to cry. He was happy. "How did this happen?" I asked.

"Endurance," He said, still shaken by His overwhelming happiness. "You came to the Secret Place."

I pulled up my pillow to my chest as I had done so many times. I wanted to hear more. He has and always will be the best Storyteller ever.

CHAPTER 37

It Is Finished

And I am certain that God, who began the good work within you, will continue his work until it is finally finished on the day when Christ Jesus returns (Philippians 1:6).

It is by His stripes I am healed—healed of fear, failure, and math. It is real, the grade is a B; but most of all, He is real. He speaks and tells me things I do not know. I have birthed a new confidence not only in myself, but also in Him. He is real. He loves me and wants the best for me, even if that is a math class. Don't lose sight of Him in the unexpected things, even an Algebra night class.

"I'm sorry for ever doubting," I said.

"Oh, Child, it is OK," He said. "You were only learning. I appreciate you staying with Me," He said.

His words were sweeter than they had ever been. They had a sound to them like a wind chime clinging in the breeze. I know my Father's voice. It wasn't about the math. Amen.

"You have known the answer all along," He said softly.

"What, my Lord?" I asked.

"It is Me," He said. "I hold the key to all Truth. To behold the treasure takes time—not time at the local bar or time with the executives climbing the corporate ladder. No, time with Me. It is only when that time is taken that all else will be peaceful. You have been faithful, and I am proud. Turn and take this to the masses. They are tired and in need of sweet dreams. I will be waiting in the Secret Place for each one of them."

"Yes, Father, I will go," I announced.

This had been raw, unrehearsed emotions, to say the least. I had opened up allowing myself to be nothing short of transparent. It was as if my hurts, fears, and shortcomings were plastered on the largest billboard, high above the busiest interstate, for all to see. But that would be OK, I thought. For by God's strength alone, I would hope as Luke had instructed in chapter 22 verse 32, that I had turned back and strengthened my brothers and sisters. As those that went before us have provided us with great examples, we too can glean from one another. As I gathered my things, my laptop, journal, and heart, I felt Him gently grab my hand and speak softly. "Don't neglect Me, My child, for I am no way near finished with you. Do you remember when Saul left?" He asked.

"Yes, Lord, I do."

"He went to our Secret Place," He said. "Some wounds take multiple trips."

His words brought me to my knees as I hugged Him. I never wanted to be finished. I whispered, "I love You," in His ear as I stood up.

With a loving expression, He looked into my eyes as He began to let go of my hand and said, "Now, pick up your pillow and sleep."

SWEET DREAMS

"It is from our time your sleep will be sweet," He continued. "In the event you are restless or tormented, I am always waiting. Come in, close the door. I hope you have seen the relationship between the onion and sleep."

"Yes, Lord, I saw that unfold," I said. "I also see that my demand for it to stop unfolded by peeling the onion. I know that if I have a Nebuchadnezzar night, You wait for me in the Secret Place for a Daniel relief. I may have a restless night of sleep, but I have been given tools and most of all a Craftsman to address the issues."

I sensed the end was near. I wasn't ready to stop.

"Stop," He shouted. "No way. We could never stop...as long as you are willing."

"Oh, Father, I am willing."

"Then be obedient, the final heavenly strength."

"Lord," I cried out. "I want it to go on forever."

"Oh, dear child, how about eternity?" He said. "That is about as forever as there is."

I looked up into His eyes and began to cry, "Please don't forget me...You are my everything."

"Oh, baby girl," He embraced me, "the best is yet to come."

I wasn't sure exactly what He meant, but I would trust Him. Like the apostle Paul had said, "You have taken care of me before and currently. Why should I believe You wouldn't continue?"

He leaned over and whispered in my ear, "Sequel." My eyes got big.

"Dena, get onboard," He said. We were at an amusement park. The roller coaster was about to leave the gate.

As the announcer called to the conductor to trip the switch to release the roller coaster cars, He looked at me and said, "Well done, good and faithful servant."

Before I could respond, our car left the gate.

I heard the Holy Spirit say, "It is better if you lift your hands." Then I heard Jesus say, "Enjoy the ride...that is how it was meant to be."

FULL CIRCLE

"It all comes back to the Secret Place...it is the beginning and the end," He said. "Each generation meets Me there. We talk, we share, laugh, and cry, whatever is necessary. Through their actions their children see Me, and *their* children see Me, and so on it goes through the generations. Keeping the coin visible, you keep Me alive in your blood line and in their hearts, one heart at a time in the Secret Place. I am waiting."

I closed the pages to my journal as I leaned back in my lounge chair on the lanai. It was surreal how time spent in the Secret Place had revealed so much. I knew I would never be the same; and honestly, I couldn't imagine going back. I had to have more of Him. My life was different. It was His, and I would be back tomorrow for another story.

"Good night, Lord," I said as I adjusted my pillow to the contour of my head. "Sweet dreams."

"Sweet dreams," He replied as I drifted peacefully into slumber. I knew He would be there when I awoke. He is the Keeper, Healer, and Creator of my dreams.

About Dena Hoover

Over ten years ago, the Lord called Dena Hoover to quit her job and step into full-time ministry. While attending a women's Bible study at a local Christian bookstore, He brought godly women into her path to prophetically speak the mantel over her life. Confirmed by the Holy Spirit, she has since led Bible studies in her home, churches, and bookstores.

After a season as a women's ministry director, God called her to begin In Remembrance of Me Ministries. She currently has written Bible study material, along with several books.

Dena is an anointed writer, speaker, and counselor. Her heart aches for God's people to be free and to live in the power for which Jesus died on the cross. Anything less is not the abundant life we are offered.

Dena is a devoted wife, mother, and grandmother. She and her husband, Dan, reside in Fort Myers, Florida, where they enjoy outdoor activities, watching football, and enjoying each other's company over a cup of coffee. She counts it a blessing to be surrounded by her daughter, son-in-law, and granddaughter.

Active in her community, Dena has organized and spoken at the National Day of Prayer in Estero, Florida, and participated in Meet You at the Pole events. Dena's ministering has taken her to Nicaragua, where she preached the healing power of Jesus Christ.

It is Dena's heart to serve the Lord, leaving no stone unturned. She believes each person has a specific purpose and calling, and desires out of her past hurts and present healing to encourage others to live theirs out. From her personal experiences with rejection, sexual abuse, betrayal, and a battle with skin cancer, she knows Her Redeemer intimately and desires to introduce Him to you.

CONTACT

If you would like to invite Dena to speak in your area, church, community group, bookstore, or other arenas, please contact her at Godsway@inremembranceofme.org or call 239-313-0009.

Dena is an ideal speaker for:

- Women's Retreats
- Women's Conferences
- Guest Speaker for churches
- Mother and Daughter events

Mailing Address:

PO Box 4599

N. Fort Myers, FL 33918

www.DenaHoover.com

In the right hands, This Book will Change Lives!

Most of the people who need this message will not be looking for this book. To change their lives, you need to put a copy of this book in their hands.

> *But others (seeds) fell into good ground, and brought forth fruit, some a hundred-fold, some sixty-fold, some thirty-fold* (Matthew 13:8).

Our ministry is constantly seeking methods to find the good ground, the people who need this anointed message to change their lives. Will you help us reach these people?

> *Remember this—a farmer who plants only a few seeds will get a small crop. But the one who plants generously will get a generous crop* (2 Corinthians 9:6).

EXTEND THIS MINISTRY BY SOWING
3 BOOKS, 5 BOOKS, 10 BOOKS, **OR MORE TODAY,**
AND BECOME A LIFE CHANGER!

Thank you,

Don Nori Sr., Founder
Destiny Image
Since 1982